A History of
STOURBRIDGE

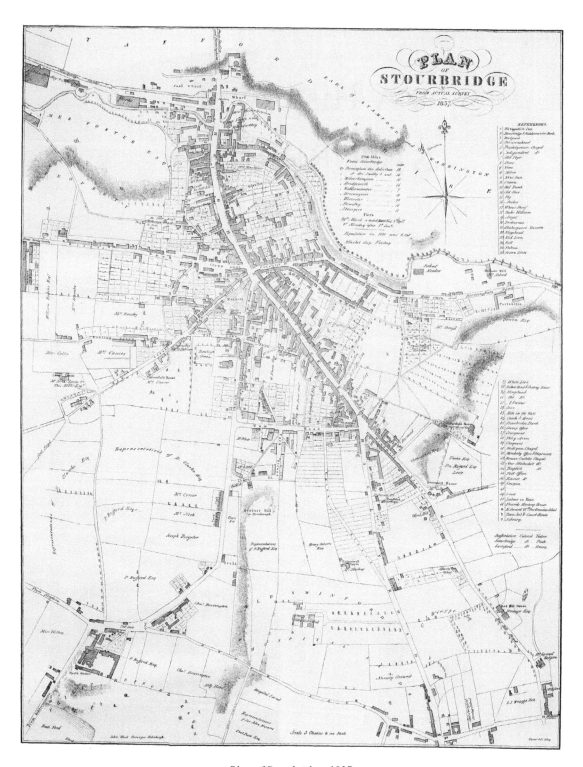

Plan of Stourbridge, 1837.

A History of

STOURBRIDGE

Nigel Perry

First published in 2001
Paperback ediiton first published in 2005
Reprinted in 2019

Phillimore is an imprint of
The History Press
97 St George's Place
Cheltenham
GL50 3QB
www.thehistorypress.co.uk

British Library Cataloguing in Publication Data.
A catalogue record for this book is available from the British Library.

ISBN 9781860773808

Printed and bound by
TJ International Ltd, Padstow, Cornwall

Contents

List of Illustrations

Frontispiece: Plan of Stourbridge, 1837

Acknowledgements

I am extremely grateful to the many persons who have given me so much assistance and encouragement in putting this book together, including David Hickman (Principal Librarian) and Marilyn Ferris (Local History Librarian) at Stourbridge Library, Roger Dodsworth (Keeper of Glass and Fine Art) at Dudley Museum and Art Gallery, Peter Boland and John Hemmingway (archaeologists with Dudley Council Urban Design and Conservation Team), Mrs. K.H. Atkins (Archivist of Dudley Libraries Archives and Local History Service), Robin Whittaker (Senior Assistant County Archivist) at Worcester County Record Office, Sian Roberts (Head of Archives) at Birmingham City Archives, Dominic Farr (Assistant Librarian) at the William Salt Library, Stafford, Mrs. Frances Neale (Archivist) at Wells Cathedral Library and the Rev. Greville Cross, Rector of St Mary's, Oldswinford. I would also like to thank Col. Iain Swinnerton for his helpful comments on an earlier draft of this work, which focused on local Stourbridge family history, and Roy Peacock for his knowledge regarding the Saxon period and earlier. My late cousin, Homery Folkes, gave me the benefit of his expert architectural knowledge and other memories of the town in the 20th century, gained during his long association with the area.

A very special word of thanks must go to Mr. Jack Haden, who has devoted so much of his life to recording local events both past and present. His extracts from local newspapers for the years since 1850 were vital for the later chapters of this book. He also read an earlier draft of the book, as well as some of the current chapters, and gave me much additional information. Finally he provided me with a large number of photographs and other memorabilia with which to illustrate the text. May I also express my gratitude to my wife, Diana, for all her support and understanding during the writing of this book and for reading the various drafts.

Illustrations numbered 8, 9 and 13 were produced from the Hagley Hall Collection (references 347135, 382960, and 347128) in Birmingham Reference Library, by kind permission of the Viscount Cobham DL and Birmingham City Archives. Illustrations numbered 12, 29, 31, 38 and 103 were reproduced with the permission of the Worcestershire Record Office from the originals in their custody. In addition the kind permission of the Rector of St Mary's was given to use illustrations 1, 5, 19-23, 25, 26, 33, 44, 64, 81 and 83; the majority of these documents are now in Worcestershire Record Office on permanent loan. Stourbridge Library is gratefully thanked for permission to use illustrations 2, 7, 10, 14-17, 24, 30, 32, 34, 37, 41-3, 45, 46, 48-54, 56, 57, 59-62, 65, 66, 68-73, 75, 77-9, 82, 85, 86, 89, 90, 92-5, 100-2, 104, 105, 107-9, 114-19, 122-9, 131-3, 136 and 137. Dudley Museum and Art Gallery gave permission to use a copy of Edwin Grice's painting for the book's dust jacket, and also for illustration 67. Mr. Jack Haden kindly allowed me to use illustrations 11, 18, 28, 39, 40, 47, 55, 58, 63, 74, 80, 84, 88, 91, 96, 99, 106, 110, 111, 120, 121, 130, 134, 135 and front and back endpapers. The Public Record Office is custodian of illustration 6 (reference CP 25/1/259/11 no.17). Illustration 3 is reproduced with the permission of the Dean and Chapter of Wells Cathedral. Mr. Robert Price kindly gave permission for illustration 36. My thanks are also due to Nigel Taylor for his notation on map illustration 31.

The poetry of history lies in the quasi-miraculous fact that once, on this earth, once, on this familiar spot of ground, walked other men and women as actual as we are to-day, thinking their own thoughts, swayed by their own passions, but now all gone, one generation vanishing after another, gone as utterly as we ourselves shall shortly be gone like ghost at cock-crow.

G. M. Trevelyan, *Autobiography of an Historian* (1949)

Introduction

Whilst I was researching my family history in the Stourbridge vicinity, it quickly became apparent that no general book on the history of Stourbridge has been published for nearly one hundred years. From the many different sources and documents collected over the years, I have attempted to fill this gap. The area of Stourbridge featured in this book covers the ancient manor of Oldswinford; this includes the town of Stourbridge and hamlets of Lye, Wollescote, Swinford, Norton and Wollaston, all of which were within the County of Worcester until 1974. The manor differs from the ancient parish of Oldswinford in one important respect—it excludes Amblecote, which has seen a completely separate manorial history.

Although the book commences with the pre-history of the Stourbridge area, the name Stourbridge itself first came into existence sometime in the 12th or 13th century. When people refer today to the town of Stourbridge, they often assume that the village of Oldswinford has always been a part of it. But for many hundreds of years up to the end of the 19th century the town of Stourbridge and the parish of Oldswinford were two separate administrative areas. Before the 15th century their roles were completely reversed, with Oldswinford being the centre of administration and Stourbridge (or Bedcote, as it was then known) subservient to it. Local government reorganisation during the past century has resulted in the gradual blurring of the boundaries that once enclosed the ancient manor of Oldswinford.

The administrative area of Stourbridge lay, until the creation of the County of West Midlands in 1974, in the north-eastern corner of Worcestershire and this had been true for the previous thousand years. The county town of Worcester lies some 21 miles to the south. The ecclesiastical parish of Oldswinford had been part of the Diocese of Worcester for a similar number of years and remains so today. Immediately to the north of the river Stour was the county of Stafford (with its county town some 30 miles away), and some 10 miles to the north-west towards Bridgnorth is the county of Shropshire. To the east of Stourbridge lies the industrial Black Country, with the town of Dudley some five miles distant. Within the eastern perimeters of Stourbridge can be found the industrial iron and clay belt that has been so important to local industry, these natural resources having played a vital role in the history and development of the town. Further to the east, at a distance of some 12 miles, lies the prosperous city of Birmingham.

The manor of Oldswinford forms a peculiar elongated shape stretching three miles from east to west, with the village of Oldswinford lying somewhere near the centre of its narrowest part. Major factors in this shape are the geographical features of the surrounding landscape. Hilly ground rising to some 600 feet dominates the eastern boundary from Oldnall to Foxcote and Wollescote, and a further natural boundary is formed to the west by the 400 ft. ridge running from Wollaston in the north to Norton in the south, aptly named The Ridge. The northern boundary is denoted by the

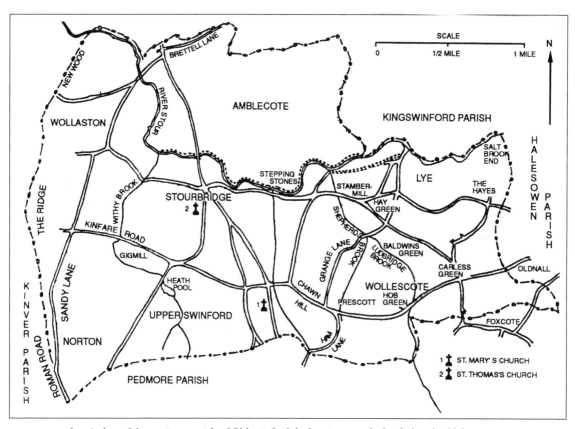

1   *A plan of the ancient parish of Oldswinford, before it was sub-divided in the 19th century.*

river Stour, into which flow several streams from the surrounding high ground. Rivers have always been important landmarks and assumed their names at a very early date in history. The Stour is no exception and in the Middle Ages was spelt Stur, giving some clue as to its pronunciation at this time. The word probably derives from the Celtic *stir* or *storm* meaning rapid or turbid (compare the German *Sturm*); there are several other waterways in the country with the same name. Upon occasions the raging river Stour caused tremendous damage to the numerous mills and other buildings along its banks. To the north of the river lies the settlement and ancient manor of Amblecote.

I

The Stourbridge Area in Early Times

Pre-History

During the first two decades of the 20th century mammalian remains were discovered near the gasworks in the sandstone north of the river Stour. Amongst those remains were the bones and teeth of the mammoth elephant, bison, rhinoceros and hippopotamus dating to a warmer period between ice ages.[1] Evidence of human activity in the Stourbridge area dates back some 10,000 years to the Mesolithic period, although before Saxon times any settlement would have been of a very temporary nature. Sometime after 3000 B.C. settlers from Spain and Portugal arrived on the Atlantic coasts of Britain, bringing with them cattle, sheep and seed corn and travelling over higher ground, this being the start of the Neolithic period. On the eastern boundary of Stourbridge in the Oldnall Farm, Foxcote and Lutley Gutter areas can be found evidence of Neolithic activity and a number of ancient flint objects have been discovered in the fields there. Tribes followed the ancient ridgeway that crossed the higher ground from Wychbury, Foxcote and Oldnall towards Cradley and it was from there that the Stourbridge area was eventually settled.

Further waves of tribes followed, making their way up the Severn Valley from the south-west. By the fifth century B.C., iron instruments were being used. As well as living in open

---

Stourbridge through Time: 48 to 1086

c. 48	Romans conquer local tribes
c. 100	Roman Road constructed
c. 409	Romans leave the area
c. 577	Saxons capture local Hwicce settlements
680	Diocese of Worcester formed
736	Charter granting land at Sture in Usmere into monastic use
c. 900	Earliest church in Oldswinford probably built
c. 954	Charter granting land in Swinford
*c.*1016	Amblecote and Kingswinford annexed to Staffordshire
1066	Norman invasion
1086	Domesday Survey mentions Oldswinford

---

villages, tribes were building forts on the hilltops. These forts were used as temporary refuges in times of danger, and were therefore not inhabited all the time. The defences were initially small wooden palisades, but had become quite elaborate by the time of the Roman invasion. One such fort was just south of Stourbridge on Wychbury Hill. Covering in excess of seven acres, it had a series of steep banks and two ditches. Its small summit enclosure is now densely overgrown by ancient trees and has never been fully excavated. Several other Iron-Age hill-forts existed in the area, including those at Clent, Kinver and Barrow Hill near Pensnett.

At the time of the Roman invasion, the area to the south of Stourbridge was the northern-most area of land occupied by the Dobuni tribe, and was probably the site of many a skirmish with the Cornovii and Tomsaetan tribes to the north and east. The Dobuni occupied a vast tract of land, from Wiltshire and Somerset in the south to Herefordshire and Worcestershire in the north. They were well organised and comparatively civilised for that era, issuing silver coins from 30 B.C. to A.D. 10 that enabled them to trade with mainland Europe. It is interesting to surmise that the distinct change in dialect between Stourbridge and Kidderminster to the south-west originated from the tribes of that period.

The Romans

The Romans under Claudius invaded England with some 20,000 men in A.D. 43 and made their base in London. They reached the Stourbridge area some five years later and after stubborn resistance and bloody skirmishes disarmed the local tribes from their hilltop at Clent. The invasion did not result in any significant settlement, but finds of Roman pottery have been made in the vicinity of Oldnall Farm. The nearest Roman towns were at Wroxeter (Viroconium) to the north and Gloucester (Glevum) and Cirencester (Corinium) to the south. The British population, numbering between 500,000 and 1,000,000 at that time, remained overwhelmingly Celtic. In 211 Britain was divided into two provinces; this district was part of the military province, evidenced by a substantial military fort some five miles away at Greensforge. In 409 the Romans ended their rule of Britain and local warriors stepped into the vacuum left.

Before the year 100 the Romans built a military road running from Droitwich (Salinae), an important salt production centre in the Iron Age, to their camp at Greensforge and on-wards to Wroxeter. That road passed along the western boundary of Stourbridge from Norton to Wollaston, its ancient route being shown on the latest Ordnance Survey map of the area. Although County Lane and part of Sandy Lane at Norton were part of that route, the road did not follow the line of Sandy Lane from Westwood Avenue through to High Park Avenue (the latter being part of an 18th-century turnpike road). Instead it followed the Ridge Top, close to the later parish boundary. The route then crossed Dunsley Lane just above its fork with Gibbet Lane (an area now called Round Hill), bisected the Wollaston to Stewponey Road near High Park Farm and forded the river Stour near where Prestwood Drive now crosses it. After the Romans eventually abandoned their defence of this area at the beginning of the fifth century, the importance of the Roman road slowly declined and played no further part in influencing the pattern of highways that grew up over the next thousand years.

The Saxons

In the mid-fifth century, Saxons began to settle in Britain. They first arrived in Kent and by 500 had settled in Wessex. In 577 the West Saxons captured Gloucester, Cirencester and Bath, the homeland of the Hwicce people whose influence would have spread up the Severn Valley to the Stourbridge area; at various times during the next hundred years the Hwicce were under the rule of either Wessex or Mercia. The population of the country as a whole probably halved between the departure of the Romans and the arrival of the Normans in 1066. The hill-forts may still have been used at times of unrest, but the seventh century was basically peaceful in this area and small homesteads and villages were built on the higher banks above the Stour and on the smaller hilltops of the area. Family groups became more close-knit in Saxon times and new hamlets were carved out by the clearing of virgin land with plough teams of oxen; two or three unfenced fields would have surrounded those homesteads. Any Celtic place-names existing in the area at that time were replaced by Saxon names. At the heart of each Saxon district was a manor house or tun, run by a local official. The hide became the unit of land, being originally sufficient land for one family to cultivate using one plough, which on average amounted to about 120 acres. The hide also became a unit of taxation and ownership of five hides could render a landowner liable to military service. In about the year 650, hides were grouped into administration areas called Hundreds, the Stourbridge district becoming part of the Clent Hundred. Soon after that local manors became units of jurisdiction, the Saxon over-lord assuming responsibility for the inhabitants living within his lordship. The word manor simply meant a dwelling place, and this explains why one quite often finds a village or town served by more than one manor.

The origins of many local names in the Stourbridge area date from that time. One feature that is immediately apparent is a series of place-names ending in 'cott' or 'cote'—Foxcote, Wollescote, Prescote, Pircote, Bedcote and Amblecote. The Saxon origin of this ending was merely a cottage or smallholding, and could conceivably be taken as evidence of the way in which the Saxons started to move down from the higher ground. Foxcote is mentioned in the 10th century as Foxcotun, meaning the Foxes Cottages. Wollescote probably obtained its name from an Anglo-Saxon person named Wulfhere. Bedcote was the area around the present town centre district of Stourbridge and its name probably originated from the old English female name Bettu (or Betta/Bettica). Amblecote also derives from the female name of Aemela.

Other local place-names suggest vital clues in the search for the Saxon origin of the area. The suffix 'ton' in Wollaston meant a stockade and indicates a settlement from Saxon times. The first part of this name possibly relates to a Saxon forename such as Wulfgar (one Wulfgar was our first Christian king of Mercia from 639 to 675). The hamlet of The Lye has a name that also suggests early origins, because the Saxon word *ley* meant a clearing or farm consisting of untilled pasture ground. This could suggest that Lye developed as a settlement slightly later than the early place-names ending in 'cote'. Oldnall sits high above the Stour Valley on the eastern boundary of the parish and manor of Oldswinford. The Saxon name Oldenhall occasionally indicated that an ancient Saxon chief had built his stronghold on that particular site, but a more likely derivation for this name is from old English *olde* and *halh*, meaning an old long narrow valley. It is quite probable that Oldnall was the first site in the area to have a more permanent settlement, from which people moved out to the other parts of the manor of Oldswinford.

2   *Red Hill looking in the direction of the town, c.1910.*

Tracks grew up to link the various cotes or hamlets and through routes became established linking other local villages of importance. Until the 13th century the town of Stourbridge (or Bedcote as it was then known) was no more important than any other hamlet within the manor of Oldswinford. The Saxon road system would not, therefore, have had its focal point in the centre of Stourbridge, but near the crossroads where Glasshouse Hill now meets Red Hill (and where the *Labour in Vain* public house now stands in Oldswinford). This theory is backed up by the fact that two main connecting routes ran through the manor in early times. One ran from the ancient hill settlement of Kinver eastwards towards Halesowen, following the present Dunsley Road, South Road, Heath Lane, Glasshouse Hill, Chawn Hill, Wollescote Road, Brook Holloway and Oldnall Road. The second route ran south from Kingswinford to Clent, which was the seat of the Hundred Court. That track crossed the narrowest part of the manor following the present Lower High Street, Upper High Street, Church Street, Red Hill, Church Road and the footpath past the former White Hall towards Hagley Road at Pedmore. The route appears more pronounced on maps before 1800 than on modern maps. On those early maps Church Street was a straight-line continuation from Stourbridge High Street, and it is likely that Hagley Road was developed somewhat later than Red Hill. The other point that might mystify the reader today is that Church Road now ends abruptly at Oldswinford church. Before the new chancel was added to the church in 1898, this track did continue straight past the old White Hall. The former importance of Church Road also explains the position where the mother church of the manor was built, as at that time it would have fronted onto a major through route and would have been close to the original centre of Oldswinford village.

This was an era when the English were being converted to Christianity. Although some Romans were already Christians, the religion gained little hold at that time. But in 597 St Augustine's mission arrived in Kent and in 601 he was enthroned as first archbishop of Canterbury. The church was then united through all the English kingdoms. A diocese was founded at Worcester in 680. Minsters or monasteries were also founded and those institutions ranged from Benedictine houses to simple communities of priests. They were often controlled by families of noble patrons and became the early parochial system, pre-dating most parish churches (including the mother church of Oldswinford). Priests and monks travelled around preaching to local communities (often under a preaching cross) and performing Christian baptisms and burials. The system of church taxes called tithes developed at this time.

Most charters of the period were grants to churches. By a local charter in 736, Aethelbald, King of the South English (or Mercia), granted land with fields, woods, fisheries and meadows at Sture in Usmere to his faithful companion Ealdorman (or Earl) Cyneberht for the establishment of a monastic estate.[2] The grant stated that the estate 'is bounded on both sides by the river [Stour] and has on its northern side the wood which they call Kinver, but on the west another of which the name is Morfe'. Usmere was the name of a province in Mercia before counties were formed. The place-name Sture was probably a large area lying close to the river Stour, bounded by Stourbridge and Kidderminster and including the present-day Ismere in the middle. A note at the end of the charter referred to another estate within the wood of Morfe named Brochyle being granted to the same earl for religious use. Both woodlands were within the ancient Kinver Forest which included land that stretched as far as the Oldswinford boundary and it is therefore open to conjecture whether that was the area called Brockhill on the hillside to the south of Brook Holloway. The Danes later destroyed the monastery and no trace of its remains has ever been found.

Viking Raids

In 789 the first Vikings (a word meaning pirates) attacked the south of England, followed by further raids on the north-east a few years later. The Oldswinford area of Mercia did not come under Danish rule until about 874 and therefore escaped the worst excesses of destruction and devastation. Five years later Alfred the Great cleared Danes out of all Mercian territory west of Watling Street and life here returned to normal, the area never becoming part of the Danelaw. Local battles, however, did still occur; a battle between the Mercians and West Saxons took place near Tettenhall in about 910 and a fort was built at Bridgnorth in the next few years. There were also pirate raids up the river Severn during that decade.

The area known as Swinford originally consisted of some 12 hides in Worcestershire and included the places we now know as Kingswinford, Amblecote, Stourbridge, Oldswinford and Pedmore. In 954 King Eadred (who was the grandson of Alfred) invaded Northumbria and killed the last king of York. In around that same year he granted to the local lord (or thegn) Burhelm a small estate of six hides in a place called Swine Ford by the local inhabitants. Included in its six hides (three each for the manors of Pedmore and Oldswinford) were all its fields, pastures, meadows and woods, with all rights attached except the duties of building defences and bridges. It is signed by Archbishops Oda and Oscetel, Bishops Cynsige and Adulf, and noblemen Athelstan, Athelmund and Alhelm. This is the earliest written document that

3 *The Liber Albus copy of King Eadred's 10th-century charter concerning land in Swinford, written partly in Latin and partly in Anglo-Saxon.*

can be shown to relate to land in the manors of Oldswinford and Pedmore.[3] By the time of the Norman invasion in 1066, however, the manors of Pedmore and Oldswinford were under the ownership of two different persons.

The boundaries of land in this charter were described as starting from the Swine Ford (on the river Stour), proceeding east to Pecg's Ford (the pig's ford), from there to Deopanford (or deep ford) and finally to Deonflincford, before turning away from the river to follow the line of the modern Salt Brook. Exactly where those fords were situated nobody will ever know, but it is likely that they were situated near where the river is now crossed by bridges. The ford of the swine was probably on the road from Oldswinford to Kingswinford at the bottom of Lower High Street Stourbridge, with the other fords being at Bagley Street, Dudley Road and Hayes Lane at Lye. Evidence of a former Roman road in the manor is afforded by the word *Straete* (or made-up road) and of the ancient track from Kingswinford to Clent by the word *Strete.* The only made-up roads at that time were those remaining from the Roman occupation period. Other surviving landmarks mentioned in the charter were Cudan Dene (the hollow of cuda and possibly the modern Lutley Gutter), Foxcotun (Foxcote), Broce (the brook or possibly Brockhill), Walacrofte (the walled croft), Eostacote (possibly an error for Preostacote meaning priest's cottage) and Aclea (oak wood or leasow).

The prefix 'Old' was then added to that part of Swinford south of the Stour, to distinguish the area from the five hides of land known as Swinford Regis or Kingswinford north of the river, which still belonged to the king. But both manors were still called Suineforde in Domesday Book in 1086. Kingswinford continued as a royal manor under completely different ownership from Oldswinford and both manors have subsequently changed hands in their entirety whenever a change in ownership has taken place. Both Swinfords were initially in the county of Worcestershire, which was in existence by the year 1000. The Hundred (created some three hundred years earlier and by then a subdivision of the County for administration purposes) had its own court. Below the Hundred the population was organised into groups of 10 households called Tithings, responsible for their own law enforcement. There followed a turbulent period in the history of the locality when Aethelred (King of Mercia and known as The Unready) died in 1016 without heirs. Aeuic, Sheriff of Staffordshire, then seized Amblecote and Kingswinford from the heirs of a deacon of the church at Worcester named Aethelsige and both those areas north of the river became part of Staffordshire. By 1066 the one hide of land known as Amblecote was under separate ownership from its larger neighbours.

A local Saxon thegn probably built the mother church of St Mary's, Oldswinford early in the 10th century. Because the bounds of the parish included Amblecote on the north side of the Stour, the parish is likely to have been carved out before the 954 charter. This follows because the then thegn would not have included Amblecote in his parish if it had been under separate ownership from his own manor of Oldswinford. He would also have been unlikely to build churches both in Oldswinford and Pedmore (within one mile of each other) if both areas of land had been under common ownership.

Norman Invasion

Rapid growth in the population meant that major administration changes were taking place by the turn of the millennium. These were to stay in place for many centuries afterwards. Before the Norman invasion in 1066, Oldswinford's three hides were owned by Wulfwin, Pedmore's three hides by Thorgar, Amblecote's one hide by two unnamed men of Earl Alfgar and Kingswinford's five hides by King Edward himself. The invasion would probably not have caused any military action affecting the common man in this area. But the Saxon lords of the manor were replaced by King William's favourites and new taxes raised. Under King Aethelred a highly efficient annual tax system had evolved to meet the cost of keeping the Danes at bay; this was called the Danegeld and was based on the ownership of hides of land. In 1085 Wil-

4 *Domesday Book entries for Swinford and Pedmore in 1086.*

liam, faced with a threatened Danish invasion, raised a large army of foreign mercenaries, billeted them on landowners 'each according to his land', and levied a large Danegeld to pay for their services. Many disputes broke out as to who owned land and commissioners were sent out to ascertain the true ownership, asking questions about the number of hides, ploughs, people, woods, meadows, mills and fishponds and an estimate of their value. The survey was probably just an update of earlier Saxon ones, which themselves have not survived. The resulting Domesday Book became the equivalent of a legal bible, carried around by judges on their circuits for the next few centuries to help determine disputes about ownership and taxation.

The Domesday entry for Suineford related that there were three hides of land valued at six pounds. Acard now held the land from William FitzAnsculf, his tenant-in-chief. The area had only one plough on Acard's personal demesne (land owned and farmed by the lord of the manor himself). Living within the manor were a priest, five villeins (villagers with a not insubstantial holding of land, but who were obliged to perform a variety of services), 11 bordars (smallholders or cottagers of inferior status with only a little land and seven ploughs between them) and two serfs (slaves with no land and in effect the personal property of the lord of the manor). In addition there was a mill valued at five shillings (which would almost certainly have belonged to Acard) and a league (or mile) of woodland.[4] From this survey one can build up a picture of a small community with probably fewer than 100 men, women and children, their status varying according to the amount of land held by each of them. Of the surrounding manors Acard also held Pedmore in 1086. A man named Paganus (or Payne) held land at Amblecote and Cradley from William FitzAnsculf and King William obviously still held Kingswinford directly.

Domesday Book made no mention of our present town of Stourbridge. The birth of the town had to wait for at least another century.

II

Stourbridge in the Middle Ages

Domesday Book to the Arrival of the Black Death

In the years immediately following Domesday Book, the face of Stourbridge was completely unrecognisable from the way it looks today and no buildings have survived from that era. The settlement of Bedcote, as it was then known, lay sprawled on the steep banks above the ford that enabled passage across the river Stour. The incline of the present Lower High Street away

---

Stourbridge through Time: 1086 to 1485

1199	First known rector at St Mary's, Oldswinford
1218	Halesowen Abbey founded with its Grange Farm at Oldswinford
1255	First documented use of the name Stourbridge
1275	Forty inhabitants in Oldswinford pay tax
1285	Bernard de Bruys becomes lord of Oldswinford manor
1292	Stafford family own land and mill in Bedcote
1322	Oldswinford manor passes to Joan Botetourt on death of John de Somery
1327	Only 19 inhabitants of Oldswinford paying tax
1349	Black Death kills some 40 per cent of local inhabitants
1350	Legal enquiry held at Bedcote into rioting at Worcester Priory
1366	Bedcote owned by Lutley family and becomes sub-manor of Oldswinford
1386	Joyce Burnell inherits Oldswinford on death of Sir John Botetourt
*c.*1390	St Mary's church tower probably built
1407	Ownership of Oldswinford split on death of Joyce Burnell
1416	Bedcote owned by Stafford family
1417-19	Joan Beauchamp purchases majority share of Oldswinford manor
1430	Chantry chapel and school built in Lower High Street
1435	Manor of Oldswinford passes to Sir James Butler, later Earl of Ormond
1461	King grants majority share of manor to Fulk Stafford
1463	Sir James Scott acquires majority share of manor
1481	Manor given to Dean and Canons of St George's, Windsor by King
1482	Edward IV grants a market charter to Stourbridge
1485	End of Wars of the Roses

5   *The 14th-century tower of St Mary's, Oldswinford.*
The spire was a familiar landmark, but removed in 1992.

from the river was far greater than it is today as it wended its way towards the crossing with the present Coventry Street and Crown Lane. Single-storey wooden cottages with panels of wattle and daub would have lined the narrow roads on either side of that ancient crossroads. Many of those buildings had just one room (the hall) but sometimes this was extended to encompass a pantry for the bread and a buttery for any drink. There were open fires in the halls and straw on floors and fleas would have bred in the bedding. Virtually no trace of any building would have been found at the southern end of the present High Street. Because of the importance of the river at that time, there was probably a track along the river's southern bank leading to the manorial mill and onwards towards Lye along the track that became Mill Street. Part of that track was later called The Cliff because of the steep gradients of the banks of the river and the cave dwellings nearby. The Lutley family of Enville were the earliest recorded lords of Bedcote, but the Stafford family owned the neighbouring manor of Amblecote from as early as 1292.[1] By 1317 the Staffords were accumulating significant land in Bedcote, including Bedcote Mill.[2] The site of the manorial hall of the lord of Bedcote has never been located, but this would have been the only structure built of stone.

There were no dwellings along the track between Bedcote and the then more important centre of Oldswinford (now Church Street and Red Hill). The cottages of the residents of Oldswinford lay between the present crossroads at the bottom of Glasshouse Hill and the church at the end of Church Road, backing onto the stream to the east. The church at the time of Domesday Book would almost certainly have been a small wooden structure, only being rebuilt in stone during the next two centuries. The earliest recorded incumbent held office in 1199 and the stone tower (the oldest part of the present building) was built towards the end of the 14th century. The FitzAnsculf family, who were overlords of the manor of Oldswinford, came from Picquigny near Amiens in the Departement of Somme, France. The manor passed later to the Paganel and Somery families, but was sub-let at certain times. In 1212 the tenant was the Earl of Salisbury and in 1235/6 Ralph de Merston. In 1285 Bernard de Bruys (whose wife was Agatha) became tenant and in 1290 the manor was worth nine pounds. Bernard de Bruys was succeeded by his son (another Bernard) in 1300/1, who in turn surrendered the manor to John de Somery in 1320/1. When John de Somery died, an Inquisition Post Mortem was held on 5 September 1322 to determine his rightful heir.[3] This disclosed that he received a total rent of £9 18s. 8d. from the tenants of the manor and that he also held the right to present the parson of the church (called the advowson). There were 31 free tenants (those who owned the freehold to their land) in the manor who paid rent of between 3s. 6d. and 6s. 0d. a year to their lord. One free tenant, however, quaintly paid only 'one barbed arrow at the Feast of St John the Baptist'. The average landholding was between one eighth and one quarter of a hide. Mention was also made of eight customary tenants with eight half virgates of land (a virgate was a quarter of a hide), paying in total 38s. 8d. yearly at the two terms of the year (25 March and 29 September). John de Somery's youngest sister Joan, who was the widow of Thomas Botetourt, inherited the manor (together with Northfield and Cradley), but she died in 1338. Her son John, who being a minor did not take control of the manor until 1340, was later knighted and died without an heir in 1386.[4] There has never been any consistent way of spelling the name Oldswinford over the centuries but most historical references do spell it as one word, including the early medieval sources that referred to it as Oldeswynford. Only during the 17th century was it commonly denoted as two separate words.

One mile to the west of Bedcote lay the hamlet of Wollaston, which like Bedcote was settled on ground above the river Stour. Wollaston was inhabited at that time in the area between the river and the present junction of Vicarage Road and High Street, with the centre of the hamlet at that point. The present *Barley Mow* public house was supposed to have been an ancient family residence.[5] The residence of the most important family was probably situated on the site of the 17th-century Wollaston Hall to the east of the village centre and near the present Apley Road. Although not officially having the title of a manor, Wollaston remained a separate administrative part of the manor of Oldswinford in several ways. Only one family at any one time owned the land in the hamlet and, in common with Bedcote and the other hamlets of Oldswinford, Wollaston had its own common fields. The first documented reference to Wollaston was in 1240, when William de la Platte and his wife Hawise conveyed land there to Peter de Prestwood.[6]

Wollescote, The Lye, Wollaston and Swinford were collectively referred to as The Hamlets. The hamlet of Lye lay one mile to the east of Bedcote and it too was settled in a position above the river Stour along the present Dudley Road towards the central crossroads at Lye Cross, around which would have been a scattering of cottages. The track leading eastwards from there terminated as soon as it reached common land at Lye Waste. Unlike some of the other hamlets of Oldswinford manor, Lye never obtained sub-manor status. To earlier generations it was always known as 'The Lye', denoting the original Saxon meaning of 'the clearing'. Simon de Lega (i.e. of the Lye) paid tax in 1275, and in 1311 Robert de la Leye obtained certain land from Bernard de Bruys, lord of the manor of Oldswinford.[7] Because Lye lay over coal seams it grew quite rapidly in the Middle Ages.

The hamlet of Wollescote (which was smaller than Lye) also never became a sub-manor of Oldswinford, but remained autonomous within the manor. Walter and Agnete de Wolfrescote paid tax there in 1275, and later the hamlet's name contracted to Wolscote (before it obtained its present format in the 18th century). The main residence of Wollescote lay high on a hill above the Shepherds Brook, a stream that emptied its waters into the river Stour at Stambermill between Bedcote and Lye at the site of an ancient mill. (The old form of Stambermill was the Saxon *Stanburn* meaning stone brook; in 1275 Adam de Stanburn lived there.) Between

Wollescote and Lye lay Pircote Grange (now simply known as The Grange), a district which had a fascinating history. The name derived from Perry, which in turn denoted pears. Covering basically the area where the Grange Estate can be found today, the land was given to Halesowen Abbey on its foundation in 1218 to be used as a farm to supply the monks with food. In 1275 Richard de Pyrecote was paying tax on land there and in 1291 the Grangia de Pyrcote contained one carucate of land (about one hundred acres) valued at 10 shillings with a fixed rent of 2s. 6d. a year.[8] John de Lutteleye (lord of Lutley which lay between Enville and Bobbington) owned land there in the mid-14th century. In medieval times, there were other areas in the manor of Oldswinford which were relatively more prominent than they are today, including Oldnall and Foxcote which have both lost their importance over the years. Oldnall was written as Oldenhalle in 1275, and references two centuries later are made to Oldehalegrene with a rental of one shilling a year. (Only in the 16th century did the name contract to Oldnoll and Oldnall.) Foxcote was mentioned in a document of 1290.[9]

In contrast Bedcote began to grow at a much faster rate than its immediate neighbours. The reasons for this were primarily connected with its residents beginning to undertake a greater amount of trade than people living in the neighbouring hamlets. From early times coal, clay and iron were being mined and goods were being made from those raw materials. Bedcote was ideally placed on an important convergence of through routes between Coventry to the east, Wales to the west, Chester to the north and the Severn Valley to the south. In addition the river at that time was a powerful force through Bedcote and provided power for the manorial mill. Once the first bridge across the river Stour was built to replace the ford at the bottom of Lower High Street, the name Stourbridge began to replace Bedcote for the central area of the town. The exact date when that bridge was constructed is not recorded, but it was depicted as having four arches and was reputed to be extremely narrow. The first documented evidence for the name of Stourbridge was in 1255, when it was spelt Sturbrug in an Assize Roll (an Assize was a royal declaration or a decision of an assembly as in the case of rents).[10] That spelling indicates that until quite recent times the name Stourbridge was pronounced quite differently from what the ear is accustomed to hearing today, although the ancient pronunciation does still survive in the name of nearby Stourton. In a taxation roll of 1333 the name was written as Sturbrugg and in 1358 as Storebrugge.[11]

By the early 14th century local tracks linked the main hamlets of the manor of Oldswinford to each other. A highway from Stambermill to Oldnall was mentioned in 1311,[12] joining up Bedcote and Hay Green to Careless Green via the present Cemetery Road and Belmont Road. Another early track linked Pircote Grange and Prescott to Foxcote, Oldnall and Halesowen Abbey; much traffic must have frequented that road in medieval times. Other lanes connected Oldswinford to Stambermill, Hob Green (Wollescote) to Pedmore, and Wollaston to Amblecote. The liability to maintain highways at that time lay with the owners of the land over which the roads passed, but a major problem for the medieval traveller was the extreme narrowness of many of those tracks. One of the earliest Acts relating to road maintenance was the Statute of Winchester in 1285 which imposed duties upon the manorial constable to ensure that an area of some 200 feet was cleared of bushes and undergrowth on either side of a main highway. Another problem was mud on the highway, and if the roads became 'foundrous', the ancient voyager had the legal right to seek a safer way, even if this was across cultivated fields.

At the time of Domesday Book in 1086 there were probably fewer than 100 persons living in the manor of Oldswinford. Between Domesday and Elizabethan times no record exists allowing an estimate of the population, but national records indicate that the number of inhabitants in southern England trebled in the 12th and 13th centuries; this was accompanied by a major amount of land reclamation. The first major check to local population growth came between 1312 and 1322 when persistent rain led to harvest failures and several years of famine. That Great Famine was accompanied by pestilence, and some 15 per cent of the local population died at that time. It was then briefly followed by a baby boom.[13]

Prior to the second half of the 13th century the population was so small that people tended to use only Christian names. Gradually the name of the hamlet where an individual lived was appended to a Christian name, representing the origin of the earliest surnames. Less commonly a person's Christian name was suffixed by the description of his occupation, by the name of his father or even by a nickname. Until the middle of the 14th century the surnames of peasants were neither consistent nor fixed; one person could be called by two or more names, for example a name representing a locality and by a nickname. In Stourbridge of 1275 could be found names indicating location such as Simon de Lega (of The Lye), Walter de Wolfrescote (Wollescote), Adam de Stanburn (Stambermill), John de Foxcote, Richard de Pyrecote (Pircote Grange), Sarra de Bettecote (Bedcote), Walter de Bosco (of the wood) and Thomas de la Gorste. Other names suggested occupations, examples being William Patchet (the pedlar), William Coco (the cook), Richard Bercarius (the shepherd), William Chec (tax collector) and Richard Coleman. A father's name was given in the case of John filius Nicholai and John filius Matthei. Nicknames were indicated by Henry Maudut (the accursed) and Richard Luggerhach (probably meaning thick ear).

By 1327 the pattern of names listed in the taxation rolls was broadly the same, although in some cases the prefix *atte* had replaced the Norman *de* for names indicating location, for example Adam atte Leye and William atte Lidgate. But Ralph de Stanbourne, Christina de Wolverston and strangely Henry de Muleward could still be seen. In other examples the prefix had disappeared completely as in Auncellode Swyneforde and Thomas Holberne. The occupational surnames listed were much the same as 50 years earlier, including Thomas Kech, Robert Collier and William le Coke. Legal documents executed in Stourbridge referred to the names of John Cardell in 1311,[14] and John Haterell and Thomas Patchet in 1358.[15] The earliest local surnames in the locality that showed later continuity (excluding the noble families owning local manors) were Cardell, Milward, Patchet (Paget) and Styler.

Ownership of a certain amount of land was always important, both as a status symbol and also for subsistence and survival. Customary tenants were subject to the customs of the manor rather than to the Common Law and were open to exploitation by the lord of the manor. Most of those tenants were called copyholders, because a copy of the conveyance of the land was entered in the court rolls when the land was surrendered at the manor court hearing. Even copyholders' rights varied enormously. The strongest were copyholders by inheritance who paid a fixed entry fine when they took over their land together with a small fixed annual rent. Some inhabitants were copyholders who did not inherit automatically, and they were in a far weaker position as they were faced with an uncertain and often heavy entry fine on succession to their land. The weakest of all were the customary tenants who did not even have a copy of the court roll, and those poor people were called tenants at the will of the lord in Oldswinford manor rentals. Customary tenants taking up a new holding had to come to the court and pay homage and relief before receiving their copy, this being symbolically represented by the lord taking their hands between his own and kissing to show their friendship. Relief was another name for the entry fine, which in Stourbridge usually amounted to one year's rental. The death of the previous holder would then be entered in the manor roll, together with a note of the heir and the amount of relief paid. Some inhabitants were completely landless or just held a small strip of land in the common fields; they laboured for other yeomen, building up their landholding strip by strip throughout their lifetime. Other people leased demesne land by indenture from the lord, generally holding it for a term of years at a rack-rent, or for a period of several lives. Heavy obligations were imposed on Oldswinford customary tenants during the 13th century. Every year they were forced to plough the lord's demesne land for six days, sow the demesne for 10 days and give one day's special work (called boon work). Their only benefit was the free food donated on that particular special day. Customary tenants also had to mow the lord's grass, fence his garden when necessary and turn up at the three-weekly court held by the manor (that duty was called suit of court). They had to pay a heriot when inheriting land and a fee to the lord of the manor as a licence to marry off their daughters (the amount varied between 1s. 0d. and 6s. 8d. and was often evaded, resulting in a fine at the next court sitting). Their corn always had to be ground at the mill owned by the lord, who could demand virtually any payment he liked for that service. The tenant could not escape by going to live in another manor, as he needed a licence from his lord to do this; even after leaving the manor he was obliged to attend the great court once each year.[16]

Transfer of land took the form of a physical giving of possession. This was symbolised by the handing over of a sod of earth in the presence of witnesses (an action called Livery of Seisin). No legal written evidence was required at that time, although normally a Deed of Gift or Charter of Feoffment was enacted. In order to record legal title to land in the courts a fictitious device called a Finalis Concordia or Fine was used, by which the buyer sued the seller for possession of the land, but reached a final agreement before the case was actually arbitrated. Three indented copies of the document became normal, the parts of which were torn off and given to the parties concerned. In 1290 an early Fine was executed between Oldswinford residents Geoffrey de Kynsedele and William du Boys, who paid 25 shillings for one messuage and a third part of one carucate of land with appurtenances in Bettecote and Foxcote.[17]

Manorial income was derived from a variety of local taxes including rents, fines and market tolls. Many of the medieval taxes had quaint names. The *merchet* was a fee payable by a customary tenant if he wished to marry off his daughter. A *heriot* was due when land was transferred; this had developed from a Saxon liability for an heir to return the military arms, including the horse, of a deceased tenant (items that had originally been supplied by the lord of the manor). After the Norman Conquest the heriot became a man's best animal, a quite onerous and unjust burden on poorer residents. Another form of local taxation on the whole manor was *tallage* (exacted by the lord on his unfree tenants), but even those persons who had neither home nor land within the manor were caught by the *chevage*, a local poll tax. *Pannage* was paid for the privilege of tenants' cattle or pigs being allowed to roam the woods or commons. The *chirset* (or church scot and originally a contribution to the church) became a fixed

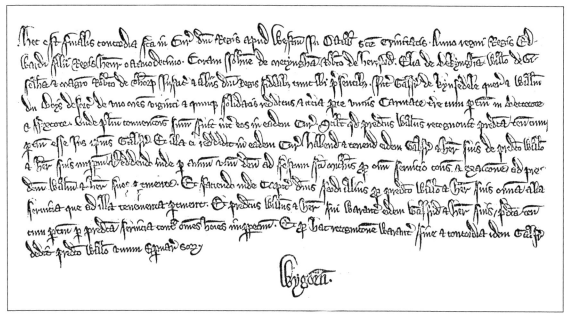

6 *A Finalis Concordia (or Fine) dated 1290, written in Latin and transferring land in Bedcote and Foxcote between William du Boys (probably the same family as the Bruys) and Geoffrey de Kynsedele.*

amount payable to the lord of the manor at Martinmas (11 November), usually in corn or eggs. The church also raised taxes which they called tithes, based on one tenth of the produce of the land. The rector of a parish was entitled to the Great Tithe, which was levied on corn, hay and wool, the vicar receiving the tithe on the remaining produce such as fruit, eggs and honey. It was the duty of the Hayward to go from door to door collecting the goods, and people refusing to pay were often excommunicated.

The king himself quickly became ingenious at raising taxes. Towards the end of the 13th century various Lay Subsidies (a general name for taxes raised on parishes between the 11th century and 1689) began to attack the movable personal wealth of Stourbridge people, with a fraction such as one tenth or one fifteenth being claimed each time. The subsidy of 1275 assessed the personal property of named individuals and some 40 persons were cited in Oldswinford. Later in 1327 a subsidy claimed 32s. 10d. from Oldswinford residents although the number paying had fallen to 19 people. One twentieth of the moveable goods of all England's laity was demanded. The purpose of that subsidy was to raise a tax to meet Edward II's costs in making war with the Scots. A change of tactic in 1334 found the king bargaining with each township or parish for a single sum, which was then allocated locally amongst the community. The quotas set for each town in 1334 stood for nearly two centuries, apart from reductions in 1433 and 1445.

The poor obviously could not afford to pay taxes and sometimes had to claim relief, if they had no family of their own to support them. Monasteries were a magnet for the poor of that time, as they provided relief in the form of money, food and medical help for anyone turning up at their gates. The closest abbey was that at Halesowen (which also owned land in Oldswinford). In 1245 a gift of one penny was given to 635 poor people on the occasion of the burial of its abbot. On each anniversary of the death of Joan Botetourt (one time owner of both Halesowen and Oldswinford manors) 20 shillings were shared out amongst the poor presenting themselves at the gates of the abbey on that particular day. It was said that the porter regularly dispensed alms and scraps from the kitchens to the needy outside its gates.[18] From Saxon times the church also gave one quarter of its tithe income to the poor.

Black Death to the Wars of the Roses
In 1349 Stourbridge was devastated by the greatest natural disaster ever to occur in its history. The Black Death plague reached the shores of England in June 1348 and eventually invaded the Midlands in May 1349. When it subsided the following August, between 40 and 45 per cent of the population of Stourbridge were dead. Whole families, both rich and poor, were completely wiped out, and many court sessions had to be devoted exclusively to registering their deaths. Burial of the dead took place in large pits, and local people still talk of such pits having been located near the north door of St Mary's, Oldswinford and under the former Oldswinford Tennis Club near the present Rectory Gardens. Although there were further local outbreaks of the plague in 1361, 1369, 1375 and 1400, these occurrences were more isolated. Some 15 per cent of the population, mainly the very old and the very young, were probably killed each time the disease struck.[19]

The Stourbridge survivors of the Black Death found that life changed immensely in the years that followed. Crop failures immediately after 1349 did not cause too much malnutrition because of the now-reduced population (which continued to decline throughout the second half of the 14th century). A shortage of manpower developed and wage earners began to dominate the farming scene, their wages doubling between 1350 and 1415 although prices remained relatively stable. Much intermarriage took place between the freemen and bondsmen classes, further blurring the distinction between the two, and licences were no longer needed to marry off daughters. Heriots, however, continued to be extracted for many more years, only gradually becoming monetary payments of between 3s. 4d. and £1 in Stourbridge (before finally being abolished in 1660). Many of the more prosperous villagers obtained their freedom from having to perform compulsory services for the lord and progressed to owning their own freehold which gave them absolute security of tenure. Those free tenants paid a token rent to the lord of the manor, which remained fixed in value for several hundred years afterwards. The decrease in compulsory services also meant that the lord's demesne was increasingly farmed or rented out. The surnames of people became more permanent and only a very small number of inhabitants now had an alias. In 1377 a new form of Poll Tax was levied at a flat rate of fourpence on every person over the age of fourteen. It was repeated in 1379 and 1381 in a kind that graduated the amount according to the occupation and the status of any person over the age of sixteen. The poor were helped in 1391 by the Statute of Mortmain which required that whenever a benefice of a church was appropriated, some of its revenues had to be reserved for the use of the parish.

The greater freedom of people following the Black Death was a major reason why the town of Stourbridge began a period of important growth. An increasing number of people were settling in the town, attracting more trade into the area. Following the large number of deaths in 1349 there was a major riot at Worcester between the townsmen and the monks of Worcester Priory; early in 1350 King Edward III's judges held an enquiry to investigate the events and punish the guilty. That opened at Kidderminster before adjourning to Wolverley and finally to Bedcote, where it was concluded. This would suggest that the area by then must have been no small place, and it was at that time that Bedcote became a separate but inferior manor to Oldswinford itself. On 9 August 1365 Sir John Botetourt, lord of the manor of Oldswinford, granted all lands, tenements, rents and services arising in Bedcote and Wollaston to Philip de Lotteley, whose family were styled lords of Bedcote at that time.[20] The significance of this event was that Bedcote (including Stourbridge) began to develop its own administrative jurisdiction and became known as the Township of Stourbridge. The manor of Oldswinford still retained the right to claim all waifs and strays, felons' goods, and escheats that were taken from the inhabitants of Bedcote and Stourbridge. A healthy rivalry grew up between the township and the parish of Oldswinford that was to continue for many centuries to come. The boundaries of Bedcote then stretched out as far as the Withy Brook at Wollaston, Worcester Lane at The Heath, half way along Red Hill towards Oldswinford to the present house called Wheelergate, and to Shepherds Brook at Hay Green and Stambermill. The name was then spelt with only one 't' as Betecote. (By the 16th century it had become Bedcott and today the only reminders of this once important name are a minor road called Bedcote Place and a group who call themselves the Bedcote Morris Dancers).

During the 15th century there was a modest increase in the number of Stourbridge inhabitants. More cottages were erected in the High Street and some of the timbers from those buildings actually survived into the 20th century. When McDonald's restaurant was built in the High Street the timbers of the building it replaced were dated to that time. The cellars of the wine merchants Nickolls and Perks on the northern corner of Coventry Street have also been dated to that century and parts of the adjoining buildings are just as old. In 1416 Sir Humphrey Stafford (known as 'Humphrey with the silver hand' because of his wealth) was actually referred to as lord of the manor of Bedcote, when he mortgaged the manor to Robert Dangel for 250 marks.[21] By 1430 there was sufficient population in the town for it to require its own chapel; the mother church at Oldswinford was at least a mile distant for the majority of the population. On 21 May 1430 the Haley family founded a chantry chapel called the Service of the Trinity in Lower High Street Stourbridge (the remains of which lie under parts of the present Sixth Form College). Twenty pence a year was given to the poor of the town out of a total chantry income of about 113s. 6d. The infirm poor who received charity there were called bedesmen (bede meaning prayer) and wore long cloth gowns of dark hue that bore the badge of the founder on the sleeve; they had to attend church regularly to pray for the soul of their founder. Income was also set aside for a small classroom for the education of the children of the poor. Stourbridge would also have had a religious gild, its members expected to make bequests to the gild in return for their names being entered on a bede-roll. The 15th century saw many new local families emerging and in 1430 names signing the Stourbridge chantry charter included Smith, Hackett, Leech, Rock, Perrott, Cowper, Hill, Poulter, Perry, Goppe, Cardell and Styler. Haye, White, Wall and Clare were names found later in the century.

In 1386 the ownership of the manor of Oldswinford had passed to Sir John Botetourt's daughter Joyce, the wife of Sir Hugh Burnell of Holdgate. Joyce died without issue in 1407, resulting in a complicated split-up of the holding which led to various disputes over the next

7 *Nickolls & Perks wine shop and the Old Bank in February 1983, at Coventry Street's junction with High Street.*

half century. One third passed to her aunt Joyce, the wife of Sir Adam Peshall, another third to her cousin, Joyce Wykes, and the remaining third to Maurice Berkeley. Joan Beauchamp, Lady Bergavenny, acquired the first two shares in 1417 and 1419 respectively. In 1435 she died, bequeathing her two-third holding to her grandson Sir James Butler (son of the Earl of Ormond), who agreed to pay 40s. a year to Maurice Berkeley for a reversionary interest in the remaining third. James Butler was created Earl of Wiltshire in 1449 and succeeded his father as the 5th Earl of Ormond in 1452, but as a keen Lancastrian he was captured and beheaded at Newcastle-upon-Tyne in 1461. His share of the manor reverted to the Crown, an event that would appear to have been repeated several times during the Wars of the Roses. In January 1462 Edward IV granted Ormond's former holding to Fulk Stafford, who died the following year without heirs. In January 1463 two thirds of Fulk Stafford's holding was given by the king to Sir John Scott, with the reversion of the remainder to Fulk's widow, Margaret, as her dower. A year later Maurice Berkeley died, his son William inheriting his father's third share before later forfeiting his estates to the Crown. Sir John Scott acquired the former Berkeley holding in 1481 before surrendering the manor to the king in exchange for other lands in July. In November 1481 the king granted the manor to the Dean and Canons of St George's Chapel, Windsor, although Margaret Stafford still had a reversionary interest at this time. By 1482 commercial activities in Stourbridge had grown so much that the town was granted a Royal Charter by Edward IV. The lord was allowed the right to hold a weekly market on a Friday together with fairs twice a year on the feasts of St Edward the Confessor (18 March) and St Augustine (28 August). (After reform of the calendar in 1752 the dates of the fairs were retarded by 11 days.) The charter was later than similar rights granted to neighbouring towns, presumably because of the late development of Stourbridge as a trading centre. As the charter was granted to the lord of the manor in person, it was he who had the right to pocket the market tolls, as well as to formulate the laws regarding trading within his manor, enforcing them through his own manor courts. Any disputes between itinerant traders were settled in a Court of Piepowders (from the Norman French *pieds poudres* literally meaning dusty feet).

Other areas of the manor of Oldswinford also developed apace in the 15th century, albeit not as rapidly as the town of Stourbridge. The Perrott family became the major landowners in Wollaston and were so-called lords of the manor there from as early as 1443.[22] Indeed they claimed a pre-conquest charter and supported a coat of arms which was emblazoned 'gules, three pears or, and a chief argent with a demi lion sable therein'. In the hamlet of Lye the Addenbrooke family acquired mills and a large amount of land in the latter part of the century. To the east of Lye Cross adjoining the boundary with Halesowen was barren common land later known as Lye Waste, which at that time was referred to as Wastehaye. At Pircote Grange John le Styler acquired land from John de Lutteleye in 1372,[23] and the Styler family continued to accumulate land there in the 15th century.

Two smaller settlements grew up between the town and Lye. One of those was Hay Green, a large triangular area just to the west of where Cemetery Road now meets Stourbridge Road at Stambermill. It had its own small pool and land there called Hay Goste was owned by Roger Orme in the mid-15th century.[24] Later in the century the Addenbrooke family acquired much of the land at Hay Green. Further to the west along the Stourbridge Road, situated at its junction with Hungary Hill and Bagley Street, lay the romantically named Highmans Green. Between 1460 and 1463 Robert Forest alias Nowell (of Cradley in the parish of Kingswinford) acquired land and properties at Hymondesgrene from the Styler and other families; Robert Forest died in 1498.[25] His son Thomas, who was keeper of Dunclent Park and bailiff of the manor of Kidderminster, gave property at Hymondesgrene and Lye in 1501 to endow a charity for the poor people of Stone.[26] (The Trust for the Poor of Stone remained in operation until at least the end of the 18th century at which time the Green disappeared when the line of the Stourbridge to Lye road was altered.)

Oldnall Green became Careless Green, a name probably originating from a family called Carles. At the foot of the hill below Careless Green was an area that is now called Ludgbridge Brook. That surrounded a stream that rose on the lower slopes of Wychbury Hill above the present Queensway, Wollescote, and descended into a wooded glen at Hob Green on the south side of Wollescote Road. In the 15th century the waste land around the stream was called Lesebrugge.[27] In later centuries the name was referred to as Lusbridge and land around it as Lusbridge Meadow.

Local Field Names

By the end of the 15th century a network of fields had been cleared around Stourbridge and its hamlets. All these fields were known by their individual names, names that in most cases had already been allocated by that time (although documentary evidence for the names tends to appear later). Quite often the fields were named either after a family who owned the land in medieval times, or because of some unusual feature of the field. Plots named after Stourbridge families give some clue as to early surnames in the parish. In most cases that particular family had ceased to own the land by the early 16th century, but there were a few cases where disposal of a field by the original family was documented. One example was a cottage on Hilles Grounde (adjoining the Mill Field at Bedcote) which was sold by a Thomas Hill to Thomas Forest in the early 16th century.[28] Another earlier example was when Richard Shepley surrendered Shepleys Land (which consisted of a tenement and half a virgate of land) together with Brayles Land (a messuage and two closes) to Elizabeth Stuerd.[29] (Those two plots remained in her family until 1632 when William Steward and his son, William, sold them to John Taylor.) Brayles Land was mentioned from as early as 1486, in which year Richard Shepley acquired the land from William Cattley at an annual rent of 5s. 4d. That plot of land was situated at Highmans Green and was later called Brayhall. Other land named after Stourbridge families included:

Walters Land in Oldswinford, including a close called Birches Woods; the Rock family owned a part of that plot;
Beardes Land situated on Chawn Hill;
Blakes Land in High Street Stourbridge (which in 1549 had three cottages built upon it);
Cardells Land on the north side of High Street Wollaston, at its junction with Vicarage Road;
Jestons Land at Lye, which eventually passed to the Milward family;
Parry's Land in Bedcote (owned by Thomas Elcox in 1549);
Tyrers Land in Oldswinford (owned by the Best family in the early 17th century);
Hartes Land in Wollescote, which later changed its name to Brade Hayes.[30]

In this category of field name can also be included the Hassold Fields adjacent to Rufford Road (once Robache Lane), Richards Fields and Cox Croft within Bedcote manor, Powlers Close near Wollescote Hall, and Foleys Meadow near the Short Heath.

Any field located near the boundary of a manor or parish often included Hayes in its name (haga in Saxon), and this was seen in field names on the eastern side of the manor of Oldswinford. Lye Waste (then known as Wastehaye) eventually became The Hayes. Similarly Hay Green was situated close to the boundary between the manors of Bedcote and Amblecote. A copyhold meadow in Lye was called Lawrence Hayes; later in 1529 William Gregory surrendered it to the use of John Cartwright at a rental of two shillings a year. Another example near the boundary with Amblecote was Coneyberry Hayes close to the river Stour on the eastern side of Dudley Road, Lye; that piece of land measured about one acre and was owned by a person named Read.

The length of certain fields was reflected in numerous names beginning with Long. Examples were Long Brockhill on the south side of Brook Holloway, Longcroft near the present Dobbins Oak Road, Long Leasow between Bott Lane and the River Stour at Lye (all of which were once owned by the prosperous Milward family), The Long Meadow by the Stour to the east of the existing Richmond Grove at Wollaston, and The Long Lands along which Brook Street was built (and which gave its name to the present school). Other names originated because of the unusual shape of the land. These included The Dog Close attached to manorial hall at Wollaston, The Four Square Harp and The Sling (also both in Wollaston). The Hook lay by the Stour at Bedcote and The Three Road Piece near the present Vauxhall Road (so named because the three tracks around its perimeter formed a triangular shape). Another variation on that theme was Broad Leasow, a close of land in Lye situated between Hay Green and Pedmore Road. (The Witton family had a long connection with part of that close being the reason why the plot had become known as Wittons Land by the 18th century.)

The hilly nature of plots was another feature that gave names to Stourbridge fields. At Wollescote the very hilly ground between Ludgbridge Brook and Wynall Lane contained fields named Birch Hill and Brockhill. Brockhill derived its name from the word for badger and belonged to the Milward family of Wollescote. It was divided into a number of fields variously named Barn Brockhill, Brockhill Meadow, and Little, Long and Nether-Brockhill. At Stambermill was to be found the ancient Gorsty Hill, probably the same area that was later named Hungary Hill (named because of the poor quality of the soil). As early as 1311 Bernard de Bruys, lord of Oldswinford, granted to Richard de la Leye a piece of waste ground in La Gorst Hill. Various references can also be found to Gorsty Meadow, Leasowes and Close. Gorsty Piece was another variation of the name on the south side of the present Junction Road near where it meets Rufford Road. An ancient close of land in that same area was named Ridge Grove (called Rigg Grove or even Red Grove in the 17th century), commemorated in the 20th century by a road of the same name. If Ridge and Red were synonymous, that could be the derivation of Red Hill which runs across a small ridge of ground between the settlement of Stourbridge and Oldswinford. A final example was Yarnborough Hill (known as Yearnebarrowe Hill Field in the 17th century when it was enclosed and seven cottages built on it). The name could indicate some previous Iron-Age remains on the hill. It later became the property of Old Swinford Hospital and is now known as Hanbury Hill (but why it acquired that name in the 19th century is not clear).

Certain other fields were named after natural features and waterways. In Wollescote there were fields named Dobbins Oak, Brook Furlong (both close to the main hall) and Crabtree Piece on the eastern side of Grange Lane. At Wollaston could be found The Washing Pool Field, and Burnt Oak was situated in the present Lion Street area. In Bedcote between Bott Lane and the Stour were located Holly Piece and at Chawn Hill was a field named Round Oak Meadow. Several Pool Leasows could be found dotted around the parish. The river Stour had many large meadows and pastures along its banks. Those included Upper Meadow on the west side of Lower High Street, and to the east of that main thoroughfare was Mill Field (owned in the 15th century by Robert Darby and later by Thomas Forest). Others were the ten-acre Bedcote Meadow and Low Lunt further towards Lye. Atcham Meadow lay between the Stour and the land given to the Poor of Stone at Highmans Green. (On that meadow could be found the 18th-century fulling mill known as the Walk Mills.)

Buildings and other features created by humans also lent their names to fields. Barn Close or Barn Piece was a favourite name, being found in every part of the manor. Hall Close and Hall Meadow described plots in both Wollaston and Stourbridge. Churchyard Field was located near Oldswinford church, land that was eventually gobbled up by the Oxford, Worcester and Wolverhampton Railway. It is difficult to imagine how some plots received their names, for example Far Hanging Piece, Hither Beanall, Isle of Wight, Land of Nod, Mount Carmel, Rib Piece, Fenny Rough, Gincreden, Hobbydebb, and not least Humble Dumbell.

III

Tudor and Elizabethan Stourbridge

Growth in Tudor and Elizabethan Stourbridge

When Henry VII inherited the throne of England in 1485 Stourbridge was rapidly becoming an important commercial centre because of its position at a crossroads on two main routes, namely the Great North Road from Bristol and Bath to the north-west, and the pre-Telford road from North Wales to London. The Wars of the Roses had just ended and it was a troubled time for the town. As part of the return to normality, the manor of Oldswinford was restored in that year to Thomas Earl of Ormond, younger brother of James who had been beheaded 25 years earlier.[1] For Thomas this was the reward for distinguished service in the war. He was a diplomat and became a member of the king's court. The manor of Bedcote also changed hands in that same year, with the Strangeways from Dorset gaining ownership.[2]

In the following year (1486) Henry VII renewed the town's market charter, originally granted four years earlier. By that time the town of Stourbridge would have already possessed its own town hall, standing at the crossroads of the two main routes. Here a number of roads converged near the present-day town clock. The town hall rested on six pillars in the centre

---

Stourbridge through Time: 1485 to 1602

1485   Manor of Oldswinford reverts to Ormond family
1486   Henry VII renews town's charter; a town hall is built at about this time
1515   Manor of Oldswinford inherited by Anne St Leger
1538   Stourbridge has 100 messuages and 30 cottages when Richard Jervois buys Bedcote
1538   Town Hall is extended
1547   Chantry is suppressed
1552   A grammar school is re-founded with income from former chantry
1563   182 families are living in Stourbridge and Oldswinford
1564   John Lyttelton buys manor of Oldswinford
1570   A second shop is opened under the Town Hall
1578   211 families are living in Stourbridge and Oldswinford
1595   Lyttelton family in dispute with Dudley family
1602   Death of Queen Elizabeth

---

8 *The 1489 accounts of the bailiff of Oldswinford, Richard Haye. Showing receipt of rents totalling £9 1s. 3d., these Latin accounts balance to the exact halfpenny.*

of the road, leaving little space for people to pass or set up their market stalls. When the manor bailiff, Richard Haye, prepared his accounts in 1489, he would have had no idea that these would still be existence over 500 years later; they are the oldest surviving details of the administration of the town, showing total receipts of £11 10s. 2d. (including arrears of rent of 21s. 5d.). The accounts describe how rent of 5s. 4d. had been lost because tenants had deserted property during the year, at Westehaye (now Lye Waste), Lesebrugge (Ludgbridge Brook) and Oldnall Green. The bailiff received wages of one pound and handed the net receipts over to William Leicester, receiver for the Earl of Ormond.[3]

The population of Stourbridge surged in the 16th century, in line with the country as a whole which showed an increase from some 2,200,000 in 1500 to 3,600,000 in 1600. A drop in the infant mortality rate combined with the fact that couples married at an earlier age in Elizabethan times were the two main reasons for that population explosion. In 1515 Thomas, Earl of Ormond died, the manor of Oldswinford passing to his daughter Anne, the widow of Devonian Sir James St Leger. Anne's son, Sir George St Leger, inherited the manor in 1532 and his son John eventually succeeded to the title. By 1538 Stourbridge had some 100 messuages with gardens, 30 cottages, 30 tofts (land where a house had once stood), two dovecotes and two mills. Surrounding the town were 1,500 acres of pasture, meadow, heathland and woodland, including five fisheries; the rental value of the manor of Bedcote (including Stourbridge) was four pounds per annum.[4] The township area was by that time firmly established as the most important part of the manor and parish of Oldswinford and the late 16th-century historian Habington wrote 'Sturbridge is now best knowne to us by a brydge over the ryver of Sture, whearunto the towne ... extendethe it sealfe in a fayre and well inhabited street'.[5] In 1538 William Strangeways sold the manor of Bedcote and Stourbridge to Richard Jervois, who was originally a poor boy from Kidderminster but made his fortune as a mercer (a dealer in silken goods) in London and became an alderman of that city. Soon afterwards Richard Jervois paid for an extension to the old town hall, which became known as 'Mr. Gervis's Hall'. Under the town hall at ground level was a market for corn and victuals and also a shop that had first been opened by Adam Wilson, a butcher, who was paid one noble each year for maintaining the clock on the town hall building.[6]

Henry VIII's dissolution of the monasteries in 1538 naturally affected Pircote Grange, the farm belonging to Halesowen Abbey. From the beginning of the century Thomas Styler was renting Pircote Grange at a rent of 38 shillings a year, and when Henry VIII's commissioners came round greedily looking at all the monastic foundations in 1535 it was valued at 42 shillings a year. On the dissolution of the abbey Pircote Grange was granted to Sir John Dudley. Between 1569 and 1573 Thomas Elcoxe and Edmund James were repeatedly fined for illegally enclosing Pircote Grange Farm contrary to normal practices, the fine being doubled on each occasion until it reached 20 shillings.[7]

The Statute of Wills in 1540 altered the way that Stourbridge land and buildings changed hands on the death of an owner. Until then landowners had been unable to devise any part of their property by Will and thus divert it from the normal course of primogeniture (by which the eldest son was heir to the exclusion of other children), except by devious legal means that involved trusts. At that time Wills were proved in the Ecclesiastical Courts of the church, which for Stourbridge people meant a journey to Worcester. If property was held in more than one county (which happened quite often because of the geographical position of the town), the Will had to be proved at the Prerogative Court of Canterbury.

This was a time of great religious upheaval for the town as the country tried to break away from the Church of Rome. In 1547 Edward VI suppressed chantries and religious gilds. The Stourbridge chantry, which had by then existed in the lower part of the High Street for a century, was allowed to keep the part of its income that was used for educating poorer children. But the poorest residents of the town suffered, because charitable income needed to support them was lost. The townspeople also lost their local place of worship and again had to walk the mile to St Mary's, Oldswinford. In that year there were some 700 'houseling people' (i.e. of age to take communion) and 2,038 persons in total in the parish of Oldswinford.[8] In 1552, however, the buildings and income that had previously been allocated by the chantry for education were used as a base to re-found a school in the town, which was named Stourbridge Grammar School.

By now it had become normal for any individual to own land in several different legal ways. In Stourbridge of 1549 there were some 30 freeholders (who had deeds), seven copyholders (holding a copy of the court roll), three tenants by indenture and two tenants who held land merely on the say of the lord. John Bradeley owned all four types of holding. These included

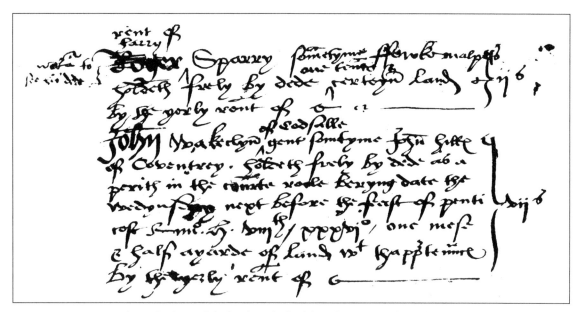

9   *A 1549 rental for lands in the lordship of Bedcote and Stourbridge.*

a freehold inn called *The George*, copyhold land in the Churchfield, land and pasture held by indenture (with a rental of the considerable sum of 40 shillings a year) and two pastures called Richards Field and Marynhome Meadow at the will of the lord. Much of his prosperity had been gained by marrying the widow of Kelland (or Kenelm) Smith who died in 1543. Similarly Thomas Hackett, William Cole, Thomas Forest, Richard Madstart and John Croft owned both freehold and copyhold land.[9]

Meanwhile the condition of the town's roads was growing steadily worse and in 1555 the great Highways Act was passed, legislation that was to last for almost three centuries. That legislation transferred the duty of maintaining roads from the lord of the manor to the parish, which every year had to appoint a Surveyor of the Highways. His main duties were to supervise the unpaid labour of the parishioners (every able-bodied person had to make himself available for four days every year or alternatively pay someone to take his place). He also had to keep records and accounts of fines and cash passing through his hands and view the roads under his control three times a year, reporting upon their condition to the nearest Justice of the Peace. His other duty was to keep a lookout for vehicles with more than the statutory number of horses. With unpaid supervisors watching over unpaid workers there was obviously no great enthusiasm to get the highways efficiently repaired; the rich avoided their duties and the poor loitered about.

In 1563 the records of the deanery showed that the number of families living in Old-swinford and Stourbridge was 182. That compared with 280 families in Halesowen and 260 in Kidderminster, although no number was quoted for Dudley as the plague was raging there at that time. In 1564 Sir John St Leger sold the manor of Oldswinford to John Lyttelton of Frankley, who was knighted two years later. A large number of new dwellings were being built in Stourbridge in Elizabethan times to accommodate the growing population. In about 1570 a second shop was allowed to open under the town hall, occupied by a draper and a mercer, but this became extremely unpopular with the townspeople who considered that it restricted the area available for the corn market. (Later in the century, on 19 March 1593, there was a minor riot during which this second shop was broken down and its timbers carried away.) Court meetings were held in the town hall's upstairs rooms, the court for Oldswinford at the northern end and the one for Bedcote at the southern end.[10] In about the year 1577 a second clock, made by a man called Watts, was installed outside the town hall and by 1578 there were some 211 heads of family in Oldswinford and Stourbridge. The count showed that the township of Stourbridge had grown into by far the largest settlement in the ancient manor by that time, containing 112 of that total. Next largest were Lye and Wollaston (29 families each), followed by Oldswinford (26) and Wollescote (15).[11] But in the last part of the century outbreaks of plague and influenza-type diseases together with the recurrence of famine again took their toll on Oldswinford inhabitants.

The Perrott family remained in Wollaston for most of the 16th century, running their watermill on the banks of the River Stour. The last Perrott with Wollaston connections was Humphrey, who sold his interests in the manor of Wollaston to George Lyddiate in 1592. Included in the deal were 20 acres of arable land, 30 acres of meadow, 100 acres of pasture and four acres of woodland in Amblecote and Kingswinford.[12] Later generations of the Perrott family moved to Fairfield (Belbroughton) and Bristol (but in 1691 John Perrott of Bristol moved back to Pedmore Hall). The hamlet of Wollaston had its own common fields. Those were merely referred to as the Wollaston Fields and were the four fields later called The Park Pieces, owned by the Foleys and covering some 20 acres near the present Kingsway. The Lyddiate family, who came from Himley, had also made their fortune in London, in this case as merchant tailors. The family bore arms of 'gules a fesse erminous between three wolves' heads or, cut off at neck'. John Lyddiate, the son of George, was a scythesmith with mills at Greensforge and Himley as well as at Wollaston. He was a very violent and troublesome man, who was often presented at court for such matters as assaulting the constable, wounding people in fights, filling in tenants' wells and blocking their rights of way. By his Will he bequeathed the manor of Wollaston to his son John for life, and then to 'such son of this said son who should be of best behaviour'; his character was obviously passed on to his descendants.

In Wollescote the Cardells were still the most important family at the start of the Tudor period. The senior line died out in about 1504 following the death of John Cardell. Elizabeth, the daughter of John and Cecily Cardell, married William Milward, the first of a long line of Milwards to live at Wollescote and its hall. Wollescote also had common fields that were called the Wolscot Feldes.

Roads, Gatehouses and Bridges
The major north to south route was Stourbridge High Street, running from the bridge over the Stour right up to the Town Gate in the street now named Hagley Road; High Street was only divided into Upper and Lower in the 19th century. The name of this road is certainly very ancient; in 1549 one Leonard Bere owned one cottage in the 'Hie Street'.[13] It is possible that at that time the lower part of the street was named Digbeth (meaning a watery site).[14] Because of its importance, Stourbridge

High Street was already paved by the 16th century, as it was decreed that 'all those living be-tween the Town Gate and the house of Thomas Jeston shall swill the pavement and the street every Friday and Lords Day to a distance of four feet in front of his house'. The street had a channel or 'gutter' that ran down its centre, which in parts left only six feet on either side for pedestrians to pass, an area that was often further reduced by traders' stalls being erected in that space. Regulations were frequently passed to deal with this situation, such as the following ordinance in May 1593:

> that no tradesman or anyone coming to the town with merchandise to sell shall erect any stall less than six feet from each side of the gutter under penalty of 6s. 8d. for the stallholder and 20s. 0d. for the bailiff or constable or tythingman if they fail to see that this order is obeyed.

Other main thoroughfares running from west to east from the central town hall were Crown Lane and Coventry Street (which led to the important medieval city of that name). Crown Lane, by now the main route from the west, was named after the ancient *Crown Inn* that stood on the south side of the road. The lane was reputed to have been so narrow that it was impossible for two wheeled vehicles to pass each other, and so low opposite the *New Inn* that one had to climb three steps from the street to enter the houses. Coventry Street was also a very ancient name, being the subject of an ordinance in 1575 that stated that 'no one shall throw ashes into the street called Coventry Street'. A further ordinance of 1595 ordained that 'all residents in the street called Coventry Street shall swill and from time to time keep in order the roads before their houses under pain of 3s. 4d.' Coventry Street continued into another ancient road called Bedcote Lane (now Birmingham Street), a name appearing in the 1549 rental of Bedcote manor.[15]

Two other roads converging on the old town hall also date from as long ago as the 16th century. Market Street, from the High Street to the present ring road, was called Rye Mar-ket because it was from there that dealings in corn took place. New Street, which has now disappeared under the 20th-century Crown Centre, was probably built in Elizabethan times, despite its name. Other historical street names which dated back to this era included Swinford Street (possibly Hagley Road) and Le Clyff (mentioned in 1590), an ancient highway with cave dwellings on one side, and a continuation of Mill Street which ran close to the Stour. Giles Hill, a passageway leading off Lower High Street, was also in existence at that time as was Angel Street (there was a Stourbridge inn called *Le Aingle* owned by Alan Wilson on his death in 1614).

Like many other medieval towns, Stourbridge had gates and gatehouses that guarded strategic approach roads, but it is probable that they had all disappeared by the end of the 17th century. On the highway from Kidderminster, near the present entrance to Mary Stevens Park at The Heath, stood Studley Gate. At an Oldswinford manor court held in 1583 the in-habitants of Stourbridge were ordered to repair their hedges between a house in Le Lane End and the Stodellgate. The gate marked the boundary between Bedcote and Oldsminford and later lent its name to Studley Court.[16] (The whole area was known as Heath Gate by the mid-19th century because it guarded the entrance to The Heath.) At the southern end of the township of Stourbridge, standing over the way into the old Middle Field, stood Le Stretegate (also known as the Town Gate). At a court sitting on 7 December 1573 John Bradeley was fined

10   *Old cottages in New Street in 1955, which were demolished when the ring road was constructed in 1968.*

11 *The Heath in c.1900, looking from Norton Road and the White Horse Inn towards Oldswinford and Stourbridge. This was the site of the medieval Stodell Gate and the later turnpike gate.*

for not sufficiently looking after that gate. At the opposite end of the town lay Le Stower Gate.[17] This might have been on the same site as the *Old Vine Inn*, adjacent to Stourbridge Grammar School, or more likely at the bottom of Lower High Street. Oldswinford also had its own gatehouses. Poulter's Gatehouse stood at the junction of Hagley Road and Worcester Lane at the boundary with Pedmore manor, although the exact site has never been proved. To complete the picture, Oldnall Gate stood on the old Halesowen road at the eastern edge of the parish boundary.

Known roads in other parts of Oldswinford at that time included the present Church Road (probably the Parsonage Lane referred to in 1582).[18] Rufford Road and Hungary Hill were called Robache Lane. Edward Bradeley was presented for not cleaning out his ditches 'in a lane called Robache Lane between a close called Ridggrove and a close called Hassold Fields'.[19] Grange Lane was known as Priests Lane for many years (a reference to the fact that it led from Pircote Grange to the abbey at Halesowen). In April 1592 Richard Mannsell was fined for not maintaining his ditches in Priests Lane at Le Lake.[20] (The name remained unchanged until the early 20th century.) Wollescote Road was known as The Churchway in Elizabethan times. It was ordained in December 1573 that 'no one shall throw into the Church Way from the house of Thomas Milward to the Gall Butts any dead dogs, cats, pigs or any other animal corpses'. Local journeys were quite hazardous at that time!

A bridge existed across the Stour at the bottom of Dudley Road Lye; it was jointly maintained by the parishes of Oldswinford and Kingswinford, which caused problems as seen in a presentment to the Worcester Quarter Sessions:

> Robarte Sheppard of the Lie in the parish of Old Swinford, shupraviser for the kinges hiewayes, presents that ... there is a bridge that is in decay, the one halfe in the parishe of Kingeswinford in the countie of Stafford, and the other halfe in the parishe of Old Swinford in the countie of Woster, which they muste mend the one halfe and we the other.

Other named bridges known to exist in that period were Lusbridge across Shepherds Brook, Wyldeybridge across the Stour[21] and the bridge across the Withybrook at the Enville Street boundary between Wollaston and Bedcote. (*Katie FitzGerald's* Inn is on the opposite side of Mamble Road to an establishment once called the Bridge Inn.)

Common Fields

The fields dominating the landscape of Oldswinford and Stourbridge consisted of long open areas of land divided into furlongs (originally a furrow length). These rectangular blocks were further sub-divided into selions, strips of land with a furrow on either side, each one theoretically capable of being ploughed in one day. This was the basis of the common field system and once a year at Michaelmas (29 September) inhabitants were allocated a certain number of strips by lot. Each field was normally subject to crop rotation consisting of wheat, rye and barley. In the 16th century most Stourbridge inhabitants held land in the common fields. For example, in 1550 it was noted that:

> Richard Madstart held by a free copie as aperith in the said courte roole (4 May 1541) eight dayes earth of arable landes lying in the Commen Feldes, and because that copie was contrary to the custom, he hath taken yt new agayn of the lord by copie for three lyves as aperith in the courte roolle wrytan in paper dated 19 day of September anno 1548 by the yearly rent of 2s. 6d.

The customs of the manor dating back to time immemorial were always very important in regulating the daily life of the manor.

Each hamlet of Stourbridge had its own set of common fields at that time. In Oldswinford itself the largest field lay between Heath Lane and The Quarry on the Pedmore boundary, across which Love Lane was later constructed. This was known in early days as the Old Field, but in the 16th century it was renamed the Middle Field. Even by Tudor times part of this common field had been enclosed and built upon, as in an indenture of 1539 William Poulter granted to Roger Kyndon a furlong of ground in the 'mydulfyld stretching upon the quarry' and one close of land 'with houses built upon', also in the common field. It is probable that another common field for Oldswinford was situated on Chawn Hill; here in 1539 Roger Kyndon was granted four buttes of ground in 'Chawnehill Fyld' and 'three dayes earth of ground in the same field upon Chawnehill'. Finally there was a common field known as Church Field, situated to the east of Red Hill between the present Red Hill Close and Junction Road (a field now crossed by the Stourbridge town railway line). That latter field was probably shared with Bedcote manor as it stretched down to the top end of Stourbridge High Street. Church Field was mentioned in 1549 when William Cole and John Bradeley owned land in it. [22] (A century later George Winchurst and others were persistently presented and fined for wrongfully enclosing the Churchfields 'neere unto the Hanginge Acre'.)

Bedcote manor also had a Middle Field (not to be confused with the one in Oldswinford) situated between Hagley Road and Red Hill. At one time that was also called Oakefield. Another well-known Bedcote common field was Catherwell Field. That covered the area between Hagley Road and Worcester Street and was probably named after a spring on the ground that had once been known as St Catherine's Well. The field was referred to in 1539 as bordering upon a quarry, probably the same 'old quarry' that was marked near Worcester Street on the first Ordnance Survey map published in 1882. By the end of the 16th century the common field system was coming to an end and much of the land had been broken up into individual plots. (Three open fields in neighbouring Amblecote manor were enclosed in 1576.)[23] Two Oldswinford common fields did survive into the following century, namely the Middle Field that stretched from Heath Lane to the Pedmore boundary and the Church Field on the eastern side of Red Hill, although in the 18th century the last remaining strips did disappear.

Major Families

In the 16th century individual residents of Stourbridge began to be recorded in more detail. A complete revaluation of property for taxation purposes was carried out in 1522. The local constable had to prepare a written survey of all men over the age of 16, the yearly value of each man's land, his livestock and the names of all strangers in the town, the place where they were born and their occupations. The so-called Loan that resulted from this survey fell

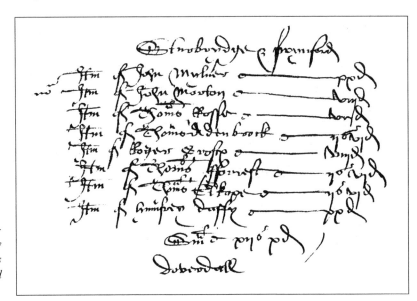

12 *The 1546 Loving Contri-*
bution taxation raised by Henry
VIII, showing the contributions
of Stourbridge and Swinford
residents.

upon all those who possessed wealth of five pounds or above, but unfortunately no written details have survived for Stourbridge. The subsequent Great Subsidy in 1524 engulfed every local worker, with even the lowest wage earner having to pay fourpence. Despite this, one third of the population escaped because they did not have any earned income at all at that time. Various poetic names were given to the subsidies of the next few years, examples being the Amicable Grant in 1525, the Devotion Money in 1543, the Benevolence in 1545 and the Loving Contribution in 1546.[24] The eight Stourbridge and Swinford inhabitants who made their contributions in that year were Thomas Addenbrooke, Thomas Forest and Thomas Elcox (paying 2s. 6d. each); John Milner and Humphrey Duffy (1s. 8d. each); John Morton, Thomas Ross and Roger Croft (8d. each).

From 1569 through to 1643 an almost continuous series of the Oldswinford manor court rolls have survived.[25] Families mentioned in the first 50 years included Archbold, Baker, Bradeley, Brettell, Cartwright, Cole, Croft, Darby, Elcox, Forest, Grove, Hart, Hornblower, Madstard, Malpas, Maunsell, Milner, Parkes, Raby, Ratclyffe, Sparry, Steward, Tailor, Tomson, Tyrer, Webb, Wheeler, White and Wildsmith (in addition to those earlier surnames mentioned on page 17). In 1538 Thomas Cromwell ordered all churches to keep a book of weddings, baptisms and burials (to be entered up each Sunday after Divine Service). Unfortunately the early registers of Oldswinford disappeared many years ago and the earliest surviving entry is for 1602. From the 1540s onwards inventories attached to original Wills for many Stourbridge persons can still be found, which describe their personal belongings room by room.[26] Inventories made before 1550 survive for Thomas Northall, Nicholas Ratclyffe, Kenelm Smyth, William Osborne, Christianne Darby, Elenore Warner, Thomas Ekulsall, Thomas Green and William Cole, all of Stourbridge, and for Thomas Warner, Edward Raby and Henry Perks of Oldswinford.[27] It is interesting that eight of the above inventories were made in the year 1544, indicating that there might have been some major outbreak of disease in that year. In 1578 the most common Stourbridge surname was Hart, represented by nine families. This was followed by Wall (six families), Beare, Pearson, Smith, Wildsmith and Wilson (four families each), and Bradeley, Briscoe, Cole, Cox, Hill, Lea, Perkes, Taylor and Wakelam (three families for each name). The spelling of surnames obviously varied, depending upon the clerk making the entry. A final 'e' was still to be found on many local surnames at that time (for example Darbye, Dunne, Mannerynge, Rownde and Skeldinge). Also any name ending in 'brook' was usually written as 'broke'.

The families influential in 16th-century Stourbridge affairs can be determined by looking at the land they owned and the offices they served (for example as churchwardens, constables, chairmen of the manor court jury, and governors of the local grammar school). The Addenbrooke family was a major force, creating wealth from mills along the river Stour. As early as 1525 John Addenbrooke was leasing a watermill (called Cradley Mill) in the adjoining parish to Lye.[28] The Lye Addenbrookes ran a mill on the site of the ancient Lye Forge and the two mills were under common ownership for many years. There was a Thomas Addenbrooke (the son of George of Romsley) on the jury of the Oldswinford court held in 1529,[29] who became one of the first governors of Stourbridge Grammar School in 1552. When Thomas died in 1555, Fulk Addenbrooke, one of his five sons, also became a governor of the school, and he in turn was succeeded on his death in 1583 by his son Thomas (1530-98), a miller who married Eleanor

Sparry of Clent. The next generation of Addenbrookes, represented by Thomas's son Henry (who died in 1618), was assessed for 10s. 8d. in 1603, the largest recorded amount in the local subsidy of that year. He owned coal and clay rights in addition to two mills within the manor (one of which was Stanbourne Mill in Stambermill and the other Lye Mill in Dudley Road).

The Hornblowers were another influential family, being scythesmiths by profession. William Hornblower was chairman of the manor jury in no less than eight different years between 1569 and 1594. The Bradeley family of Oldswinford also owned substantial tracts of land in both town and parish; their land included a croft called Hobbgrene and a freehold inn called *The George* in Stourbridge. The Elcoxe family was equally influential. Thomas Elcoxe, who lived in Coventry Street in Stourbridge, owned Green Close next to the chantry chapel and was also one of the original governors of the grammar school. The family possessed land in more than one diocese because in 1567 Thomas's Will was proved in the Prerogative Court of Canterbury.[30] Thomas' son, also called Thomas, was fined heavily several times between 1569 and 1573 for wrongfully enclosing Pircote Grange but eventually became law-abiding, being appointed bailiff of the manor in about 1591. In about 1600 he sold part of Green Close for an extension to the grammar school, but soon afterwards the family disappeared from the town. Another major landowner was the Darby family, who were recorded buying land in Oldnall in 1581 and 1583.[31]

Living Conditions and Treatment of the Poor

Wealthier inhabitants of Stourbridge in the mid-16th century continued to accumulate many more possessions than their forebears would have owned. The main room of a house at that time was the hall, in which were found table boards, forms, cushions, stools, benches, cupboards and painted cloths and canvases. The buttery and kitchen contained such implements as pewter dishes, brass kettles, skillets, pottingers, frying pans, treen platters, saucers, silver spoons, cauldrons, pot hooks, tongs, bellows, fire shovels, shaving knives, wooden tubs, pails and buckets. The chambers were furnished with feather and flock beds, bolsters and mattresses, blankets, flaxen or hemp sheets, with carpets on the walls. Also dispersed around these houses were coffers, chests, candlesticks and an occasional spinning wheel with its wool cards. In the clothing closet could be found coats, doublets, hoses, shoes, caps, shirts, jackets, gowns, petticoats, hoods and girdles.[32]

At the other extreme the number of poorer inhabitants in need of help multiplied rapidly. This was partly due to an increase in the population (caused by couples marrying at an earlier age and a fall in the infant death rate) and partly to the increasing frequency of famine and epidemics. The biggest blow was the loss of relief after the suppression of the monasteries in 1538 and the chantries and religious gilds in 1547. The effect of the disappearance of the monasteries was probably not too great, as by that time their charitable donations, representing at the most two to three per cent of their total income, were being frittered away in indiscriminate alms. Even their hospitals were in disrepute. The loss of the chantry and gild revenues had a far more drastic effect. All the income from those institutions, apart from that used for educational purposes, was diverted into non-charitable hands, and that left no other major source of funds for helping the poor.

The alternative source for raising money for the poor now became the parish, which was beginning to take on civil as well as ecclesiastical responsibilities. In 1535/6 an Act made the parish responsible for the impotent poor. The priest and churchwardens had to procure charitable donations on a Sunday. Private alms to beggars were forbidden under penalty of 10 times the amount given. In 1563 limited powers were given to magistrates to compel generous giving, and each parish had to appoint two or more collectors of charitable alms. Nine years later the office of Overseer of the Poor was created, although in Stourbridge the term Collector of the Poor survived for another 100 years. Four successive summers of atrocious weather, commencing in 1594, caused terrible famine and corn prices to soar. There followed the famous Poor Laws of 1597/8 and 1601, by which it became compulsory for the parish to appoint overseers, maintain and provide work for paupers and apprentice the children of the poor to masters wherever possible. The income to pay for this came from a separate rate levy on landowners, as well as from tithes and fines. The changed circumstances following the Reformation did, however, stimulate alternative forms of private charity. Many one-off bequests were made in the Wills of Stourbridge people. Richard Cole, who died in 1552, bequeathed four nobles (a coin worth approximately 13s. 4d.) 'to bring me to my grave and to be dolt and geven to the pore people'. Such amounts were given out at the funeral service to the poor who stood by the lychgate. A large amount of money was also raised by 'church ales' (a form of religious carnival during which bells were rung, minstrels performed and dancing, drinking and general merriment took place). The church brewed the ale for the occasion from ingredients supplied by parishioners.

Manor Administration

The authority and power of the lord of the manor was organised in the Stourbridge area through the offices of a number of local officials working for the manor courts. The lord's deputy was called the Steward, an office held by Walter Chance in Oldswinford in the late 16th century. The Bailiff looked after monetary and secretarial matters; it was he who collected the fines meted out by the courts, and guarded and sealed the standard weights and measures used for trading in the market place. These measures included an iron ell, a brazen pound, half and quarter pounds, a bushel and half bushel, a peck and half peck, and quart, pint and half-pint pots. Thomas Elcoxe was a well-known holder of this office in the late 16th century.

One of the most difficult offices to serve was that of the Constable. In earlier years this official was appointed by the manor court, but later by the parish vestry. Amongst the varied duties of the Oldswinford constable were:

> looking after the parish armour; he could not allow this to go outside the bounds of the parish without the consent of six inhabitants (under threat of a fine of 20 shillings);

> supervising the provision of watch and ward and dealing with any unrest in the manor; he could raise the hue and cry, calling for assistance from any inhabitant, but was often the subject of an assault himself;

> supervising the stocks, whipping posts, ducking stools and other sundry means of punishing offenders within the manor;

> apprehending and flogging vagabonds, prior to accompanying them on their way to the next parish;

> controlling papists and nonconformists, and reporting any persons who failed to turn up at church on a Sunday to the Quarter Sessions.

The local Stourbridge militia had to draw their armour from the parish chest in Old-swinford church. As early as 1477 an Act had been passed requiring the local population to practise their archery on a Sunday. In the reign of Henry VIII the local militia was in its infancy, and Oldswinford could only muster eight archers plus 12 other able-bodied men, of whom only four could supply their own horse and harness. The Oldswinford practice area in the early 16th century was situated in a field referred to as Le Buttes (or Le Hallbuttes) in Wollescote, probably close to the main residence of the Milwards.[33] The constable could call upon deputies in each hamlet to help him (they were called tithingmen in Oldswinford; tithingmen were originally part of a group of 10 men who were mutually responsible for the behaviour of each other and the name continued even though the custom of communal guilt was obsolete by that time).

Another officer called the Reeve looked after the cultivation of arable land, and he in turn could call for help from others such as the Hayward (who tended the woods and meadows) and the Pindar (who kept the pound for stray animals). In the market place could be found the Ale and Victual taster, the Inspector and Sealer of Leather, the Clerk of the Market and the Bellman (the tasks of these officials are described in chapter VII). Each manorial office holder had to appear at the manor court once every three weeks to give an account of any infringements of the manor rules. They also had to ensure that the accused persons actually turned up in court.

The appointment of the Oldswinford manorial officials took place annually at the Court Leet in September or October. The ale and victual taster was automatically promoted to the office of Constable in the year following his original appointment. Up to 1575 only two tith-ingmen were appointed each year, one being responsible for Lye, Wollescote and Oldnall, and the other for the town of Stourbridge and hamlets of Swinford and Wollaston. From 1576 the court elected five tithingmen, responsible respectively for the town, and the hamlets of Swin-ford, Lye, Wollescote and Wollaston. (In 1611 it became the normal practice to appoint two tithingmen for Stourbridge itself, again demonstrating the growing importance of the town as compared to Oldswinford and the other hamlets.) The Constable and ale tasters were chosen from the town of Stourbridge every other year, with the hamlets taking it in turn to provide a person in the intervening years.

The meetings of the Oldswinford Court Baron took place twice a year (at Easter and at Michaelmas) and various administrative matters were dealt with, ranging from the transfer of land to the proclamation of various ordinances concerning the inhabitants as a whole. A jury of some 15 local persons would be sworn in to give their verdicts and to assess fines. The Court Leet was held every three weeks to deal with minor offences. There was a complete breakdown in the manor court system after the second Court Baron in 1595 due to violent dis-putes between the Lyttelton and Dudley families, and that state of affairs appeared to last until 1609, no doubt producing much chaos in the area. The court sessions were held in Poulter's Gatehouse at Oldswinford up to 1564, the year in which Sir John Lyttelton bought the manor of Oldswinford and transferred the venue to the upper rooms of the town hall in Stourbridge.[34]

The unseemly antics of Stourbridge inhabitants in Tudor times included Richard Dones' eavesdropping under people's windows at night, thereby breeding 'stryfe and disorder among-ste hys naybors', Eleanor Hart of Lye 'misbehayving her tonge', and the theft of clothes that

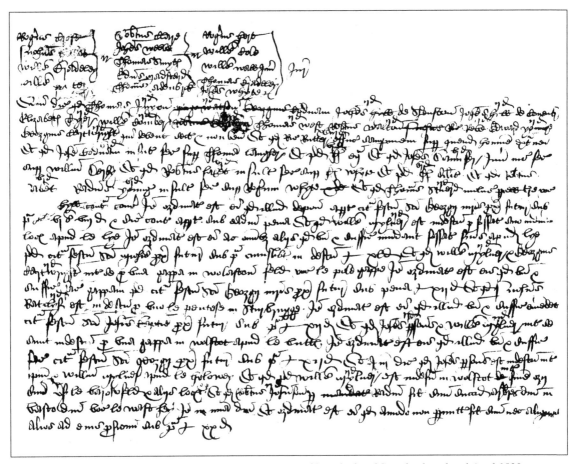

13   *The earliest surviving court roll for the manors of Swinford and Stourbridge, dated April 1529.*

were hanging on hedges. Numerous individuals were accused of assaulting each other in the town, being generally rowdy and playing illicit games such as bowls and loggats (a form of skittle-pins). In April 1578 a group of supporters of the Sparry family of Clent were accused of coming to Stourbridge market place to seek trouble with the servants of John Grey, during which they uttered the words 'yf any of them be in towne he will be slapped on the lippes'. Luckily no serious affray did take place on that occasion. Even the incumbents of Oldswinford church found themselves in trouble from time to time; Richard Mauncell was fined several times in the 1570s for playing cards and dice at a house party. The anti-gaming ordinances were very unpopular as 44 householders were fined at just one court sitting in 1585 for such offences (ten were playing backgammon, five bowls and 29 dice and cards).

One very troublesome Stourbridge family was the Madstard clan. An Edward Madstard came before the manor court as early as 1529 when he was fined for selling fish at an excessive price. Thomas Madstard, who died in 1587, was a mercer.[35] His son Richard (also a mercer) was actually referred to as 'Madstarke alias Starkmad' when he was sworn in as constable in October 1590. This reputation was apparently well earned, for he was a violent and unpredictable man. In one incident in March 1593 he pulled down a cobbler's shop that he claimed had been illegally erected under Stourbridge town hall. A later court recorded that Richard Madstard had made an encroachment on the High Street of Stourbridge when he dug up soil and erected posts, benches and stalls to the nuisance of passers-by. In September 1594 he brought a famous court case against Gilbert Lyttelton, a wild man himself and son of lord of the manor, Sir John. The case concerned the alleged mismanagement of Stourbridge Grammar School by certain governors and the wrongdoings of its masters, in particular Richard Allchurch who had been dismissed from the school in October 1590 for wrongfully selling ale but who was backed by several Stourbridge traders. The commissioners, appointed by the Council of the Marches of Wales, met in the church at Kidderminster, various witnesses being called who gave a graphic account of life in Stourbridge at that time.[36]

Punishment by the manor courts took a variety of forms. Sometimes a fine would be levied, assessed by two officers called Afferers. The standard fine for an assault was sixpence, but this was often increased by the value of the weapon actually used in the assault! At other times the punishment would be physical with the use of stocks or pillories (in which the offender was secured upright), and for the ladies a ducking in the goomstools or cuckingstools. The town stocks had been a common sight from at least the early 15th century, when every village and town had to provide them by law; they were sited near the lychgate of Oldswinford church and in the market place in Stourbridge. In October 1582 the inhabitants of Oldswinford were ordered to provide a goomstool and pillory, for which the lord of the manor had to donate the necessary timber. The stocks often had their locks smashed and could even be physically removed by drunken inhabitants, but each time they were faithfully rebuilt. Offenders were often left in the Stourbridge stocks for three whole days and nights, but in 1604 Nicholas Craftes had been there for only four or five hours when one of his friends broke open the stocks and rescued him. The friend was then arrested by the Constable, who was in turn assaulted by a woman described as 'the chief maintainer of many vices in our town'. If the court had to remove the liberty of a Stourbridge inhabitant on a longer-term basis, he was led down the six stone steps into one of two dungeons under the old town hall, with only a bundle of straw for his comfort.

The lord of the manor could claim the goods of any felon living within his precincts (this was called the right of escheat). An example occurred at Stourbridge in October 1580. John Berde, late of Stourbridge, had been hanged for murder at Leicester, and the Oldswinford manor jury was required to testify regarding his possessions. These were listed as 'a cubbarde, chyre, foure treen platters, a coffer, a peyre of bedstedes, an earthen chafyngedishe, a hande-yron, a staffe, a canvas, a fyer shovle, a payle beinge a gallon, a cutting borde, a form and an olde coveringe'. It was also a felony to take one's own life, so when John Moore hanged himself at Oldswinford, his goods valued at 7s. 11d. were forfeited by the Constable.[37]

IV

The Seventeenth Century in Stourbridge

Life before the Civil War

The beginning of the 17th century saw exciting events taking place in Stourbridge, when the town was briefly involved in a national plot. On 8 November 1605 the escaping traitors involved in the Gunpowder Plot arrived at Holbeach House some five miles north of the town; the house was then owned by Stephen Lyttelton. When the law caught up with them, Robert Winter was shot through the arm by a crossbow bolt, but escaped with Stephen Lyttelton and they were both eventually captured at Hagley some weeks later. Thomas Percy was also shot at Holbeach by a musket ball, dying three days later from his wound. Other less fortunate individuals were captured alive at Holbeach and taken to Stourbridge gaol before being removed to the Tower

---

Stourbridge through Time: 1602 to 1714

1605	Gunpowder plotters gaoled at Stourbridge
*c.*1610	First foreign glassmakers start production at Stourbridge
1617	Wollaston Hall is built
1625	Nicholas Sparry purchases manor of Bedcote; almshouses built in High Street
1627	Richard Foley moves to Stourbridge from Dudley
1642	Prince Rupert stays in Stourbridge with Richard Foley during Civil War
1643	Prince Rupert makes Wollescote Hall his headquarters
1651	Charles II flees through town after Battle of Worcester
1661	Thomas Foley purchases manor of Oldswinford
1665	Plague in the town
1666	First Quaker Meeting House in Scott's Road
1667	Thomas Foley founds Old Swinford Hospital
*c.*1690	The Heath Glassworks built
1696	A new south aisle is built onto St Mary's Church
1698	The Independents build their first chapel on corner of Coventry Street
1699	Oldest surviving survey of manor of Oldswinford
1700	A new rectory is built at St Mary's
1711	First mention of annual horse-racing week at Stourbridge
1714	Death of Queen Anne

---

in London to await their terrible fate. One Wollaston resident eventually benefited from the events; it is recorded that Mr. Lyddiate bought valuable timber from Holbeach House after the subsequent investigation into Stephen Lyttelton's title, and that was probably used some ten years later on the construction of the new Wollaston Hall.

The population of Stourbridge in the 17th century continued to suffer from the natural phenomena of famine and plague, although no records appear to have survived to enable one to estimate the overall number of persons or families living in Stourbridge during the early years of the century. The wealthiest inhabitants at that time can be seen from a lay subsidy taxation roll of 1603. Henry Addenbrooke (land valued at £4), Thomas Milward (£3), Edward Bradley, Thomas Walton, Thomas White and Widow Wakeley (£1 10s. each), with William Horneblower and Richard Bradley (£1 each) were the major landowners in the area. In addition Richard Wheeler, Richard White, Owen Foster, Edward Best, Nicholas Baker, John Sparry, Thomas Harrison, Richard Smart, John Hassould and John Rock each had goods valued at £3 each.

The influence of the Addenbrooke family over Stourbridge affairs declined in the 17th century. Henry Addenbrooke's widow (née Gertrude Spratt) became associated with the glass industry when she leased land called Colemans to Paul Tyzack, the first glass manufacturer to set up at Stourbridge in c.1610. One of Henry's nine sons, Nicholas Addenbrooke (born 1603), married into the Sparry family and sold much of the family land to the Foley family in mid-century. Nicholas's brother, Roger Addenbrooke (1612-71), married Ann Brettell in 1639 and went to live in Kingswinford. It was he who was the father of John Addenbrooke BA (1652-1724), who made an endowment and gave his name to the famous hospital at Cambridge. The senior line of the Addenbrooke family might have died out altogether in the following century if Mary, the daughter of Jeremiah Addenbrooke (who in turn was a grandson of Roger) had not married John Homfray in 1758. Their son eventually took up the arms and name of Addenbrooke as a condition of his inheritance.

By the early years of the 17th century the Sparry and Baker families had reached the peak of their influence on Stourbridge affairs. In the previous century the Sparry family had acquired fame when Roger Sparry of Clent (1504-48) was Yeoman of the Bedchamber to Henry VIII; he acquired property in Stourbridge from Fulk Malpas in 1518, although he never apparently lived there. Roger Sparry, a mercer and the first of his family to live in the Stourbridge area, was probably descended from a brother of that Roger of Clent. Both Roger of Stourbridge, who died in 1601, and his son John, who died in 1643 (also a mercer), were governors of Stourbridge Grammar School. As described on page 46, John Sparry conveyed almshouses in Stourbridge High Street to a charity in 1632.[1] John's eldest son Nicholas, who purchased the manor of Bedcote in 1626, was also of a charitable disposition, giving back to the grammar school the chantry chapel in Stourbridge High Street. This made amends for the fact that it had escheated to the lord of the manor some years earlier due to an unfortunate legal error. As soon as Nicholas Sparry had bought the manor of Bedcote its court meetings were merged with those of Oldswinford. Nicholas's brother Ambrose Sparry was a dissenting minister at Wolverhampton and Martley before returning to take the post of headmaster of Stourbridge Grammar School, first serving in office from 1633 to 1648. In November 1651 he became involved in the Pakington Plot, when Sir John Pakington made false accusations against local Presbyterians in the area. He was imprisoned for a time, but was able to take up the Stourbridge headmastership for a second term from 1666 to 1675, dying in 1679. Another brother, Edward, carried on the family business as a mercer in the town.

The Baker family was similarly involved in the running of Stourbridge Grammar School at that time. The earliest mention of the family in 1529 is of a Nicholas Baker, who was a smith and had substantial possessions in Oldswinford and Bedcote.[2] Many subsequent members of his family were governors of the school, including Nicholas (c.1552-1604), the latter's nephews Gregory and John, and grandson John who died in 1678. Another of Nicholas's grandsons was the Reverend Joseph Baker MA who was headmaster of Stourbridge Grammar School from 1648 to 1651 and died in 1668 aged 42. Joseph's second wife was a wealthy lady named Anne Swynfen and the couple are commemorated by a monumental inscription on the west wall of the nave of Oldswinford church. The terms of his Will created Joseph Baker's Exhibition, a charity that was implemented from 1692 until it was merged with other grammar school charities in 1876. Later in the century a mercer called Richard Baker provided a Quaker Meeting House for Stourbridge dissenters at the rear of his house in Coventry Street. The Baker family later moved to Hertfordshire.

The most notable family event in the 17th century was the meteoric rise of the Foleys from the status of small yeomen nailers at its commencement to immensely wealthy gentry owning vast estates of land in Herefordshire, Worcestershire and Staffordshire by its end. The founder of this great fortune was Richard Foley (1580-1657). Born in Dudley, where he was mayor in 1616, he moved to Stourbridge in 1627, in which year he bought a tenement from John Sparry, probably the Brick House in Stourbridge High Street (now the *Talbot Inn*).[3] In the same year he leased Hyde House near Kinver for 21 years, and by 1629 had built an engine house and slitting mill there, being the first machine in the area capable of slitting iron for nail rods. In 1630 he acquired the manor of Bedcote from Nicholas Sparry. He is said to have acquired the nickname of Fiddler Foley, supposedly having twice disguised himself as an itinerant musician to acquire industrial secrets from Sweden. His second wife was Alice, the daughter of William Brindley of The Hyde near Kinver. From the huge profits he amassed during the Civil War, he continued to purchase large amounts of land in the Stourbridge area, much of it from the Addenbrooke family. He was buried in Oldswinford church in July 1657.

A group of families whose wealth was based on the cloth industry began to make their mark in 17th-century Stourbridge. Best known amongst these was the family of Hickman who lived in Kinver during the 16th century. John Hickman was a clothworker who died in May 1623 leaving 20 shillings for the poor of the town of Stourbridge. Richard Hickman who died in 1657 owned houses on Yearnborough Hill. He had the satisfaction of seeing all his daughters marry successfully, one to Benjamin Newbrough (a wealthy Dudley clothier), another to Edward Jeston (another clothier of Stourbridge), and a third daughter to John Tristram, a Belbroughton physician. Richard's son Edward married Dorothy Addenbrooke (whose mother was a Sparry), and so the Hickmans became related to just about every other important Stourbridge family. Richard's grandson Gregory Hickman (1651-90) settled in Green Close House, which was on the site of the 20th-century grammar school library in Lower High Street. It was that Gregory's son, another Gregory (1688-1748), who purchased a large piece of land in Lye from the Addenbrooke family, ground that became very valuable for its fine clay and was to provide a basis for the family fortune from the brickmaking industry later in the 19th century.

14 *The Hemplands and Round Court near the town centre; these interesting buildings were formerly used by the town's clothiers and were demolished in 1911.*

Other clothing personalities included Jasper Newbrough who moved from Dudley to Stourbridge at the same time as the Foleys.[4] Both families became associated with the management of ironworks at Wolverley in the 1660s. The Scott family began their association with Stourbridge in 1667 when John, a yeoman farmer of Chaddesley Corbett, moved to the town. His son William was a clothier and his grandson William was an original trustee of the dissenting congregation in Stourbridge. In later years a third generation named William (1698-1766) married into the Hunt family, leased the Town Mill in 1734 and converted it into a fulling mill. The Jeston family originated from Kinver and became haberdashers, bedders, clothiers and upholsterers. Roger Jeston, who died in 1622, built up a large personal fortune in London as a member of the Haberdashers' Company. The family was actively buying up land in Oldswinford just before the Civil War, including land at The Heath. On one and the same day in December 1681 John Jeston married Mary, the daughter of Paul Henzey, and Edward Jeston's daughter Rose married Edward Henzey, thus establishing the Jeston association with the glass industry.

The other striking change to the family make-up of Stourbridge was the arrival of several wealthy but secretive immigrant glassmakers. During the first years of the century the parish registers record a number of foreign-sounding surnames in their pages. These belonged to men from Lorraine who had been tempted to England during the previous century to practise their secret skills of glassmaking. In the early 17th century they had been forced to use pit coal rather than the dwindling supplies of wood for their production and the area between Stourbridge and Kingswinford was ideal for their purposes. Names such as Francis Conculyn, Peregrin Henzey, Jacob de Howe, Daniel Tittery, Zachary Tyzack and Jeremiah Bago began to be scattered amongst the entries in the registers.

Paul Tyzack, the first glassmaker to arrive in Stourbridge, was descended from the noble family of Du Thisac who left the woods of Bohemia in the early 15th century and trekked to the Darney Forest in the Vosges mountains of France. Paul had a reputation as an honest and just-dealing person, but is said on one occasion during the Civil War to have had all his deeds stolen by soldiers. He died in 1665 and his son Paul made a good marriage to Joyce, the daughter of John Lyddiate of Wollaston Hall. Joshua Henzey (1600-60) a member of another major glass family, married red-haired Joan Brettell (1590-1672) in 1618 and set up a works across the Stourbridge boundary at Amblecote. His son Paul Henzey (1627-93) married Ann Tyzack and was churchwarden at Oldswinford for the 1672/3 year, an occasion he celebrated by having his initials inscribed in gold leaf in the church registers. Later female members of the Henzey family intermarried with the Jestons, Pidcocks and Dixons who were only too willing to carry on the glassmakers' art when the Henzey male line died out. Some other fine foreign craftsmen also appeared in the registers later in the century. From 1644 onwards these included the oddly named Julius Caesar Rackett (a member of the Rachetti family from the province of Mantua in the Lombardy area of Italy), Abraham, Jacob and Benjamin Visitalias in the 1650s and Onesiphorus Dagnia in the 1670s; all these were skilled in making glass vessels rather than broad glass.

Wollaston Hall, where the Wheelers and other local families lived for some years, was one of the most beautiful homes in the area and typical of the way the upper classes adorned their houses and gardens. The half-timbered house had a date of 1617 carved upon one of its gables, but was built on the site of an earlier building from which only a castellated tower

15 *Wollaston Hall, c.1905. This picturesque building was constructed in 1617 and demolished during the 1920s.*

remained. The building had nine bedrooms, three dressing rooms and three attic rooms above the ground floor. The entrance hall opened onto a massive oak-well staircase with a domed roof, and the wood-panelled dining room had an open chimney breast. Its gothic design was fronted by two pillars surmounted by two lions rampant. From a lodge at the entrance ran a long avenue of sycamores. In the extensive grounds were ancient sculptured figures, rose pergolas, kitchen gardens, orchards and woodland walks. Running between the hall and land called Mount Carmel was a strip of ground called The Rough that was 'traversed by a winding path, exhibiting through several avenues in different directions, a pleasing prospect of the subjacent vale'.[5]

Serious crimes at that time were tried at the Worcester Quarter Sessions and cases involving Stourbridge people make interesting reading.[6] Thomas Walton of Oldswinford made several appearances there. In 1606 he killed some of Richard Westwood's cattle and assaulted his own wife with a pike nearly killing her. A warrant was again issued for his arrest in 1610, when he was described as 'an evil doer, fighter, quarreller and common disturber of the peace'. In 1612 William Waldron, a victualler and tithingman of the town of Stourbridge, was accused of rescuing a cut-purse named Adam Jones from custody and of giving him shelter. In 1619 John Wildsmith, a blacksmith of Oldswinford, came before the bishop on suspicion of stealing a sheep and two loins of mutton (a capital offence at that time). In 1620 a Stourbridge locksmith, John Huntbach, was indicted for keeping a house of gaming, where cards and other unlawful games called 'shovel board' took place. John Pearson and his wife Ann appeared in 1628. John was accused of being 'a common drunkard, sorcerer, slanderer, quarreller and fortune teller', and Ann of cursing her neighbours, threatening to cut off a pregnant woman's nose and violently using a piece of timber to strike another woman who had a child in her arms at the time. Fulk Knowles was charged in 1637 with immoderately beating and misusing his apprentice, Owen Brown; the court was told that nobody could actually testify what had become of Brown. Those found guilty of such crimes were committed to prison in the Bridewell at Worcester, which in those days was inside the castle. The county gaol at Worcester was also referred to as the House of Correction. Stourbridge inhabitants were often sent there for other crimes such as running away from their families and stealing iron belonging to the parish. In 1625 the constable of Oldswinford and Stourbridge, John Compson, reported that 'we have no recusants; rogues and beggars have been punished according to the Statute; we have no unlawful gaming; we do provide for the poor; drunkards are daily punished'. Nine persons who kept common alehouses were also named.

Constant disagreements concerning land had to be sorted out by the manor court. The numerous small paths that wound their way around the strips of land were often blocked, either intentionally or by accident. In 1622 it was reported that 'John Raby hath stopped up a way with a paire of nayles thereby causing Thomas Milner to carry hys mucke farr about another way'.[7] Again in 1639 it was ordered that 'Humphrey Jeston shall keep a sufficient way at the end of his gardens or remove his pales further into his garden, that there may be a good way for people to passe, before the 25th day of March next, uppon payne to forfeyt makying default 10s.'.[8]

Important features of the Stourbridge landscape at that time were the commons. The population had the ancient right to graze their animals, although legally the land belonged to the lord of the manor. As with the open field system, control of the commons gradually passed from the manor court to the vestry during the century. If people encroached on the commons without permission they were promptly fined. In September 1627 Thomas Smythe was fined sixpence for enclosing pasture land called Richards Fields in Bedcote manor at a time when it should have been common. The major commons in Stourbridge were Stourbridge Common (including The Heath), The Short Heath, High Park and Lye Waste. Stourbridge Heath or Common stretched from the present Mary Stevens Park towards Norton and the Roman Road at Wollaston. The name heath implies an elevation to a marsh, the marsh in this case being centred around a stream that ran through Mary Stevens Park to Gigmill at Norton. The Short Heath lying near the present Witton Street (named after the Witton family who later owned much of the land on the common) was separated from The Heath itself by the brook that ran towards the Gigmill. Its 28 acres was situated within the manor of Bedcote and therefore belonged to the township of Stourbridge, whereas The Heath lay in the manor of Oldswinford. High Park Common was used by the people of Wollaston, and was an area of high ground that included the present High Park Avenue and land to the west of the manor rising up to the parish boundary.

At the beginning of the 17th century Lye Waste on the eastern boundary of the parish had only a few scattered cottages and little importance other than as a common on which the people of Lye could graze their animals. In October 1627 Samuel Addenbrooke 'surrendered one meadow of land at le Waste Hayes with ditches and hedges, on which is recently built one cottage, to the use of Henry Addenbrooke and his wife Elenor'. By October 1638 fines were being levied at one court sitting on no less than 10 persons for encroaching on Lye Waste, namely 'John Perkes de Lye, William Bach, John Buffery, William Hill, John Westwood, William Round, John and Thomas Sidaway, John Milward and Henry Addenbrooke'. Legend has it that after the Civil War a group of wandering people settled there, and little could be done to turn them away, despite the strict laws against outsiders settling illegally in the parish. Those people would have found the Waste completely unsuitable for cultivation, as the soil was rich in clay, and that probably caused them to turn to nailmaking as an occupation. They did however find the clay very useful as a material for building their first houses when mixed with straw and stubble.

Administration in the early 17th Century

In the final years of the 16th century many of the civil duties of the manor courts were transferred to the jurisdiction of the parish. In particular the parish became responsible for the care of the roads, the provision for the poor and local militia matters. The officers in the parish who shouldered these new burdens were the churchwardens, overseers of the poor and supervisors of the highways, who were each elected annually by the parishioners at the Easter Vestry. The appointment of the latter two had to be approved by justices of the peace at Quarter Sessions. Anyone elected was obliged to serve in an unpaid capacity for a period of two years, although in exceptional circumstances they could be excused by a Tyburn Ticket, awarded to a person who had apprehended a criminal.

The office of Churchwarden was a very ancient institution. Besides keeping the accounts for the parish (those for Oldswinford survive from 1602), churchwardens were responsible for presenting to the church authorities any inhabitants who were guilty of bad behaviour. They also had to pay the parish clerk, keep the peace at parish meetings and look after the church fabric. Some had an assistant called a Knocknobbler, who was responsible for removing dogs which misbehaved during the divine service; he used a pair of wooden tongs for the purpose. The following extracts from Owen Foster's parish accounts in 1606 give some idea of the variety of duties performed by churchwardens at Oldswinford:

For horse meat at the visitacon	...	iid
For taking out of the grave two children	...	viiid
Paid for Wytsen farthings	...	xviiid
For the Artycles	...	viiid
For washing the surpesses 6 tymes	...	iis
For painting the churche and whit lyme to whitten hit	...	xlvs

Finance for the parish at that time came from a variety of sources. Oldswinford church continued to be a major owner of land (called glebeland) in the 17th century and received the rents from it. In 1635 an inventory of that land was copied into the parish register, showing that it lay on both sides of Grange Lane, in the area of Love Lane and on the western side of Red Hill. But the main source of income was the levy of a parish rate. Parish rates were based on the value of property owned by each inhabitant and the earliest general rate listed in 1603/4 totalled £7 14s. 0d. The amounts levied tended to vary quite drastically from one year to another and depended mainly upon the current condition of the church fabric. £13 10s. 0d. was raised in 1609/10 (of which £6 came from the township of Stourbridge) and much of that was used to repair the steeple. The same amount was levied in 1625/6 when a bell was renewed and the church was painted. This income was supplemented by interest (normally at 12 per cent per annum) on capital lent out by the parish in the form of bonds, which were secured by the churchwardens in the grammar school chest at Stourbridge. Some 14 of those loans to the smaller traders in the parish and township were in existence and are listed in the churchwardens' accounts of 1653/4. The holders were Richard Allchurch (£6 5s.); John Smart, Gilbert Gill, Robert Raby, Edward Raby, Margaret Smith, Isaac Smyth, John Perks and Thomas Hart (£5 each); Richard Horneblower and Henry Allchurch (£2 10s. each); Thomas Mills, Edward Southwick and John Manning (£1 5s. each).

Another source of income consisted of pew rents. With the old form of mass giving way to services with long sermons in the 1540s, the congregation could no longer be expected to stand for the whole length of the service and pews began to be built in churches. It was the duty of the churchwardens to allocate those pews, and the right to occupy a particular pew became attached to individual properties in the parish. Wollaston Hall had seats allocated to it in the loft of Oldswinford church in the 17th century. On the death of the owner of a property, the right to use a certain pew passed to the new tenant, rather than to the owner's heir.

The parish officer who had to shoulder the burden of looking after the needy was called the Overseer of the Poor. The costs of their care continued to grow at that time, which meant a poorhouse had to be considered for the township of Stourbridge. It had its origin in the Poor Law Acts of 1597 to 1601, which allowed a parish to erect separate lodgings for old or sick paupers at the ratepayers' expense. Stourbridge eventually responded to that legislation by the conversion of one house into two almshouses for orphans and poor people at the top end of the town's High Street (backing onto Court Street and near where Pargeter's furniture shop stands today). These were established soon after 1623 as a result of legacies of £10 each bequeathed by William Seabright of Wolverley and London (who died in 1620) and by Lawrence Palmer of Alcester.[9] John Sparry actually owned the building, which had a frontage of nine and a half yards onto the High Street. Sparry then conveyed the property to the original 15 trustees of the Stourbridge Almshouse Charity in a deed dated 13 November 1632.[10] Those trustees were all well-known Stourbridge personalities: the parson Richard Hottoft, John Lyddiate, Nicholas Addenbrooke, Richard Foley, Jasper Newbrough, George Winchurch, Thomas Milward, John Baker, Gregory Baker, John Taylor, John Compson, Richard Hickman, Richard Cox, Edward Archbold and Thomas Deavell. Very little is known about how many persons were housed there or about the running of the almshouses in the 200 years in which they operated. (The almshouses ceased to operate in 1838, and in June 1839 the property was leased to Henry Bate for 99 years; by 1913 the trust consisted of four houses, the income being used for out-relief to widows and orphans living in the town. In March 1938, when the lease finally ran out, the premises were sold to Marsh and Baxter. The trust still exists today.)

A poor rate or levy, first allowed by the 1597/8 Act, was to become the major means of supporting the poor over the next three centuries. It was not until 1616 that a 'lewne' (a local dialect word for a levy or rate) was first raised for the parish of Oldswinford, generating a mere eight pounds. The burden of the poor levy on local landowners increased dramatically as the century went on, especially in years of war, famine or disease. During 1625 infection broke out over the whole county which resulted in taxes for the poor being extraordinarily high. In the Civil War years £48 a year was raised from the poor levy (and that figure later increased to £97 in 1664/5, £73 of which came from the town of Stourbridge whose inhabitants were in distress due to the plague).

With the cost of poor relief constituting such a large burden on the finances of local parishioners, each parish became particularly watchful regarding the settlement of strangers within its boundaries. In the first half of the century strict enforcement of the laws against harbouring strangers was expected from the manor courts. From the earliest times migrant labourers had to be pledged by those freeholders who employed them on the manor, and the freeholders faced a heavy fine if they broke the rules. The Oldswinford manor court made pronouncements such as the following:

4 April 1627—Francis Brooke received John Jackson and his family into his home contrary to the law, and was ordered to 'avoyd the said Jackson and his family before the next court leete, under penalty of twenty shillings, or give security for the discharge of the parish';

24 April 1634—William Ames, Elenor Hornebloer (widow) and Isabel Wall (widow) received and gave hospitality to rogues and vagabonds, and were fined 12d. each;

29 October 1637—'that the constable, churchwardens and overseers shall give warnings to any stranger that shall att any tyme come to inhabit within this parish, within six dayes either to depart or give security to the parish. The constable and some other officers shall make diligent searche once every month for all strange inhabitants, under payne of forty shillings per officer'.[11]

It can be seen that the manor and the parish were working closely together at this period. The security mentioned above normally consisted of a bond of indemnity. Prior to 1731 the top half of these bonds was written in Latin and the bottom half in English. The Latin section gave the names and occupations of persons putting up the security for the stranger concerned and stated the sum of money in which the guarantors were bound. The English section described the circumstances for which the parish was seeking protection. Each year the churchwardens handed the bonds on to their successors.

Many individual Stourbridge benefactors continued to be very generous to the poor. The tables of benefactors in the west porch of St Mary's, Oldswinford show that funds were donated for the purposes of food, education, erecting almshouses, apprenticing children, maintaining widows or simply providing cash for the needy. Inhabitants making major endowments in the 17th century included:

George Winchurst—6s. 8d. per annum to 20 poor people of the town, payable on Good Friday out of rent from Bedcote Meadow;

William Seabright—£3 0s. 8d. a year for providing 14 penny worth of bread every Sabbath Day (William Seabright was also responsible for the endowment of a free grammar school at Wolverley and for many other charitable works in Worcestershire parishes);

John Sparry—15 shillings a year to 15 poor persons on Easter Day and Christmas Day;

Nicholas Archbould—£20 for the poor (the Archbould family had important connections with Worcester);

John Lyddiate—£10 for the poor;

Thomas Oliver—the interest on £20 for 20 poor widows and householders of the town annually on the Feast of St Thomas;

Richard Foley—£20 to be let out annually by the governors of the Free Grammar School of Stourbridge to four or more 'poor young beginners' at one shilling in the pound interest, which interest was to be paid to the poor every Easter Even;

John Compson—£5 for the use of the poor;

Dorothy Hickman—the interest on £20 yearly to 20 poor people;

Richard Hottoft (the parson of Oldswinford)—£10 for the poor.

The third parish officer was called the Supervisor of the Highways. In 1634 the supervisor for the parish of Oldswinford, Richard Hickman, was prosecuted at the Quarter Sessions for refusing to serve and for obstructing the highway from Stourbridge to Bridgnorth by digging a ditch across the road. For most of the century there were two supervisors, one each for the parish of Oldswinford and the town of Stourbridge. From 1674, however, the parish elected a separate supervisor for each of the hamlets of Lye, Wollescote, Wollaston and Swinford. In 1691 the financing of the system was put onto a sounder footing with the adoption of a permanent highways rate, but the four days enforced labour was increased to six.

Inhabitants of the time had a positive obligation to clean their own part of the highway. Water had to be thrown onto the street in dusty weather to a distance of four feet in front of a person's house, and the pavement had to be swilled every market day and Saturday, making sure that the central gutter was left unblocked. The manor court published ordinances to make sure that the streets were kept clean. In September 1627 it was decreed that 'no man shall laye any mucke or compost in the streete except he remove it within five dayes after, uppon payne to expecte for any default 5s. 0d.'. At the next court in April 1628 Clement Cowper suffered the stated penalty as he had 'layd mucke in the streete of Sturbridge'. In October 1642 no fewer than 10 people were fined 3s. 4d. for 'ridlinge ashes and layinge shovelinges in the street'. Butter sellers had a habit of littering the streets with broken pots, and in April 1632 an ordinance was passed that 'butter sellers that brecke earthen pottes shall take the broken pottshardes that any of them doe breake and are broken by them away orth of the street the same day in payne for any default 3s. 4d.'. It was equally important for each Stourbridge tenant to clean out his ditches regularly to avoid unnecessary flooding and to keep gates, hedges and fences in good and constant repair. Deliberate destruction of the highway was yet another travel problem. In October 1640 it was ordered that 'whosoever shall digge and carry away any stone or gravell out of the high way above Colles Howses betwixt the lane of Nicholas Sparry and Thomas Mylward shall forfeyt and pay the sum of 5s. 0d.'. Travellers in the more rural parts of the parish had to be very careful not to damage growing corn as they made their way through the field tracks. In October 1680 it was ordered that 'all who come to this town with horses travelling through the grain fields shall bind, that is shall tayle their horses from the feast of the annunciation of the blessed marie the virgin until all the grain shall be carried from the said fields under penalty of 12d for each offense'. Local industry also had a destructive effect on the local roads, especially after the use of wood gave way to coal in the 17th century. The old packhorse trains were superseded by heavily loaded broad-wheeled wagons carrying coal to Lye and other forges, each horse load carrying five to six hundredweight. The roughness of the roads caused problems to the growing local glass industry; the sheets of glass were carried by men on foot who were called 'crate-carriers' and in 1636 the manor court referred to an assault on one of these unfortunate individuals.

Danger from fire and water was yet another hazard. Fires were caused because of the common use of wood in buildings and the close proximity of houses to each other in the town's narrow streets. In April 1629 the manor court of Bedcote ordered that 'Thomas Bach, one of the tenants of this manor, who hath a little cottage or rather a hovell wherein one William Yonge dwelleth in Bedcote Lane, shall amend and repaire the said cottage and buyld up a more sufficient chimney for the preventing of danger of fyer, or poole down the same under payne of 20s.'. The other natural element that proved a hazard in the past was water. Excessive floodwater from the fast-flowing river Stour created problems over many years for the inhabitants of the town. One of the worst occasions was the May Day Flood in 1623. Dud Dudley saw his ironworks at Cradley and Lye ruined, causing him to dispatch a messenger to warn the people of the town. Despite his efforts the inhabitants suffered considerable damage and had to move to the top storeys of their houses.

Civil War and Commonwealth

The unsettling events of the Civil War in the middle of the century made life particularly unpleasant for local inhabitants. The Civil War years saw many movements of troops, both Royalist and Parliamentary, through the Stourbridge area. In October 1642 the Royalists led by Prince Rupert marched from Mere near Enville to the property of Richard Foley at Stourbridge staying there three days; Richard Foley was reputed to have been cunning enough to supply both sides in the Civil War with his iron products. The year 1643 saw a short military encounter on Stourbridge Common after a force of 250 dragoons under the leadership of the jovial Colonel 'Tinker' John Fox had advanced from Worcester to relieve the garrison of 300 Parliamentary men at Stourton Castle. When they came across the Royalists (led by Prince Rupert) laying siege there, they were chased away and supposedly routed on Stourbridge Common, 64 of their men being killed and 30 captured. But it appears that Prince Rupert himself was nearly taken prisoner when, riding across Stourbridge Common towards his quarters at Wollescote House, he was closely pursued by a Parliamentary trooper. He only escaped when a young lad closed the Heath gate after he had passed, his adversary not having time also to pass through. The Milward family residence, Wollescote House, was the headquarters of Prince Rupert for a time, an event that greatly impoverished the family. On his departure it is said that the Prince left his signet ring with the Milward family and when the monarchy was restored a younger member, John Milward, was rewarded by the king with the gift of a sugar plantation called the Godwin Estate on St Kitts.[12]

The war was a particularly costly time for ordinary Stourbridge people as both sides in the dispute attempted to extract their dues from the population. In August 1644 the people of Oldswinford and Stourbridge were forced to make a contribution of £19 10s. 0d. to support

Colonel Sandys and the Royalist troops, no doubt only one of many such payments to maintain peace in this area. The conflict also disrupted the normal recording of events, and the following note appeared in the Oldswinford parish registers:

> That in the yeare 1649 and in the later end of the last yeare 1648, by reason of some neglecte in the parish clerke, and others that had their children baptised privately and out of the Parishe, the precise tyme and day of many of the Christeninges, Buryinges and Weddinges cannot be certainely knowne. But afterwardes uppon the enquiry of the Clerke, they or many of them are here set downe and registered as near the tyme as could be knowne.

After the Battle of Worcester on 3 September 1651, Charles II was reputed to have fled through Stourbridge on his way to Boscobel. The story states that he came along the Rye Market and down the Lower High Street to Wordsley, where his party partook of some beer, bread and meat at a house before continuing their flight.[13] Many years later the king told Samuel Pepys that his party rode quietly through the town, as the Parliamentary soldiers there 'had nobody to watch, nor they suspecting us no more than we did them'. Oldswinford's puritan rector during that difficult period was Jervis (or Gervais) Bryan; he found himself being ejected from his living by the restored regime in 1662 and took a post at Birmingham until 1675; he is buried at Coventry where he died on 27 December 1689.

16 *A portrait of Thomas Foley (1617-1677), the founder of Old Swinford Hospital.*

Life after the Restoration

After 1660 life returned to a more settled state and there was great prosperity in the area; the glassmaking industry had become well established and trade in Stourbridge rapidly recovered, although the cloth industry was in decline. In the 10 years up to 1669 some eight traders minted their own halfpenny and farthing tokens and on one of those (issued by John Pratt) the town's bridge was depicted as having four arches. Many new families took up residence in Stourbridge and there was a huge growth in the nonconformist movement in the second half of the century.

By the end of the 17th century Stourbridge High Street was lined with the private dwelling houses of more prosperous inhabitants, including the Foleys, Allens and Whorwoods.[14] The *Talbot Hotel*, by then named the Brick House, indicating the changing nature of materials used in houses during the century, was the residence of the powerful Foley family. In 1661 Thomas Foley purchased the complete manor of Oldswinford. Wollaston remained in

17   *The earliest plan of the manor of Oldswinford, surveyed in 1699 by Josiah Bach.*

Lyddiate hands until the mid-1670s, when its manor and hall were also sold to Thomas Foley for £5,000. The whole Stourbridge district had thus become united under Foley ownership, and they used their wealth to found Old Swinford Hospital in 1667 (more is said about this school on pages 164 and 165). In 1677 an attempt was made to improve the accessibility of the town when the Worcestershire engineer, Andrew Yarranton, began a project to improve the Stour between Stourbridge and Kidderminster. This involved the excavation of an artificial channel, the remains of which can still be seen at Stourton, but the undertaking ran into financial difficulties and had to be abandoned.

A survey of the area drawn up in 1699 by Josiah Bach still survives, but that plan unfortunately excluded the township of Stourbridge.[15] The surveyors of the map were Richard Smith of Drayton, John Cocks of Churchill and Jonathan Taylor and Oliver Dixon senior, both of Dudley. (The great 20th-century Stourbridge historian, H.E. Palfrey, discovered the map in a lumber room at the offices of Rufford & Co., firebrick manufacturers, when he was employed there as a boy clerk.) The principal roads in Oldswinford at that time consisted of Hagley Road, Heath Lane, Glasshouse Hill, Church Road (which ran in a straight line through the present building and churchyard of St Mary's church), Rectory Road, Rufford Road, Hungary Hill, Chawn Hill, Grange Lane, Old Ham Lane and a lane that ran between the latter two roads from the Walker Avenue to the Drews Road junctions. (This thoroughfare had been demoted to a footpath by 1827 and had disappeared completely on later maps.)

Lye Waste was so rough at that time that it was left uncharted on the 1699 survey. In other parts of Lye and Wollescote the equivalent of the following roads existed: Wollescote Road, a wide road from Hob Green following the stream towards Pedmore (a route that has declined in importance over the years and is now only a minor track), Brook Holloway (formerly known as Ludgbridge Lane), Springfield Avenue (a minor track leading onto Lye Waste), Perrins Lane, Wynall Lane, Careless Green Road (a wide green leading towards Lye Waste), Oldnall Lane, Balds Lane and two roads leading from it to Oldnall Farm that formed a triangle, Stourbridge Road Lye (which widened as it crossed Highmans Green and Hay Green), High Street Lye (ending at Lye Waste), Pedmore Road, Dudley Road, Cemetery Road (to the west of Pedmore Road only), Bott Lane (an ancient name mentioned as early as 1574), Engine Lane (called Dark Lane in the previous century and Back Lane later in the 18th and 19th centuries) and Bagley Street.

The most noticeable difference compared with today was the fact that Lye High Street was not a through route to Halesowen; the main road to Halesowen still ran through Careless Green and Oldnall.

The importance of Wollaston, compared with the other hamlets, was diminishing somewhat at the time. Its rateable value in 1699 was only £158, compared with Oldswinford £388, Wollescote £222 and Lye £198. (Norton was not given a value as it was not considered a separate district.) The roads then existing in Wollaston were Bridgnorth Road (from the Stourbridge boundary as far as its junction with High Park Avenue), Vicarage Road (from Bridle Road to the Amblecote boundary, being the main road from Kinver to Dudley) and High Street Wollaston joining up the former two roads. The latter road followed a different course to today from its junction at Vicarage Road to the manor boundary at Amblecote, as it ran in a straight line past Wollaston Hall and down to the Stour. It is impossible to tell from the map whether High Park Avenue existed as a road at that time as it formed the limits of the Wollaston boundary on the map; it was not turnpiked until the following century at which time it assumed its present wide straight features.

In 1696 there was a major dispute about people's rights to use the Washing Pool that lay on the then important boundary between Wollaston and Stourbridge. During the court proceedings it was described as the common pool for the people of Wollaston to water their cattle and was located on the northern side of Bridgnorth Road, opposite the present Mamble Road. Mentioned as early as 1622, the land around it was then owned by the Sparry family.[16] Gregory Hickman, the Stourbridge clothier, acquired fields around the pool, and later in 1782 the Washing Meadow was featured in an exchange of land between the Hickmans and Foleys of Witley Court, from which the Hickmans obtained the Castle Estate at Oldswinford. *Katie FitzGerald's* which now stands at the ancient Withibrook Bridge location was at one time called Washing Pool House.

By the end of the 17th century the major landowners in Stourbridge were the families of Foley (including the Old Swinford Hospital land), Hunt, Milward, Tristram and Wheeler, together with the church's glebeland and the remnants of Halesowen Abbey's Grange estate. The latter gradually became referred to as Grange Ground and was owned by a Mr. Steward in 1699. Other smaller landowners included the families of Addenbrooke, Bradley, Compson, Jeston, Norbury, Norton, Perkes, Philips, Philpot, Read, Whitemore and Witton. Besides the Addenbrooke family mentioned earlier, the old families of Bradley and Hornblower were in decline during the century whilst the newer industrial and professional dynasties were in the ascendancy.

The Milward family was one of the oldest dynasties in Oldswinford. Although not prominent in the previous century, the family rose from yeoman to gentleman status during the 17th century, marrying wisely. Successive generations of Milwards were governors of Stourbridge Grammar School. Thomas Milward (1670-1724) was an attorney and married Martha, the daughter of the respected Oldswinford Rector Simon Ford. Their son, Thomas, an attorney of the Inner Temple, was the last of the male line at Wollescote. He married Prudence, the daughter of Captain Oliver Dixon (a barrister living in Dudley before his family moved to Oldswinford).

The Wheeler family was another influential family of the late 17th century, but was first mentioned in the parish in 1549 when they owned land at Foxcote.[17] By 1669 John Wheeler (1646-1708) was a local magistrate and managed Cradley Forge in the neighbouring parish. Before the end of the century he had moved into Wollaston Hall and in 1699 bought Audnam Glasshouse from Edward Bradley. His monument in Oldswinford church records that he had five daughters by his first wife, and four sons and six daughters by his second wife, and a silver flagon, donated in his memory in 1708, is still in use in the church. It was he who endowed the Wheeler Charity School in Red Hill. In 1716 his eldest son John moved to Wooton Lodge, Staffordshire. The Wheeler property and land in Stourbridge were eventually inherited by the Unwin family.

18 *The Glover and Wheeler charity school in Red Hill, built in the early 18th century, and now called Wheelergate. It passed into private hands in 1883, but was repurchased for the Stourbridge Grammar School headmaster for a few years from 1951.*

New forms of national taxation followed the end of the Commonwealth period. The Poll Tax of 1660 was the first attempt to tax a person according to his social rank; it ranged from £100 for a duke down to £5 for a gentleman and sixpence for an ordinary mortal. In 1662 the Hearth Tax was introduced, charged at the rate of two shillings per hearth on each house worth 20 shillings per annum or more and levied twice a year on all social classes except those in receipt of poor relief. That tax was eventually abolished in 1689, only to be followed in 1697 by the hated Window Tax levied on any house large enough to possess more than six windows (or other openings) and with an annual rental value of more than five pounds. It started life as a basic tax of two shillings per annum, graduating upwards according to the number of windows in a building, but was later raised no fewer than six times between 1747 and 1808. It was not finally abolished until 1851. Administration of the tax depended upon local officials.

The state of the town's health during the 17th century was influenced in no small way by the supply of drinking water. This had been provided by communal wells from the earliest of times and old names remind us of these once popular meeting places. They include Catherwell close to Hagley Road Stourbridge (originating from St Catherine's Well), Spring Well on the west side of the foot of Lower High Street (which gave its name to Spring Meadow) and Well Leasow at Oldnall Farm. Maidwell at Wollaston (close to the present Richmond Grove) caused a dispute between John Lyddiate and the people of Wollaston in 1626, when it was reported that 'John Lyddiat gent. hath not opened the well in Wollaston Field called Maydwell. He shall ridd and scoure the well in the same field within one month'.[18] Stourbridge persons who fell ill at that time stood a far better chance of having access to a physician if they were institutionalised. The parish surgeon was obliged to look after the health of the inmates of the poorhouse. As early as 1660 the parish was paying William Allen 16 shillings for medicines.[19] Old Swinford Hospital School also had its own physician, Dr. Reynolds. In 1682 the feoffees absolved him from all his arrears of rent for the Heath Land in view of the special care he had taken of the boys there over the past 10 or 11 years. Sometimes even the monarch was involved; from 1684 persons suffering from a painful swelling of the glands called scrofula would try and obtain a certificate from the parish which was needed to gain admittance to the royal presence to be touched with an angel or gold medalet. (This quaint custom of 'touching for the king's evil' lapsed after the reign of Queen Anne.)

The Anglican church in 17th-century Stourbridge had a huge influence over the day-to-day living of parishioners, but it was fighting a battle against the increasing number of nonconformists in the area. Church courts had jurisdiction over such matters as marriage, divorce, incest, fornication, adultery, drunkenness and Wills. The rector and churchwardens were always more than ready to present any member of their flock who fell foul of the strict moral code, the punishment often being excommunication. This was still a particularly severe punishment, as no member of the Anglican church was allowed even to speak to an excommunicated person, resulting in that individual becoming a social outcast. In 1682 the churchwardens of Oldswinford, Thomas Slater and Francis Parkes, made the following presentment to the bishop of Worcester: 'We present Ezekiell Partridge and Mary his wife and Sarah Reynolds for being expuled Quakers and standing excommunicated. We present George Wade and his wife for standing excommunicated.' In 1684 the parish excommunicated Ambrose Crowley, Ezekiel Partridge, Sarah and Hannah Reynolds, Richard Jones, Edward Ford and Ann Hodges for not attending

Arthur, by the grace of God Bishop of Worcester, to his beloved in Christ the Rector Churchwardens and Parishioners of the Church of Oldswinford Greeting.

Whereas, in the words of the Apostle, we ought, while we have time, to do good unto all men, especially unto them which are of the household of faith, and therefore not the least among our duties is to lend helping hands in time of need to those who endeavour to build or repair churches and places dedicated to the worship of God; and whereas there exists an area contiguous to the Town of Dudley entitled the Priory Estate whereon it is proposed to build more than 2,000 houses, of which already a number have been erected holding a population of some thousands; and whereas this district has recently been transferred by Order in Council to our Diocese of Worcester and the cure of these inhabitants is now chargeable to us and the Church in our Diocese; and whereas further we have learned by diligent enquiry that the resources of the said district are insufficient for the purchase of a Site, and for the building of a Mission Church and Parsonage House to serve their spiritual needs.

We therefore charge and exhort you in the Lord to consider favourably the request which the Curate in Charge and Chapel Wardens have laid before us, and to give freely of your alms to the relief of their necessities, as far as in you lies, so that they may bring to a prosperous end the work which they now desire to undertake, and that God may be glorified and His Kingdom extended by the Church and the Parsonage to be erected in that place. And you shall take care that all that is collected of the gifts of the people of your said parish to this end shall be duly delivered to us for the Curate and Wardens aforesaid, without any diminution, to be employed by them for the said purposes.

Farewell in the Lord.

Given at Worcester, the second day of September in the year of Our Lord one thousand nine hundred and thirty-two, in the thirteenth year of our Episcopate, and in the second of our Translation.

19 Left. *A 1932 brief issued by the Bishop of Worcester in 17th-century format.*

20 Right. *A 1680 collection from the congregation of St Mary's, Oldswinford to redeem captive slaves from Algiers.*

church. Paul Hawkes, Mary Milton, William Spittle, Elizabeth Wade, Silvester Insole, Edward Best, Joan Rider, Sarah Baker, John Tyrer, Mary Lowe and Abigail Perrins suffered a similar fate for incontinency (meaning sexual misbehaviour). Sarah Reynolds, whose name appears above, suffered particularly badly at the hands of the church. In 1674 she was a poor Quaker woman with five children who was sent to prison for refusing to pay ninepence towards the cost of repair of the steeple house at Oldswinford. It was a constant battle for the churchwardens to keep the weaker-minded members of the congregation out of the many inns and alehouses in the district. In 1616 Thomas Gibbings of Lye was presented to the Quarter Sessions for 'allowing tippling on the Sabbath Day in the time of prayer, and the parishioners are much disquieted thereby'.[20]

Oldswinford church also supported deserving causes outside the parish's own confines. The means of obtaining funds for such charity was a 'brief', a royal mandate addressed through the bishop to the minister and churchwardens at Oldswinford. The document was read out during Sunday service and a retiring collection was normally taken, although some collections were actually made from house to house in the parish. The money was then paid over to the archdeacon's clerk at Worcester. The St Mary's Book of Briefs gave details of collections made between 1680 and 1759. The first few collections included a list of each individual donor, an example being the sum of £10 12s. 11d. raised in 1680 to redeem slaves interred in Algiers by barbary pirates. The largest amounts collected were always for overseas causes, including the relief of French protestants in 1681 (£26 9s. 11d.), 1686 (£36 5s. 2d.), 1688 (£19 8s. 11d.) and 1694 (£5 13s. 0d.). The relief of Irish protestants raised £38 3s. 1d. in 1689 and £11 0s. 1d. in 1690. There followed collections for distress in Piedmont in 1699 (£11 10s. 4d.), distressed protestants in the principality of Orange in 1703 (£8 3s. 10d.), poor distressed Palatines in 1709 (£10 2s. 0d.) and for the reform of the episcopal churches in Poland and Prussia in 1716 (£11 4s. 0d.). Although collections were occasionally arranged for individual persons, the majority of money raised in the 17th century was for communities in distress, but in the 18th century the emphasis turned to the rebuilding of churches following major disasters such as floods and particularly fires.

Parish Relief in the late 17th Century

In 1662 an Act of Settlement was passed which laid down rules about the payment of poor relief. It stated that persons could be removed from the place where they were living and returned to the parish of their settlement if they were likely to become a charge on their adoptive parish. The exceptions were those who already rented property within the parish worth £10 per annum or more, owned or resided in freehold property within the parish, could give the parish security, or had already resided in the parish for at least 40 days. In 1692 a new Act stated four further ways in which settlement rights in Stourbridge could be established. Intending residents could then prove that they had served a term as a parish officer, paid local rates or levies to the parish, served an apprenticeship with a master within the parish or hired themselves for a full year to any person in the parish. From 1697 strangers were allowed to come and work within the parish provided that they brought with them a Settlement Certificate. This guaranteed that they would be taken back or relieved by the parish of their settlement if they were unable to support themselves. These certificates, variously spelt 'sotivecat', 'scortificate' or 'surticiss' by Stourbridge scribes, contained signatures of both the issuing and recipient parish churchwardens, together with the signatures of two justices of the peace. Stourbridge people with such certificates were referred to as 'out parishioners' and were constantly being summoned to meetings or to the Quarter Sessions so that the parish overseers could examine their documents; usually the stranger had to pay the parish's costs of setting up that meeting.

Persons who decided to opt out of the system altogether were treated more harshly than the industrious poor of the parish. An Act of Parliament in 1597 ordered that vagabonds should 'be stripped naked from the middle upwards and be openly whipped until the body be bloody, and then passed to their birthplace or last residence', or if this was not known to a House of Correction. The practice of whipping vagabonds was carried out strictly in Stourbridge. In the parish register on 7 January 1665 was entered: 'Elizabeth Bromley, Mary Bruckshaw and Alexander Bruckshaw were taken at Stourbridge in this parishe, as vagabonds and wandering people, and whipt according to law and sent to St George's in Southwarke, the last place of theire abode and theire birthplace.' A Removal Order had to be taken out by the parish to pass on a vagabond. Each vagrant was handed over from parish to parish and the signature of the constable of each parish through which the person travelled was appended to the order. In April 1745 Jane Harrison, a 'wandering person', and her two children were returned from Newcastle upon Tyne to Oldswinford. They left

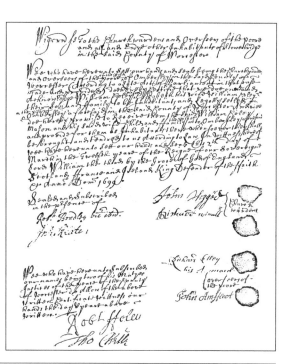

21 *A 1699 settlement certificate for a mason named William Coley and his family, issued by the churchwardens and overseers of Ombersley to the inhabitants of Stourbridge.*

22 *An inquiry by the parish in the 18th century to ascertain the father of Eleanor Richards' child. Personal details were not spared, however embarrassing.*

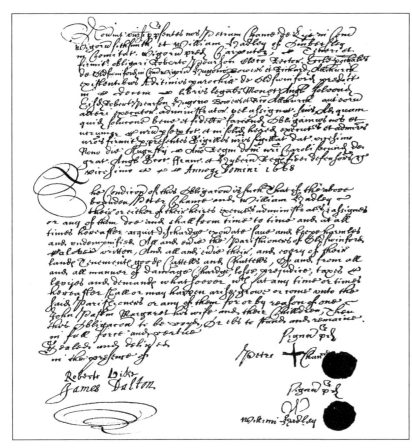

23 *A bond of indemnity issued in 1668, indemnifying the parish against any costs incurred in looking after John Paskin and his family. The top part is written in Latin and the bottom part in English.*

Newcastle on 5 April and arrived in Oldswinford on the 18th of the same month, after having been passed on by the constables of Durham, Whitewell in Derbyshire, Stretton in Staffordshire, Sutton Coldfield and Northfield (by no means the shortest route).

The attitude of the church towards unmarried mothers at that time was one of both moral reproach and of concern for the drain on the parish coffers. Their children were described in the parish registers as 'base born'. Because any illegitimate child automatically obtained legal settlement in the parish where he or she was born, the Stourbridge overseers were particularly keen to learn about such cases. They would immediately apply to the magistrates to have a formal examination of the woman concerned, with the aim of finding out the name of the father. The father normally had one of three options. Firstly he could pay for the child's maintenance, and to ensure that this was done he had to produce sureties to relieve the parish of any expense; in 1656 a Bond of Indemnity was taken out in the sum of £40 to ensure that the parish did not incur any expense regarding the illegitimate child of Alice Davies.[21] Alternatively he could marry the lady concerned and in order to give him the necessary encouragement it was not unknown for the parish to offer a cash incentive; such weddings became known as knobstick weddings and a local example occurred when Richard Jones was offered 3s. 6d. to marry Elizabeth Ellits.[22] Finally the father could appear at the next Quarter Sessions, from where he would be committed to the House of Correction at Worcester if he did not contribute to the child's upkeep.

V

Georgian Stourbridge

By the time George I came to the throne in 1714 Stourbridge inhabitants were enjoying a more settled lifestyle than they had experienced previously. The years up to 1750 saw little change in the administration of town affairs. Stourbridge was by now a prosperous market town, and was also increasing in importance as an industrial centre. Coach travel was leading to more comfortable and faster journeys, although it was still very expensive for the ordinary man. Around that time the average distance covered each hour on coach journeys was a mere five miles, although that improved to seven miles (perhaps 50 to 70 miles a day) by the end of the century. Relays of fresh horses had to be provided every few miles along the route at the numerous coaching inns of which the *Talbot* in Stourbridge was an important link in the chain. Parish surgeons continued to be appointed to look after the health of people who could not afford to pay for their own doctor to attend; they were appointed annually by the parish

Stourbridge through Time: 1714 to 1799	
1715	Rioters burn down Independents' Chapel
1724	Samuel Johnson at Stourbridge Grammar School
1729	Oldswinford parish sets up its first poorhouses
1735	St Thomas's Chapel built in Market Street
1752	First mention of a theatre in Stourbridge
1753	First Act for turnpiking of local roads
1770	John Wesley visits Stourbridge
1773	The old Town Hall is demolished
1778	Construction of new Bridewell prison in Stourbridge
*c.*1780	First Baptist meeting at Stourbridge
1780	First bank opens in Stourbridge
1782	Stourbridge commons are enclosed and a canal is built
1785	First Sunday School at St Mary's, Oldswinford
1790	A subscription library is opened
1791	Act for lighting and cleansing the town
1798	Formation of Stourbridge Local Volunteer Association
1799	New workhouse built for parish of Oldswinford

and it was their duty to care for the occupants of the workhouses. Known parish surgeons included a Mr. Briscowe between 1727 and 1739, Thomas York in 1738 and 1739 (who also appears to have been a local barber), Mr. Shaw in 1744, and from the late 1740s to the early 1770s the regular physician was John Ellis.

The First Parish Workhouse

The number of poor claiming relief imposed increasing demands on parish and township. A major change in the early Georgian years was the creation of the first workhouse for the parish of Oldswinford, almost a century after the township of Stourbridge had set up its own poorhouse. For many years the parish had paid rents for the houses which the poor inhabited and in 1728 was paying for some 10 families a sum amounting to about nine pounds a year. An Act of 1722/3, however, had encouraged parishes to build workhouses and in April 1728 the vestry was empowered to provide 'a common house or houses for lodging the poor inhabitants of the parish of Oldswinford and employing them therein, and such other methods for lodging, employing and providing for them in a common workhouse as shall be convenient'. From the following year through to the mid-1830s the parish ran its own workhouse.[1]

The first workhouse consisted of a number of smaller houses purchased by the parish specifically for the purpose and the overseers ran the scheme themselves on quite a small scale. In 1738 a much larger building was purchased at a cost of £95, the money being raised by a levy and repaid to Mr. Milward of Wollescote Hall. The exact location of this workhouse is not known, although there is a row of Queen Anne-style cottages on the western side of Church Road referred to locally as 'the almshouses'. The first governor was John Perrins (a nailer from Lye Waste) who was helped by his wife Frances; the couple were paid £9 a year with free lodgings and food. The first trustees and managers were George Wigan (rector), Gregory

24 *These Queen Anne-style cottages in Church Road, Oldswinford, may have been used in the 18th century to house the poor of the parish. Seen here in 1983.*

Hickman, Edward Kendall, Edward Milward, Joseph Best, John Spencer, John Hill, Thomas Tristram, Wildsmith Badger, Jonathan Deeley, Philip Orton, Thomas Grove, Edward Badger, Robert Quartermain, George Knowles, Anthony Crane, John Hancox, Joseph Green, Sergeant Witton, Daniel Hopkins, Caleb Robinson, Joseph Cox, Thomas Allen, Joseph Elcock and Thomas Milward. Furnishings included six beds, four blankets, four rugs, three mats, two boilers, tubs for brewing and washing, kitchen grates and vessels for beer. All persons under the age of 18 whose parents were on parish relief had to come into the workhouse, unless they agreed to be apprenticed out to local masters. A schoolroom was provided for the younger inmates. A separate apartment for the reception of the sick in mind was built later, and the accounts in 1773 mention the purchase of two locks for the 'madhouse'. Persons entering Oldswinford workhouse were required to bring all their possessions with them and surrender them to the parish, although if they later left they were allowed to take back items such as beds, cooking utensils and basic furniture. Anyone refusing to enter had his weekly parish relief stopped.

The type of work required from men consisted mainly of the local skills of nailmaking and lockmaking. It is no coincidence that the first governor, John Perrins, was a nailmaker by trade and he was required to furnish a nailshop with all the tools and implements sufficient for himself and three other workmen. The parish provided the iron. In 1740 a locksmith's shop was erected and a Mr. Perkes assisted in furnishing it. The women inmates were employed at sewing and spinning and the parish provided the wool and the spinning wheels, items that the women were occasionally allowed to take out with them when they left the workhouse. Other ladies were employed in running the workhouse itself, cooking, washing and cleaning. At first the inmates were allowed a certain percentage of the value raised from the sale of their goods and extra payments were given for exceeding the normal quota of work. It was a strict rule that nobody was allowed out without leave from the governor and one of the inmates had to act as doorkeeper; that unfortunate person became very unpopular with other inmates and was liable to be beaten up. Longer-term absence was also a problem, especially in the hop-picking season. Residents were obliged to attend prayers twice a day and wear their pauper's badge on an outer garment during the whole time they were in the workhouse. Remarkably until 1753 inmates were actually allowed to bring their dogs into the workhouse. Punishment for lack of discipline could consist of having pay stopped, or even the terrifying ordeal of being locked up for the night in a small cupboard (that was infamously called 'the dark hole') with just bread and water for the whole day. The ultimate punishment was to be turned out of the workhouse, as the person then had no means of support, but a right of appeal to the Quarter Sessions did exist.

The workhouse diet in 1749 was 10 pounds of cheese between 20 persons a week, two strikes of malt for 20 persons per month, and 12 pounds of meat boiled in a pot twice a week. In the mornings for breakfast the inmates had milk or 'peas broth' and for supper bread, cheese and a drink. It was a strict rule that everyone had to eat their hot meals together in one room, that room being named the 'publick house'. In 1741 a mill for grinding corn was bought into the workhouse and in later years the workhouse baked its own bread. The institution even had its own pigsty built and a wall four feet high joined it to the workhouse. Drink was brewed in its own brewhouse, which was fitted out in a cellar, and water was supplied from a well, although soft water had to be brought in. Malt together with hops at a shilling a pound were bought from a Mr. Egginton. The meat varied between beef, pork, bacon, mutton and even veal with an occasional treat of herrings. Groats were allowed for breakfast, and the accounts also showed the purchase of salt, treacle, and sugar. Non-alcoholic thirst was quenched by milk. Soap was used for washing clothes, but probably not for personal hygiene.

Retaining workhouse governors and their wives proved a tricky problem. John and Frances Perrins stayed for less than three years and in 1741 Jeremiah Reynolds was appointed on a yearly salary of £7 18s., payable half yearly. He was also offered two guineas a year by each parish overseer to perform the duties of overseer and to collect the rates. Reynolds was not a success, however, and was discharged in May 1742. For the next six years the governor was Henry Harris, but he managed to get himself into debt; the parish had to threaten to make him an inmate in his own workhouse unless he departed with his wife and children. Richard Smith of Wollescote was next appointed at the reduced salary of two shillings a week. He in turn did not endure the position for long because in June 1750 John Thomson of Rowley was appointed at the improved salary of £15 per annum (including four guineas from the elected overseers). John Thomson died in office in January 1756 and Joseph Green immediately succeeded him at an annual salary of £12. In 1766 Benjamin Bradley and his wife are recorded as holding the office at a remuneration of £10 a year. In 1783 Joseph Perrins (perhaps a relative of the first governor) was appointed at the reduced rate of two shillings a week.

Administration of the poor law by the overseers and other parish officials took more time and created more paperwork than any other aspect of parish life at this time. Three over-seers of the poor were still elected annually at the Easter vestry meeting, one for the parish of Oldswinford, one for the town of Stourbridge (but only up to 1740) and one for Amblecote. Management of the poor relief continued to be totally independent for each area. Separate books of account were kept and separate poor rates were levied. The removal of families from the township of Stourbridge to the parish of Oldswinford and vice versa (a journey of a mere half a mile along Red Hill) was quite commonplace as both authorities tried to keep down their costs. Great rivalry had always existed between town and parish and this sometimes broke out into bitter disputes. In 1742 an agreement was reached which said the township would receive their own poor without any lawsuit against the parish. Disputes still occurred as in 1746 the parish minuted that 'the overseers lett the gentillmen of the town know that there was a greement ... to

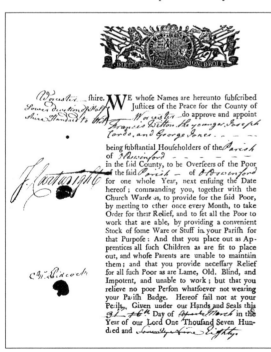

25 *A 1780 certificate for the appointment of the Oldswinford overseers Francis Witton, Joseph Cardo and George Jones.*

take or receive the poor without any trobel ... and that we will not take to Thomas Shaford ... before we will take him we shall stand a triall with them'.

Relief for the poor who were not residents of the workhouse was given by officials issuing weekly 'notes allowable'. To qualify for relief, claimants actually had to appear at each monthly meeting (unless they were too sick) and no woman was heard at a meeting if her husband was able to come himself. Notice of meetings was normally pinned in the church porch but later in the century so few people turned up that a person from the workhouse had to be appointed to walk around the parish and inform the principal inhabitants before each meeting took place. The monthly meetings of parishioners normally commenced in the vestry and then adjourned to a more comfortable venue (the *Talbot* in the years up to the 1720s, the private houses of the more important parishioners in the 1730s and the workhouse from the 1740s onwards). The following are just a few of the thousands of individual decisions from those meetings:

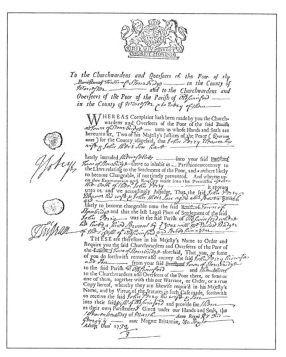

26 *An order for the removal of John Perry and family from the township of Stourbridge to the parish of Oldswinford in 1733. Although a distance of less than a mile, the two areas were under separate poor law administration.*

That ye blind boy have a fidell and [be] removed to his mother, and have 12d. for milk.
That Widow Bell's son be allowed 4s. 6d. more to buy a violin.
That Sarah Beassley's family be relieved, her children having the smallpox.
That James Richards have som straw to cover his hous with.
That Elizabeth Whithouse have a wheel.
That William Brook's wife have two shillings to support her in her lying in—her husband being a soldier.
That John Gauden's daughters be allowed to support 'em this month, they being both lame.
If widow Perrins keeps card playing, she shall have no pay from the parish.
That Skinny Robinson come to the workhouse.
That no person shall have any parish pay that keeps either dog or bitch.
That Mary Darby be taken in the workhouse, and be kept to hard labour.

Once claims for relief from the parish had been assessed, a list of recipients of regular weekly cash was displayed. At the start of the Georgian era 70 persons (some 50 were women) were receiving amounts varying from sixpence to two shillings a week.

All Oldswinford paupers and their families had to wear brass badges with the letters O.P. marked on them; the punishment for not doing so, besides being whipped or imprisoned, included loss of relief. Because of the shame attached to the badge, people naturally tried to wear it on an undergarment where it was not so conspicuous. Being aware of all their little tricks, the Oldswinford parish meeting in 1753 ordered everyone to wear their badge on an outer garment or be turned out of the workhouse. The degrading requirement to wear a badge was repealed in 1782, provided that the pauper was of good character.

It fell to the overseers actually to pay the dole money once a week. In the early years, the Oldswinford overseers made these payments from the church doors after the service and sermon on a Sunday; the poor were obliged to turn up or they forfeited that week's relief. Soon after the first parish workhouse was built, the weekly payments began to be made from that building by the master on a Friday. Every Thursday he presented a list of the weekly pay to the parish treasurer and was given the necessary money. Some people had to travel a long way to collect their dole; of the 64 people on the parish's weekly list in 1772, 13 came from the township of Stourbridge, five from Brettell Lane, two from Dudley and one each from Clent, Pedmore and Blakeshall.

Besides paying out the dole money, the overseer was also responsible for gathering in the funds. His first step was to call in a surveyor to draw up a map showing each plot of land naming owners, but such plans invariably led to many disputes. In 1743 Thomas Milward, one of the largest local landowners at that time, appealed to the Quarter Sessions against the levy made on him and this resulted in the parish agreeing to make a new assessment. Further new surveys followed in 1751 and 1759. In former years only the persons actually owning land had been assessed by the parish for poor rate, but by the 18th century tenants and cottagers were also being asked to pay their share. Levies of between sixpence and four shillings in the pound were then raised. Their collection was a tiring and hazardous task and was undertaken by the overseers themselves in earlier years. In 1741, however, the master of the workhouse took on the task of collection, the money being paid over to the parish treasurer at the end of each round.

The Last 40 Years of the 18th Century

As Stourbridge progressed into the second half of the 18th century major changes began to take place to the landscape, with fields and commons being enclosed and new roads constructed with the help of turnpike trusts. Industry prospered, helped by a new canal system, and this made many more residents comparatively better off. Growth in the population in the last few decades of the century was fairly rapid, the prosperous iron, coal and clay-based industries attracting people from a large number of surrounding agricultural parishes. In 1781 there were some 1,000 families in Oldswinford and Stourbridge, a considerable increase since Elizabethan times.[2] But accompanying the rapid acceleration in population growth was an equally rapid deterioration in living accommodation and conditions in the particular areas of Stourbridge where those new industries were developing.

The first major change to take place was the creation of the turnpike trusts. The old medieval gates of Stourbridge had already disappeared, only to be replaced by a completely new type of barrier in the form of the turnpike tollhouse and its gate. Although the first turnpike roads in the country had been built in 1663, it was not until the 20 years after 1750 that new highways really mushroomed. Individual Acts of Parliament had to be passed in order that local trusts could charge a toll in return for the right to build and maintain the roads in question, and Stourbridge had two such Acts passed in 1753 and 1772. They established

Oldswinford Gate.

Frees Coalbournbrook, Hollowsend, Pedmore, Wordsley and Colistreet Gates and Bars.

Horse ...	..	...
Chaise	...	...
Gig	E	...
Waggon	...	..
Cart	...	...
Cattle		

13 day of *May* 1854

Hay Green Gate

Frees Park, Halesowen, Gibbet Lane, Lye Cross, Bedcote and Hayes, Gates and Bars.

5 day of *July* 186

s. d.

Horse	
Gig. &c.	
Waggon	.5
Cart	

Produce the Ticket or pay the Toll.

LYE GATE

Frees Prescott, Farthings Lane, Woodside, Level, Merry Hill, and Grange Gates and Bars
186

Horse *July 5*	
Waggon ...	
Cart	
Chaise	
Gig	
Asses	
Pigs	
Sheep	
Beast	

Produce the Ticket or Pay the Toll.

GRANGE GATE

Frees Prescott, Farthings Lane, Lye, Woodside, Level, and Merry Hill Gates and Bars
186

Horse	
Waggon *nine*	
Cart	
Chaise	
Gig *26*	X
Asses	
Pigs	
Sheep	
Beast	

Produce the Ticket or Pay the Toll.

Brettell Lane Gate.

26 Day of *May* 1863

s. d.

Carriage	..	..
Cart ..	..	..
Waggon	..	..
Horse ..	..	..
Cattle ..	..	..
Sheep ..	..	..
Pigs ..	..	..

Frees Nether Trindle, Princes End, corbyn's hall, round oak, kingswinford Queens Cross, Badgers Bank, Pensnett, and Tipton, Gates and bars.

Produce this ticket or pay the toll.

27 *Tickets issued by the turnpike gates in the Stourbridge area in the 19th century.*

the Stourbridge District of Roads, which made it possible to appoint a paid surveyor for the first time. To finance the project loans could be raised on the security of the tolls and much money was raised in that way from local Stourbridge glassmakers such as the Rogers, Hill, Pidcock and Grazebrook families and from the new banking companies that some of these families had formed.

The first road to be turnpiked ran from the old town hall in Stourbridge to Wordsley Green via Cobourn Brook. Joseph Pool of Stourbridge was appointed clerk to the trustees.[3] The purchase of land was negotiated and turnpike houses were built, their windows jutting out in a characteristic way onto the roads they were guarding. There followed the turnpiking of the road leading to Bromsgrove (with a branch running from Oldswinford to the Birmingham to Kidderminster turnpike road 'at the Clap Gate near the Spout'). On 21 July 1762 the first meeting of the trustees took place at the *Talbot* to enforce the turnpiking of the route from Stourbridge to Colley Gate.[4] William Pool was appointed the first clerk and treasurer at £10 a year and Harry Court was made surveyor of the road for a salary of £20 a year. It was only to be expected that surveyor Harry Court would receive large financial benefits from those turnpike schemes, and in 1767 the Stourbridge Gate was farmed out to him at a rate of £141 a year, which he then farmed out to others at a profit. The Stourbridge Gate had been erected on the Stourbridge to Lye road between a barn belonging to John Iddins and a close of land called Coxcroft (in the possession of Thomas Northall) and the scheme was completed by the erection of a turnpike house. The first gatekeeper was appropriately named John Barrar, who in addition to his weekly wage of about one shilling was allowed threepence a week towards candles (but not during the summer). A later rail was erected at The Hayes, and a Mr. Pardoe was paid four shillings a week to maintain it.

By 1782 further turnpike gates were sited at: Birmingham Street near its present junction with Mount Street; Hagley Road, Oldswinford, near its junction with Worcester Lane; the start of Norton Road at The Heath, near the present gates to Mary Stevens Park (and possibly on the same site as the old Studley gatehouse); the top of Chawn Hill at its junction with Grange Lane (land adjoining was called Turnpike Leasow at that time).

In 1789 the road leading from *The Fish Inn* at Amblecote to Iverley Hill on the Norton to Kidderminster road was turnpiked. This ran via High Street Wollaston, High Park Avenue (variously known as Dudley Road in 1782, Gate Hangs Well Road in 1851 and High Park Road in the 1880s) and Sandy Lane, Norton. In the 1780s Bridgnorth Road was also extended from its High Park Avenue junction up and over the Ridge Top.

Coach travel benefited in a major way from the new highways. From the *Talbot Inn*, Stourbridge in 1781 one could take the Diligence to the *Crown Inn* at Worcester or to the Bell at Wolverhampton (the complete return journey taking a whole day). On three days a week people could take the Post Coach, on its way from Holyhead to London, arriving in London at lunchtime on the following day. The cost for the journey was 27 shillings (or half of that amount if you were sturdy enough to travel on the outside of the vehicle). Stourbridge had possessed a post office from early in the 18th century; recorded postmarks on letters in-cluded 'Stowerbridge' in 1712, 'Stouerbridge' in 1733, through to the present spelling from 1775 onwards. By 1792 the cost of a journey to London had increased; Rufford & Co. were charging 31s. 6d. inside their coach or 21s. 0d. on the outside.

At about the same time as the earlier turnpikes, there was a proposal in 1776 to construct a new canal system, promising an important improvement in the transport of local industrial products and enabling the opening up of new trade and more distant markets. One hundred years after Andrew Yarranton's abortive attempt to construct the area's first canal, an Act of Parliament was passed to enable a new company to build a canal connecting Stourbridge with the Birmingham Navigation at Brierley Hill and the Staffordshire and Worcestershire Canal at Stourton. There was enormous speculation in the newly offered shares, which by 1792 attracted an unbelievable premium of £350 per share. An initial capital of £30,000 was raised from shareholders who included many of the wealthy glassmakers (Edward Russell, John Pidcock, George Ensall, Thomas Hill, Thomas Raybould as well as the clothier William Scott). The talented John Brindley carried out the initial survey and the canal was built in 1782, despite many objections from interested parties, not least the town's road carriers. (The canal was later extended into Lower High Street in the years 1830 to 1834.) From paying a dividend of £9 in its first year, the Stourbridge Canal Company prospered and reached a peak in 1848, then paying a dividend of £70 a share.

The turnpikes resulted in other changes to the local roads of Stourbridge. The most important happened in 1773 when the ancient town hall or market building, which for centuries had stood awkwardly in the middle of the High Street blocking its major junctions, was taken down. It was then possible to widen the openings of the roads leading from it. Crown Lane was widened, partly with the help of £1,000 donated by Lord Stamford, towards whose home at Enville Hall the road led.[5] (It was only renamed Enville Street a century later.) New Street only ran as far as the present Lion Street (a name which first appeared at that time). Rye Market (running from Bell Street to Worcester Street) was renamed Church Row on the completion of St Thomas's church in 1736, and finally became Market Street in the late 1800s. A footpath ran from the church to the top end of the High Street. At times during the 18th century Coventry Street appears to have had the alternative name of Pig Street, because of the pig market located there. In 1708 it was referred to as 'Pegg Street or Coventry Street', and in 1742 a John Horton was mentioned as living at John Hind's 'in ye pig lane'.[6] Coventry Street led into Lower Lane on the route to Lye, and running off it to the south was the notorious Angel Street.

Stourbridge High Street at that time reflected the changing conditions of the town as a whole. Throughout the 18th century many timber-built properties were fronted or replaced by brick-built houses for the richer merchants. In the 1760s a house called Stourhurst was erected on the eastern side of the lower part of the High Street. This was followed 10 years later by the Foster family home next door, built in red brick with stone dressings, with Gothic windows and ogee mouldings with a double curve terminated by a fleur de lis. This style was known as Strawberry Hill Gothic (after Horace Walpole's house at Strawberry Hill, Twickenham). The Foster home, now numbered 7 Lower High Street, had its own coach house attached as did many other important residences at that time.

A detailed plan of Stourbridge was drawn up in 1781, the oldest surviving map of the town centre.[7] The following year the whole parish (excluding Amblecote) was mapped by Mr. Blackden of Loxley, Staffordshire and the Stourbridge surveyor, Harry Court, showing roads and fields in great detail, with the owners marked on the map itself.[8] They were paid £47 7s. 10d. for their

28   *18th-century frontages at numbers 7 and 8 Lower High Street, taken in 1977. The closest building is Sandford House (formerly offices of the Stourbridge Water Board), whilst the furthest is Stourhurst.*

effort. In about 1800 another plan of the town of Stourbridge was sketched by John Scott for the manuscript volumes of his memoirs of the Rev. James Scott.[9] Other Stourbridge roads on maps at that time included:

King Street (this became Queen Street in Victoria's time);

Mill Lane (called Mill Street by 1801 and now obliterated by the ring road);

Giles Hill (an ancient footpath that can still be found in Lower High Street);

Windmill Street (so named because of the windmill that used to stand on the summit of its hill where Ibstock Drive is now found). When St John's church was built in 1860 its name was changed to Church Street. In 1816 an army barracks was sited there which housed French prisoners of the Napoleonic War;

Halfpenny Hall Lane (named after the building that stood close to the present Redhill School on the northern side of the road. This became Junction Road on the opening of the old Stourbridge Junction railway station in 1852);

Hagley Road (variously called Hospital Lane and Hagley Street later in the 19th century);

Talbot Street (named Back Lane in 1837 and Talbot Back Lane in 1851);

Theatre Road (newly constructed in about 1780 and alternatively named Theatre Row, Seven House Road and Theatre Street in the 19th century);

Bell Lane (which became Bell Street around 1890);

Bowling Green Road or Lane (which was gradually extended throughout the 19th century towards Wollaston); Hempland (a series of courts that were originally settled by the weaving community);

Heath Street (only the Lion Street end in 1781; by 1882 it had been extended through to The Heath side);

Worcester Street (Heath Road in 1851).

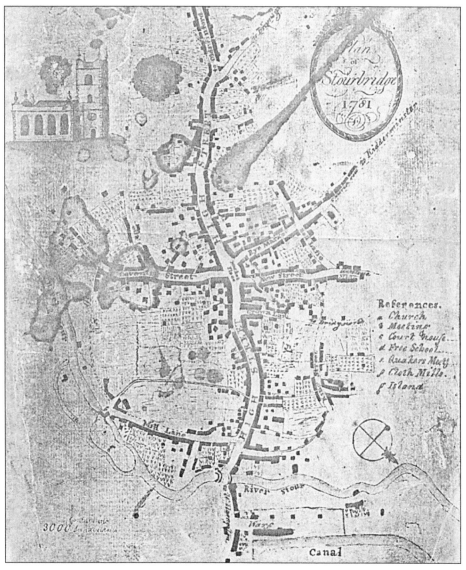

29   *The earliest surviving map of Stourbridge town centre, drawn up in 1781.*

30 *A view of Stourbridge published by the historian Nash in 1782, looking from meadows near Wollaston Hall. Towards the horizon, from left to right, it shows the Grammar School tower, the Church Street windmill and St Thomas's tower.*

The major development in the last 20 years of the century was New Road (also known as Kidderminster Street until about 1860). In 1832 it contained some well-built modern buildings and two places of worship.[10] New Road was extended as far as Market Street in 1801, but now forms part of the Stourbridge ring road. Court Passage also appeared at that time, being variously known as Court House Lane and Court House Road. In the last two decades Scotts Road (known as Mission Road) and Bradley Road (called Bank Street for some years after the opening of the Stourbridge and Kidderminster Bank in 1834) were also built, together with the distinctive triangle of roads at the southern end of Angel Street (at one time known as the Three Road Garden). In Oldswinford and Wollescote little change took place in the 18th century. St Mary's Lane was now clearly a road. Love Lane, previously a track into the old common fields, was developed as far as the first bend on the top of the hill. Field Lane was the first new development in the early 1800s. The main housing in Wollaston was still centred near the junction of Vicarage Road and High Street.

Enclosure of the commons was another major change to hit the Stourbridge landscape in the 1780s. In the early 18th century the last of the open fields had been enclosed by private agreements, but the commons had to await private Enclosure Acts that were enacted in 1780 and 1782. The four main commons were divided into enclosed plots of land; they consisted of Stourbridge Common (including The Heath), The Short Heath, High Park and Lye Waste amounting to some 700 acres in total. These commons all previously belonged to the Foley family as lords of the manor. The freehold was either sold to the tenants, exchanged for other pieces of land, or granted as compensation to those persons who had lost their grazing rights. A large part of High Park Common was allocated to Thomas Hill who fenced it and planted it with trees for the protection of game, the estate later being sold to the Earl of Dudley.[11] Enclosure of the open fields and commons around Stourbridge certainly benefited the town, for it was the key to more efficient farming and put funds into the local community as large landowners began to buy out other residents with only smallish holdings.

Every Rogationtide a party of church officials and parishioners used to beat the bounds to inspect the markers of the glebeland of the church, and this became a somewhat festive occasion. The parish provided food and drink for those who went on the walk. Such was the importance of upholding these bounds that a complete description of the boundaries of the parish was copied into the Oldswinford church registers at various times. The glebeland belonging to the church was included in the Enclosure Acts above and the rector given compensation for his lost tithes. The new owners of the land had to pay for the additional fences and any necessary new buildings; this cost the Oldswinford rector £1,427, which he raised by allowing the Enclosure Commissioners to sell off 82 acres of his newly acquired lands.

The area of Stourbridge most affected by enclosure was Lye Waste. It was there that many newly arrived families used to squat, living in their mud huts; they were makers of nails, chain, anvils, vices and bricks, and miners of coal and clay. Back in 1725 families claiming poor relief and living on Lye Waste were ordered by the parish to come to the next parishioners' meeting in order that their children could be placed out as apprentices. Only one family actually turned up, much to the consternation if not surprise of the overseers. William Hutton wrote in 1782:

> If the curious reader chooses to see a picture of Birmingham in the time of the Britons, he will find one in the turnpike road between Hales Owen and Stourbridge, called the Lie Waste, alias Mud City. The houses stand in every direction, composed of one large and ill-formed brick scoped into a tenement, burnt by the sun, and often destroyed by the frost. The males naked, the females accomplished breeders. The children at the age of three months take a singular hue from the sun and the soil which continues for life. The rags which cover them leave no room for the observer to guess at the sex. Only one person upon the premises presumes to carry a belly, and he a landlord. We might as well look for the moon in a coalpit as for stays or white linen in the City of Mud.[12]

Following the 1782 enclosure of Lye Waste more than 100 inhabitants exchanged their squatters' rights for small freehold plots. The commonest names of the families were Brooke, Chapman, Heathcock, Hill, Knowles, Pardoe, Pearson, Perry, Round, Taylor, Walters and Wooldridge. The area very quickly became known as 'mud city' as hardly one house in fifty was not made from mud and thatch. A multitude of new roads began to cover the common, leading off the new turnpike road to Colley Gate. These included Cross Walk (Cross Walks Road) and Crabbe Street. Chapel Street was built between Pedmore Road and the Lye High Street.

As a result of the influx of new families into the Stourbridge area there was a substantial change in local surnames, and by now the most common surname in the parish was Hill. Besides surnames such as Harris, Jones, Richards, Davis and Tailor (which can be found in most other parts of the country), the area had many local names that were prolific. Those included Brookes, Knowles, Pardoe, Skidmore, Westwood, Bache, Cartwright, Pearson, Perkes, Perrins, Robins, Round, Sidaway, Wood and Wooldridge. All of those names are still well represented in the area today.

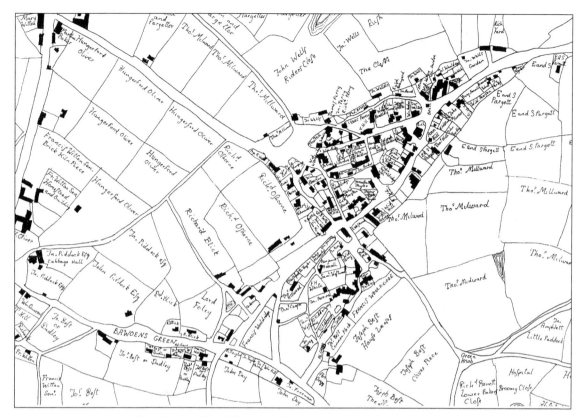

31 *A map of Lye Waste in 1782, drawn up for the Enclosure Act.*

Law and order in Stourbridge was strengthened by the construction in 1778 of a new Bride-well; the previous prison under the town hall had been demolished with the main hall in 1773. Ten guineas was paid to Oliver Dixon as a contribution towards its construction, being provided in the proportion of 2:2:1 by the parish, town and Amblecote respectively.[13] The new building was probably the small prison later mentioned as being situated in the court house at the top of the High Street Stourbridge, and affectionately called 'the cage' by the local people.[14] The local militia provided further backup for the parish constables. Prior to 1757 service in the militia was mainly based upon a man's property and wealth, but from 1757 to 1831 inhabitants were subjected to a compulsory ballot to choose which of them would have to give their services each year. In 1781 Moses Heathcock of Stourbridge was unlucky enough to be chosen to serve in the county militia. He managed to persuade Richard Dancer to serve in his place for the then current payment of £10 (half of which was found by the parish). Insurance against such an expense was often taken out by those individuals who could afford to, but it was quite normal for the parish to pick up the bill. As well as the compulsory militia, volunteer military associations became quite common during the period of the French Wars between 1793 and 1816. By 1798 Stourbridge had its own Local Volunteer Association of Cavalry, consisting of about 110 gentlemen organised into two 'corps' and covering a radius of about seven miles around the town. Each man had to provide at his own expense a horse, arms and uniform (which consisted of a blue frock with velvet collar of the same colour, a white kerseymere waistcoat, leather breeches and a plain red hat). The yellow buttons on their dress bore the letters 'S.A'.

As the 18th century drew to a close, the first signs were manifesting themselves of major changes to the system of administration of town and parish. In 1791 an Act of Parliament was passed to enable the lighting, cleansing and watching of the local streets. Amongst its provisions were that: any person possessing a house with a rental value of £40 or with a capital value of £800 could be elected a commissioner; lamps were to be provided to light the streets of the town (under the control of the commissioners); constables were to be appointed to keep a night watch from watch-boxes. The first meeting of the new commissioners took place at the *Crown Inn*.

The provision of medicine for the sick continued to improve. By the 1790s the parish surgeons were Mr. Freer and Mr. Evans. Their duties included compulsory attendance at the monthly parish meetings, in order to pronounce upon the medical condition of applicants for parish relief. They had also to provide medicine and perform a limited amount of surgery, because there were no hospitals in the area at that time. The Oldswinford surgeon occasionally had to act as a midwife. The financial reward for his services to the parish varied between £4 and £6 a year, but by 1800 the remuneration had increased to £10. Like other Oldswinford parish officials, however, he was usually paid very irregularly (sometimes a year in arrears) and had the greatest difficulty in getting any money at all from his employer, often being told to wait until yet another levy had been collected from the parishioners. A sad medical case occurred in September 1769 when widow Price applied for support for her son, Richard, who whilst on his own suffered a fit, fell onto a burning fire and was burnt in a most terrible manner. The parish surgeon, Mr. Ellis, had to travel to Dudley to see him nearly every day for several weeks, and was forced to claim an extra allowance for undertaking that arduous task. Richard apparently survived his ordeal,

By his Majefty's Permiffion.

STOURBRIDGE
LOYAL VOLUNTEER ASSOCIATION.

APRIL 23. 1798.

RESOLVED, and we the undersigned, do agree to form ourselves into an ASSOCIATION of CAVALRY to consist of one Hundred, or upwards, for the Defence of our most gracious King (whom God long preserve,) our happy Constitution, and the protection of the Town and Neighbourhood of Stourbridge: to assemble together from time to time, according to Law, and to act in aid of the Civil Magistrates.

THAT such Association be under the Direction of JOHN ADDENBROOKE ADDENBROOKE, Esq. the High Sheriff of the County of WORCESTER, and the HONOURABLE EDWARD FOLEY, one of the Members for the same County.

THAT each of us shall at his own expence provide himself with a proper Horse, Uniform, Arms, and Accoutrements; and be Trained and Disciplined.

THAT the Association, when complete shall be separated by Ballot; one half to serve under the Direction of the High Sheriff, and the other half under Mr. FOLEY.

THAT any Gentleman being desirous of quiting this Association, he shall be at full liberty so to do, upon his first giving a Month's Notice to either of the above-named Gentlemen.

THAT the Uniform shall be a Blue Frock with a velvet Collar of the same colour, White Kerseymere Waistcoat, Leather Breeches, and a Plain Round Hat, Yellow Buttons, with the letters S. A.

THAT upon our Honour, we engage to attend the above-named Gentlemen, or either of them when required in Defence of our King, our Constitution, and the Town and Neighbourhood of Stourbridge: but it is understood that not one of us shall be obliged to go a further Distance from the Town of Stourbridge than Seven Miles.

THAT any further Regulations, not altering the preceding Resolutions, may be made at a General Meeting, by a Majority of the Association then present.

GOD SAVE THE KING.

John A. Addenbrooke.	William Ambler.	John Wilkes.
Edward Foley.	Thomas P. Foley.	Francis Hobson.
Richard Brettell.	Thomas Hill.	Benjamin Robins.
Francis Homfray.	Edward Hill.	Edward Oliver.
Richard Hickman.	Dudley Bagley.	Michael Grazebrook.
T. W. Grazebrook.	Joseph Robins.	Francis Rufford, Junior.
Thomas Homfray.	Charles Hopkins.	Edward Westwood.
George Briscoe.	William Harris.	John Hollington.
Waldron Hill.	Benjamin Cox.	John Moore.
Benjamin Littlewood.	Arthur Harrison.	Thomas Lea, Junior.
Francis Walker.	Thomas Hampton.	Thomas Wood, Junior.
William Hunt.	John Richards.	Thomas Alport.
Thomas Hill, Junior.	Jeston Homfray.	Charles Dickinson.
Samuel Bate.	George Homfray.	John Scott.
James Pitman.	J. Honeybourne.	Thomas Stokes.
Nathaniel Smith.	John Compson.	William Gosnell.
John Pidcock.	Serjeant Witton.	John Amphlett.
Edward Dixon.	George Stokes.	Herbert Jenkins.
George Collis.	Joseph Chillingworth.	William Evans.
John Causer, Junior.	Thomas Brooke.	William Wight.
William Brown.	John Witton.	Thomas Wight.

32 *A poster advertising the rules for the Stourbridge Loyal Volunteer Cavalry in 1798.*

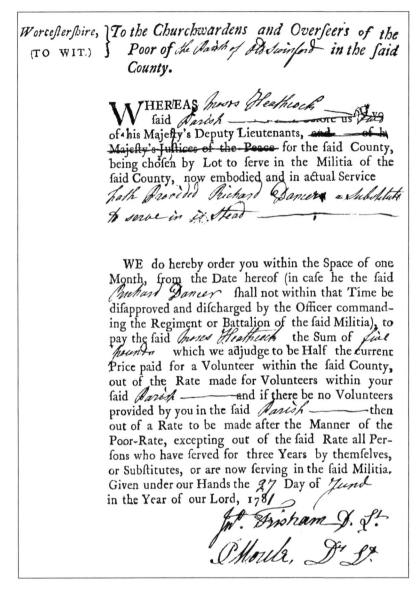

Worcestershire, } To the Churchwardens and Overseers of the
(TO WIT.) } Poor of *the Parish of Old Swinford* in the said
County.

WHEREAS *Moses Heathcock* ~~said Parish~~ ~~before us two~~
of his Majesty's Deputy Lieutenants, ~~and~~ ~~of his~~
~~Majesty's Justices of the Peace~~ for the said County,
being chosen by Lot to serve in the Militia of the
said County, now embodied and in actual Service
hath Provided Richard Dancer a Substitute
to serve in it Stead

WE do hereby order you within the Space of one
Month, from the Date hereof (in case he the said
Richard Dancer shall not within that Time be
disapproved and discharged by the Officer command-
ing the Regiment or Battalion of the said Militia), to
pay the said *Moses Heathcock* the Sum of *five*
pounds which we adjudge to be Half the current
Price paid for a Volunteer within the said County,
out of the Rate made for Volunteers within your
said *Parish* ———— and if there be no Volunteers
provided by you in the said *Parish* ————then
out of a Rate to be made after the Manner of the
Poor-Rate, excepting out of the said Rate all Persons who have served for three Years by themselves,
or Substitutes, or are now serving in the said Militia.
Given under our Hands the *27* Day of *June*
in the Year of our Lord, 17*81*

Jno. Trisham D. L.

P. Moule, D. L.

33 *A 1781 order to reimburse Moses Heathcock (after he had been chosen by lot to serve in the county militia) for half of his costs in substituting Richard Dancer.*

and 18 months later John Ellis was paid an extra £3 for his superb devotion to duty. Another alternative for sick people lay with the various druggists and their products. In October 1773 Mr. S. Cotton informed his friends and the public that he had opened a shop next door to the *Talbot*. There he provided an assortment of teas, chocolate, coffee and sugars; likewise an assortment of choice drugs, oils, colours and brushes. He stated that 'farriers and cow doctors could depend on being served with best drugs upon reasonable terms'.

The parish regularly provided other benefits. In addition to weekly cash payments, certain occasional payments were given to the poor, and these were called 'by-pay'. They included cash for persons who were temporarily sick or out of work and grants of materials such as iron and cloth to enable people to work at home. Coal, shoes and other items of clothing were given, especially in the winter months. In 1775 a total of £1,200 was collected to support the parish's 220 paupers, a number that had increased three or four fold since the beginning of the 18th century. Over half of those recipients were from the town of Stourbridge.

Parish administration continued to have its problems. Utter confusion reigned in 1785 when one of the elected overseers, a farmer from Wollaston, William Egginton, was declared bankrupt. James Belcher, the parish constable is recorded as claiming costs of £1 15s. for apprehending Egginton and conveying him to Worcester Gaol. The parish had lost £74 due to the incident, and opposed Egginton's liberation from gaol until he repaid the money. Neither did the collection of the poor rate go smoothly. Certain inhabitants always made certain that they were out when the collector came around, which necessitated the parish ordering that 'no person be called upon more than twice for each levy (provided they be at home) and if not then paid, to be distrained upon immediately'. Some landowners paid their levy in kind and there were always people who would or could not pay their levy. According to the parish accounts in 1784, uncollected levies amounted to £203, enough to cover the parish's weekly payments for the ensuing six months.

Prominent Families in the 18th Century

Families that rose to prominence in the 17th century still tended to be the major landowners at the end of the 18th century, but many more inhabitants were property-owning compared with a hundred years earlier. The wealthiest families were still the Foleys (including land owned by the trust set up for the Hospital School), Hickmans and Milwards (who by now owned the Grange Ground). Not inconsiderable land was also held by John Amphlett, Joseph Hancox, Francis Hill, the Kynnersley family, Hungerford Oliver, Thomas and William Pargeter, Richard Phillips, Thomas and Benjamin Pratt, Thomas Rogers, Francis Unwin and Francis Witton (including his company). The rectors of Oldswinford still owned large areas of land. On the 1782 survey of land almost one hundred different names were listed, but many of those were now sub-tenants of their land. Other inhabitants who made contributions to the life of the Stourbridge district, although not major landowners, included Edward Kendall, John Biggs, Wildsmith Badger and Francis Homfray. The wealthy had to pay a variety of national taxes during the 18th century, levied on personal possessions such as carriages, clocks, watches, dogs, servants, guns, hair powder, horses, silver plate and even armorial bearings. But in 1799 the Income Tax, so familiar to everyone today, was introduced to finance the long war against France.

Of the many branches of the Hill family in Stourbridge, Francis Hill (who lived in a three-winged house at Foxcote) was the most influential. In 1816 he bought further land in Oldswinford from the then bankrupt George Stokes. Another wealthy Hill branch originated from the Tiled House at Bromley near Kingswinford, where they worked a blade mill. Elizabeth Hill of that branch married Humphrey Bachelor, owner of the Dennis Glasshouse at Amblecote, which she inherited on his death. In 1762 the Dennis property passed to her nephew Thomas, the son of Waldron Hill and Elizabeth née Tyzack. Besides their considerable interest in the local glass industry (companies that were the forerunners of Thomas Webb and Corbett Ltd.), Thomas and his partner William Waldron formed their own bank-

34 *An 1854 portrait of Samuel
Rogers (1763-1855), poet and
banker.*

ing company in Stourbridge in about 1780. Thomas Hill used his great wealth to build and
endow Christ Church, Lye in 1813, his grandson Henry being its first incumbent. Thomas
died in 1824 aged 87 and is commemorated by a memorial on the west side of the north
aisle of St Mary's, Oldswinford.

The Rogers family also became involved in banking in Stourbridge, in addition to their
earlier interests in the flint-glass and bottle industry. Thomas Rogers was the grandson of another Thomas, a Welshman who died in 1680 and who married Anne, the daughter of Daniel
Tittery of the old Hoo Glasshouse at Holloway End. Like his father, Thomas Rogers junior
lived at The Hill in Amblecote (on the site of the present Corbett Hospital), but eventually

left the district for Newington, Middlesex and Cornhill, London. He had two sons, Daniel and Samuel (a banker and poet), and five daughters, all of whom died at White Hall, Oldswinford without ever marrying.

The Witton family had resided in Oldswinford parish since at least the second half of the 16th century, an Eleanor Witton having tenure of land called Stonecroft on The Heath in 1633. In 1778 Edward Russell, owner of The Heath Glassworks at the time, died and left his property to his three nephews Francis Witton, Richard Russell Witton and Serjeant Witton. Serjeant Witton decided to live at Heath House, but in 1801 he became bankrupt and a sale took place at the *Talbot* in Stourbridge disposing of the house, pool, glasshouse and other adjoining property. The Witton family were strong nonconformists. The Badgers were another well-known Stourbridge family of that period. An earlier Wildsmith Badger was a scythesmith who, with his wife Phoebe, leased land from Samuel Foley at The Hayes Lye in 1674. Pits were sunk on the land and his son John had a pool and dam sited there in 1760. This family also lived at White Hall for some years, but by 1768 John Badger had become bankrupt and was forced to sell the property.

Francis Homfray was the first of his family to settle in Worcestershire. He came from Wales near Rotherham and established an ironmaking plant in the Stourbridge area. His son Francis (1674-1737) was married initially to Mary Baker who died in 1715, and then to Mary Jeston, by whom he had four sons. One of those sons, John Homfray (1731-60), went to live at Wollaston Hall. In 1758 John Homfray married Mary, the daughter and heir of Jeremiah Addenbrooke, and their only son John (1759-1827) inherited the estate of Over Sapey from Edward Addenbrooke in 1784, assuming the arms and surname of Addenbrooke and becoming High Sheriff of Worcestershire in 1798.[15] The Hunts of Oldswinford gained prominence when Samuel Hunt, an attorney, married into the Jeston family. This family remained solicitors in the town of Stourbridge until late into the 19th century. A fine memorial is positioned high up on the sanctuary wall of St Mary's, Oldswinford to William Hunt, who was killed in 1843 at the early age of 42 by a fall from his horse.

Older families continued to prosper. Gregory Hickman purchased Wollaston Hall in 1731 and by 1754 his son Edward (1724-1802), a lawyer, had moved into Oldswinford Castle, also purchasing the land around it. Edward's grandson was Captain Richard Hickman (1792-1855), the last of a long line of the family to be prominent in Stourbridge affairs, and he was a partner in a large brickworks at Hay Green. Oldswinford Castle itself was probably built in the late 16th century; a rather fine Tudor fireplace was uncovered when it was converted into flats in the 20th century. It remained the family home of the Hickmans for many years. The Scott family successfully continued with their clothier trade. William Scott IV (1721-92) carried on the family's dissenting tradition by providing funds for the building of the Presbyterian Chapel in Lower High Street in 1788. After his death at Great Barr in 1792, his family donated money for the construction of Lye Unitarian Church.

The daughter of Thomas and Prudence Milward, also named Prudence, married Hungerford Oliver of the Grange, Oldswinford (whose ancestors originated from Bristol in the early 18th century). But the Milward fortune was largely dissipated by Prudence and Hungerford Oliver's son Edward in the early years of the 19th century; he was reputed to have been an incurable gambler. The family home of the Milwards was Wollescote Hall, which stood in a

35   *A watercolour of Oldswinford Castle, c.1825.*

36   *The 17th-century Wollescote Hall, c.1950.*

magnificent position on the northern side of Wollescote Road overlooking Lye and Hob Green. The building dated from about 1660, although it incorporated some timber-framework from previous Milward occupation as the site had been inhabited since as early as the 12th century. Thomas Milward added a new bay on the western side in about 1760. Wollescote Hall was later sold in 1848 to Stephen Hipkins, a brewer, who converted the attic into a second storey in about 1850. Financial problems caused the sale in 1861 to Elizabeth King (who owned mines) and she lived there for the remainder of the century.

Early Years of the 19th Century

Detailed records, which supplemented the church registers, began to be kept after 1801, when the first national census of population was undertaken; this event has taken place every tenth year since (with the exception of the war year 1941). The Oldswinford overseers William Perrins and William Cooksey carried out the parish census in 1811; it involved house-to-house enquiries, for which they were jointly paid three guineas. The results of that census showed that the parish had 905 families living in only 881 houses, and a total population of 4,380 persons (which excluded the township of Stourbridge). Only 10 per cent of inhabitants were now engaged in agriculture, but 82 per cent were in some other trade, leaving eight per cent with no employment at all. Census returns for the town of Stourbridge indicated the number of inhabitants as 3,431 in 1801, 4,072 in 1811, 5,090 in 1821 and 6,145 in 1831.

The 19th century opened with many disturbances in Stourbridge, owing to the high price of food. The colliers were rioting and the 7th Dragoon Guards had to be called to restore order in April 1800.[16] During the first two decades of the century, people suffered great distress due

---

Stourbridge through Time: 1800 to 1837

1800	Stourbridge Ironworks built by John Bradley & Co.
1803	Prophetess Joanna Southcott lives at Oldswinford rectory
1810	Congregational Chapel built in Lower High Street
1812	Fire damages grammar school tower
1813	First local newspaper
1816	Scott's Charity School is opened
1817	43 per cent of population on parish relief after end of Napoleonic Wars
1825	Board of Improvement Commissioners set up for town
1827	New Market Hall erected in Stourbridge
1828	Stourbridge Lion steam locomotive is built
1829	High Street is macadamed
1831	Dispensary set up in New Road
1833	Gas Company is formed
1835	Stourbridge Mechanics Institute founded
1837	Oldswinford and Stourbridge workhouses close when new Wordsley workhouse built

mainly to the continuing wars with the French. Five years earlier, in 1795, £1,000 had been raised at the *Talbot* towards providing cheap corn for the poor, and in 1813 a similar sum was raised at a public meeting to establish a soup shop for their relief. Despite the hardship the poorer inhabitants did enjoy the festivities that followed the peace with France in 1814; an ox was roasted and many sheep were dressed and shared amongst them. But the years immediately after the war were even harsher. In 1816 over £100 was raised from further collections for the support of a soup establishment and in 1817 no fewer than 1,868 persons (representing 43 per cent of the population) were receiving parish relief. A mere 158 landowners and tenants could contribute towards the poor rate. A local petition was presented to the House of Commons committee on the poor laws, which complained that the poor rate was four times as high as it had been at the start of the war and requested assistance for Stourbridge. By 1818 matters were beginning to return to comparative normality with only 13 per cent of the population on relief. The parish had to resort increasingly to taking out distress orders to collect their rates, and sometimes other means of raising money to support the poor were resorted to, in particular public subscriptions. Shops providing soup and bread at reduced prices were a continuing feature of the 19th century, and in 1829 a permanent building for that purpose was erected in the north-west corner of the new Stourbridge market place.

With many more people being cared for by the parish workhouse, it was decided in 1799 to build a new 'House of Industry'. The building was situated on the western side of Hagley Road, near its junction with Worcester Lane (a plot later occupied by a laundry company). A sum of £250 was borrowed from each of the Stourbridge bankers Hill & Co. and Rufford & Co., the capital being secured on the workhouse and repayable in half-yearly instalments of £50 to each lender. The parish appeared to remain heavily indebted to the banks over the next two decades and in 1820 an extra rate of three shillings in the pound was collected to pay off the arrears. Problems with workhouse governors continued in the early 19th century, commencing with the appointment of Joseph Cardo in 1807 (by now paid eight shillings a week). In addition a governess named Mrs. Giles had already been in office for several years at that time. Within 18 months Joseph Cardo was discharged, as he had 'taken an unwarrantable liberty in having his maintenance in the workhouse, in direct violation of his agreement and order of 5 May 1807'. The position was advertised again and this resulted in William Cooksey being appointed in January 1809 at an annual salary of £20. Cooksey got into great debt in 1813, and according to the vestry minutes great mismanagement had taken place in the workhouse. On examination of his accounts it was found that he owed the parish the large amount of £80. He also failed to pay over all the taxes that he had collected in that year, an omission that landed him in Worcester Gaol in 1816, but the parish thought so well of him that they recollected the taxes and petitioned for his release. Following this William Rogers and his wife were appointed governor and governess (Mrs. Giles being retired with a parish annuity of £10 for life in recognition of her long service). An attempt by the Rogers to have their son boarded at the workhouse so that he could attend the free school in Stourbridge was firmly squashed by the parish. By March 1815 Rogers was also over £70 in debt and agreed to give up his goods to the parish in part payment, quitting his job the following month, his wife being allowed to continue until December. In November 1816 Joseph Spittle and his wife were given the position at the inflated salary of £30. This time the parish was luckier with

37   *The market hall and Market Street, Stourbridge in the 1830s.*

its choice, for Joseph was still in office in 1829 when he was appointed constable for parish affairs in addition to his post as governor.

The administration of the township of Stourbridge (but not the parish of Oldswinford, which was still governed by a Parish Vestry) underwent important changes in the 1820s. In 1825 an Act of Parliament put the town under the control of a Board of Improvement Commissioners. This had powers to regulate the market, build a new market place and control the lighting, cleansing, watching and paving of the streets. To be a commissioner, an inhabitant was required to own property with a value of £1,500. As a consequence the Board became almost exclusively composed of local gentry, professional and businessmen who took their duties lightly, attending meetings only when it suited them. Much of their time in later years was spent abusing each other at meetings. The good news for the inhabitants was that rates were limited to three shillings in the pound, and the commissioners did not run up any large debts.

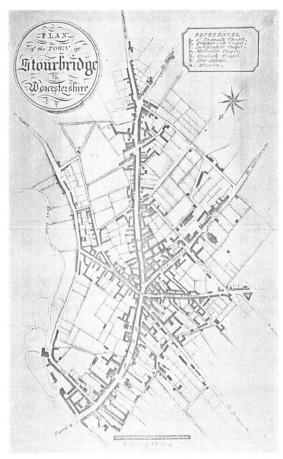

38 *A plan of Stourbridge drawn by John Scott in 1802.*

A new market hall was duly started, built to a design by John White. Numerous small properties between Market Street and New Street were demolished to make room for that complex, and the building was finally opened on 5 October 1827 at a cost of £20,000. Covered stalls filled the sides of its quadrangle interior, and this must have compared very favourably with the triangular shape of the previous building, the centre of which had been used as a fruit and vegetable market and shambles. Part of the new market hall was soon enclosed for the purpose of a Friday Corn Exchange, the rather bleak building also being used for larger public meetings, concerts and dances.[17] More intimate functions were held at the *Talbot* or *Vine* hotels in High Street.

The health of the rapidly rising population began to cause concern. In 1820 the parish was already making donations to institutions outside their boundary, such as the five guineas per annum paid to the Birmingham General Hospital. After the cholera epidemic in 1831, the various medical men of Stourbridge got together at the *Talbot* on 15 November and formed the Stourbridge Board of Health to protect inhabitants from the disease. The cottages in the town were all limewashed, the Board paying for this to be done if the occupants could not afford it themselves. Beggars were suspected of being the chief source of infection, now that their treatment was less harsh than in the previous century; the public flogging of women had been outlawed in 1817.

Crime was on the increase at the time. In 1812 a local newspaper reported that 'the depredations committed in the vicinity of Stourbridge are without example; there is scarcely a night passes but robberies or attempts take place'. It was at about this time that a Mr. Robins from Stourbridge was robbed and murdered whilst making his way back home across Dunsley Heath; the criminal concerned was the infamous William Howe (alias John Wood). On 20 March 1813 Howe was hung in chains in the wood where the crime took place (now known as the Gibbet Wood). His body was fastened into a square framework by his hands and feet, and several days later it fell to Dr. Downing to transport the body back in a sack. Also in 1812 a man named Charles Wall threw a young girl, Sally Chance, into a pit of lime, where her body was consumed. After Wall's execution at Worcester, his body was brought back into the custody of the same Dr. Downing in Stourbridge, who put it on public display;

huge crowds came to see the body, much to the disgust of some of the townsfolk. Afterwards Downing was reputed to have preserved the complete skin of the felon. A large number of other crimes were treated as capital offences at that time. Execution was the fate of those found guilty of sheep and horse stealing, coining and forgery, highway robbery and house breaking as well as treason, murder and rape. Many of those executions would actually have taken place in Stourbridge in former years. The last execution at neighbouring Stafford for a crime not involving murder took place in August 1833 and the last person to be hanged there in view of the public was William Collier in July 1866.

Further improvements were made to local roads in the first three decades of the century. The final Turnpike Act to affect Stourbridge was passed on 11 April 1816; this set up four turnpikes on the road from Stourbridge to Bridgnorth. Further turnpike gates had earlier appeared in Dudley Road (just above Lye Forge) and on the bend in Grange Lane close to its present junction with Croftwood Road. Tolls were normally charged for every head of cattle and every horse, chaise, gig, wagon or cart, although local cart traffic was exempt from toll. The Oldswinford gate charged one penny a horse or wagon, and this freed gates and bars at Coalbournbrook, Hollowsend, Pedmore, Wordsley Heath and Collis Street from any further charge. In 1823 the Turnpike Commissioners considerably improved Lower High Street by reducing the slope between the lower and upper parts and soon afterwards public subscriptions were requested in order to flag High Street, Rye Market and other streets as far as funds would permit. Over £1,000 was raised in six months and work commenced in 1829, the central ramparts being macadamed.[18]

39   *A watercolour of Stourbridge viewed from Amblecote, painted by Thomas Creswick (1811–1869), before Amblecote church was erected. The church in the centre is St Thomas's.*

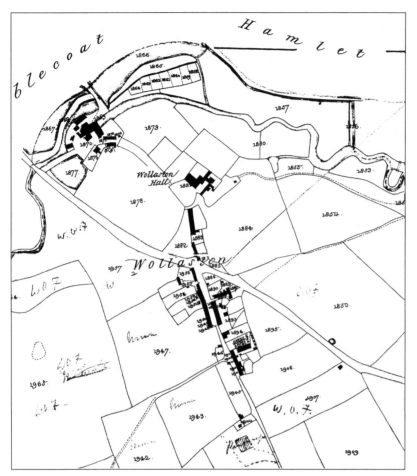

40 *A plan of Wollaston from Brettell and Davies' survey in 1827.*

Various new surveys of the area were also carried out in the early years of the 19th century. After Harry Court's son Richard had made a new survey in 1814, the parishioners threw out his map. They complained that 'the map only gave one valuation for each landlord, even though his holding might be spread over several plots of land; the names of the landlords and tenants were incorrect in many cases; the whole valuation was confused; and there were numerous instances of inequality contained within the valuation'. In 1827 John Orme Brettell and John Davies made a superb survey of the parish of Oldswinford (excluding the town centre and Amblecote) to a scale of four chains to one inch for poor law rating purposes. These two men were remunerated at a rate of seven pence for every acre (a total of £120) and the parishioners successfully adopted their survey in 1829. It was rescued by a vigilant member of the general public when a local solicitor was having a clearout of his papers some years ago.[19] Although roads were not named, the occupier and owner of each plot of land were fully referenced in an accompanying book.

VI

Victorian Stourbridge

Radical Changes before 1850

The first few years of Queen Victoria's reign witnessed immense change and improvement in living conditions for many residents of Stourbridge. Families were abandoning their country parishes for the better wages and prospects offered in industrial areas where the industrial revolution was in full swing; for the first time many people began to work in large factories. At the same time a great revival in religious worship was seen and the number of small chapels mushroomed. Later chapters deal fully with both the growth in industry and religious revival at that time.

The 19th century in Stourbridge saw a threefold increase in population (at least) and in 1837 the government began to record births, marriages and deaths on a national scale through local registries, thus providing a record of the entire population of the country. The number of people living in the town of Stourbridge increased from 6,145 in 1831 to 8,332 by 1851. But

---

Stourbridge through Time: 1837 to 1879

1837	Accession of Queen Victoria
1839	County Police Force is established
1840	New bridge is built over river Stour in Lower High Street
1843	St Mary's Church, Oldswinford is rebuilt
1848	Stourbridge School of Art opens
1851	Rufford & Wragge Bank goes into liquidation
1852	Stourbridge is connected to the railway
1855	High Street is lit by gas
1857	Town is served by piped water and obtains its town clock
1861	St John's Church is opened
1866	Town Commissioners are reorganised into three wards
1867	Railway line to Birmingham is completed
1872	The town hosts the Worcestershire Agricultural Society Show
1876	Victoria Hall skating rink opens in Stourbridge
1878	Volunteer Fire Brigade is formed in Stourbridge
1879	Branch railway line to Stourbridge Town is built

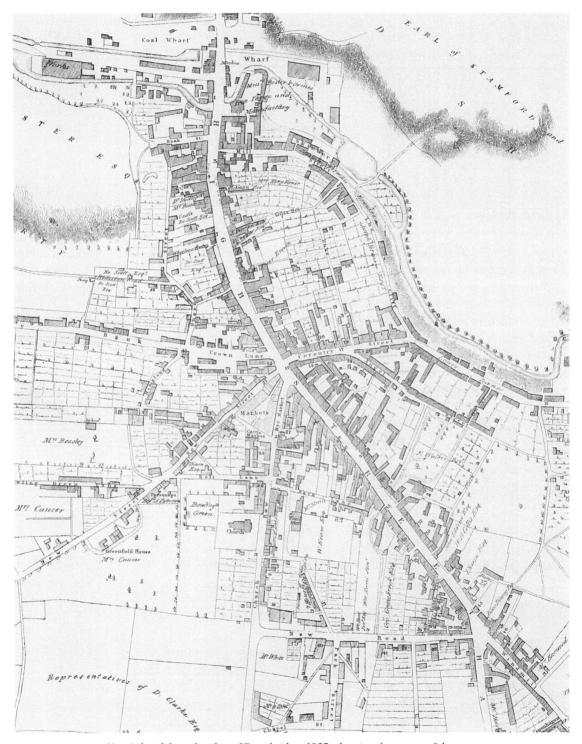

41   *A detail from the plan of Stourbridge, 1837, showing the centre of the town.*

most growth took place outside the town centre on the industrial eastern side of the town, rather than in Oldswinford, Norton and Wolla-ston where the buildings were more residential in character. As the population increased in Lye, the slums grew worse. In 1841 Lye and Lye Waste were almost one continuous series of humble dwellings and workshops, interspersed at intervals with others of a more respectable appearance.[1] By that time 4,000 people were living on Lye Waste. Most of their housing still consisted of mud huts, the floors being of clay and the roofs thatched. Lye people referred to each other by their nicknames, such as Old Latchet, Smacker, Firelock, Squirrel, Growler, Taypot, Pighook, Slapfoot or Pay-cock, indicating a unique and close-knit society. The dreadful poverty, scantily dressed children and billows of black smoke emanating from the small forges in the nailers' back gardens gave rise to the saying that 'the Lye and the Waste and Careless Green were the three worst places that ever were seen'. Other populous areas nearby were Careless Green (41 pages of entries in the 1851 census) and Chawn Hill village (31 pages of census).

42   *A mud house in Cross Walks at Lye, still inhabited in 1943.*

The town centre of Stourbridge was improving in appearance, however. Its High Street contained some fine private residences, generally kept in excellent repair with elegant fronts and rambling interiors, interspersed with the more modest offices of professional men and shop premises. High Street, Coventry Street and Market Street formed the main business district of the town but one did not have to walk far out of the centre to find rows of dreary cottages. The worst were in Enville Street, Beauty Bank, Birmingham Street, Angel Street, Church Street, Hagley Road, Worcester Street and The Heath, where the massive glassworks cone was the sole survivor of the world-famous glass industry within the boundary of Stourbridge.

Major changes took place in local and national administration in the twenty years leading up to 1850, caused in no small way by the greater franchise granted by the Reform Bill of 1832 and the Municipal Reform Bill of 1835. That legislation was accompanied by the founding of trade unions, co-operative societies, friendly societies and similar organisations for the self-improvement of working men. The middle class was becoming a major political force and the pace of change was slowly beginning to have an effect on living conditions. Many outbreaks of smallpox, typhoid and cholera occurred due to the crowded living conditions. A dispensary in New Road had previously been established in 1831 to look after the medical needs of the poor (as long as they were not on parish relief), supported by subscriptions and

43   *The Stourbridge Board of Guardians in 1901.*

donations. It then moved to Hagley Road, and in the 1840s was open between 9 a.m. and 10 a.m. on four days a week, caring for 600 or 700 persons a year. House surgeon there in the middle of the century was William Lascelles Norris. Another cholera scare resulted in the Public Health Act of 1848. At work the Factory Act of 1833 enforced inspection of factories, in 1842 the Mines Act forbade women and children under the age of 10 from working underground, and the Ten Hours Bill of 1847 did something towards limiting hours of work, all of which helped the downtrodden workers of Lye. In 1833 John Swift and five other partners established a small gas company and a manufacturing plant was built on the two-acre Coney Close site on the eastern side of the main road at Holloway End, Amblecote. This in turn led to the first proper lighting of the streets, shops and churches of Stourbridge (as well as in Pedmore, Amblecote and Wordsley) and the introduction of lighting into some private homes soon followed. The gas plant was incorporated by an Act of Parliament in 1855, promoted by the enterprising currier William Akroyd, who was chairman for a short time.

The problem of looking after the poorer members of the community continued to tax the authorities. In 1833 Chadwick's enquiry into workhouse conditions reported that the Old-swinford workhouse was managed by a Select Vestry, but attendance at their meetings was very irregular, the accounts were in great confusion and the workhouse was in a filthy state with little order or discipline. In 1834 the Poor Law Amendment Act stated that towns could no longer provide outdoor relief to the able-bodied, so that those who could not look after themselves had to attend a workhouse. In 1836 Oldswinford and Stourbridge combined with the ancient parishes of Kingswinford and Halesowen to form the Stourbridge Union, with its workhouse at Wordsley. In line with the township workhouse, the Oldswinford parish work-house closed down in about 1837, the year in which the Wordsley workhouse was enlarged at a cost of £2,179. The affairs of the new Wordsley workhouse were managed by a Board of Guardians 24 strong (in addition to the 10 ex-officio guardians); they were responsible for the poor from Amblecote, Brierley Hill, Quarry Bank, Cradley, Cakemore, Hasbury, Hawne Hill, Illey, Lapal, Lutley and Quinton. The inhabitants of these latter hamlets faced a very long walk indeed when taking up their places in the workhouse. Some further help for poorer folk was obtained in 1846 when repeal of the Corn Laws gave more stability to food prices.

Public administration of local roads was addressed by the 1835 Highways Act; that abolished unpaid labour and parishes were encouraged to unite into 'highway districts'. They could then employ a paid district surveyor, and a measure of compulsion to do this was added by a later Act in 1862. Even in the middle of the century the cleaning of the streets of Stourbridge was generally ne-glected, as watchmen carried out that duty but only when they felt fit to do so. The annual expenditure on repairs for drainage, cleans-ing etc. was estimated to be a mere £100 in 1847.[2] Streets were more effectively policed following the setting up of a formal county police force in 1839, which soon took over the peacekeeping duties formerly performed by the parish constable and town watchmen.

The Tithe Commutation Act of 1836 commuted tithes to cash payments, and detailed maps with lists of landowners were drawn up for each parish at that time for the Tithe Redemption Commission. (The 1935/6 Tithe Act finally abolished the tax, and compensated owners for their lost rentals.) The Marriage Act of 1836 removed an insult to the religious feelings of Dissenters and Roman

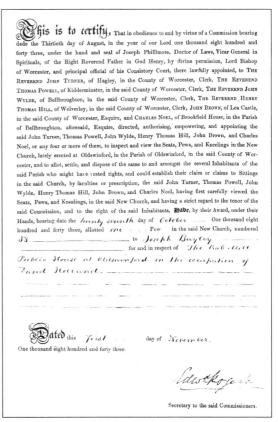

44 *An 1843 pew rental agreement for a seat belonging to the* Crabmill Inn *on the rebuilding of St Mary's Church, Oldswinford.*

Catholics, as it enabled marriages to be taken by a non-Anglican parson for the first time. Pew rents were the cause of many disputes, but only limited relief was given at that time. When Oldswinford church was rebuilt in 1843 there were 110 numbered pews on the ground floor and a further 42 in the lofts. New box pews were erected in the rebuilt church, and a committee of four clergymen and two laymen had to be formed to sort out the new seating arrangements. By that time, 756 out of 1,432 sittings in the church had become free; it was not until 1921 that all the seats at the evening service were declared free of rent.

One area where little progress was made before 1850 was with the supply and the disposal of waste water. Homes still had to rely either on wells in their own gardens, communal wells or a water cart for their water supply. Because local water was considered to be too hard for washing clothes and not fit for cooking, much of it still had to be purchased from water carts at a cost of half a penny for five or six gallons. By 1850 these carts were supplying nearly 1,500 dwellings in Stourbridge at an average cost of more than half a penny a day. In 1847 Hob Green (which lay at the foot of Brook Holloway and had been owned since 1782 by Edward Hickman, a lawyer and land proprietor of Oldswinford Castle) was suggested as a site suitable for a reservoir to provide the town with running water.[3] The area included a pool, orchard and five other enclosures totalling about seventeen acres, but nothing came of the proposal.

Disposal of waste water was another difficult problem. Since Tudor times an open sewer had run down Stourbridge High Street, and no doubt other streets had similar arrangements. There were also open sewers coming out of the passageways off High Street, and waste water was often thrown from the windows of the cramped rows of cottages. The 1791 Stourbridge Act had failed to have much impact on the worst slum areas. In 1847 these were Mill Street, Duke Street, Angel Street, Lower Lane, Crown Lane and The Hemplands. Mill Street was very unhealthy because of its narrowness and low-lying position by the river Stour, this not being

45 *A Dutch-style gable-ended building in Angel Street at its junction with Birming-ham Street, c.1910. The street housed a large Irish comm-unity.*

helped by the skin works nearby. A privy serving several houses there opened directly onto the street, so that no modest female could make use of it. Soft water could only be fetched from an open stream 200 yards away by trespassing on other people's land. Duke Street had a drain for part of its length, but the houses were not connected to it. Thirteen houses there shared one water pump, and in one adjoining court there were large pig sties and muck holes. Angel Street at that time contained mainly Irish immigrants who lived in dilapidated houses consisting of one room up and down; they were badly overcrowded and known as Irish lodging houses. It was by far the worst street; open gutters ran close to doors and windows of homes and ground floors were below street level so that drainage ran into them. Crown Lane was not drained at all and as the houses were also below street level they too were often flooded. In addition a large hole for the reception of manure was described as a great evil there. The wells in Beauty Bank had sewage flowing directly into them and the stench was atrocious. Even recently-built roads such as Union Street had been constructed without any regard to sanitary conditions; it was undrained and the process of cleaning out privies was going on in the middle of the day, leaving a great heap of disgusting matter in the street.[4] The traveller along New Street, Coventry Street and Birmingham Street could see gutters filled with household slops and decayed vegetable matter.

Expansion of the local road network gathered apace from that period onwards. Stourbridge High Street was a major beneficiary of Victorian skills. In 1840 the local turnpike trust built a replacement bridge with only one arch, which was considerably wider than its predecessor.[5] At the same time the approach to the town from the north was much improved in appearance and convenience by the re-siting of three houses further back from the road.[6] Additional streets were constructed around the town centre. These included Smithfield (where the new meat and cattle markets were held), Union Street, Summer Street, Park Street, Mount Street, Duke Street, Chapel Street and Field Road (the Church Street end of Parkfield Road). Foster Street, after many years of being a footpath into Angel Street, was made into a road, and named after the town's leading industrialist of the period, James Foster. Footpaths connected Angel Street to Lower Lane, one being descriptively called The Gullet. Parts of Coventry Street were equally unsavoury and brothels were known to have existed there during the Victorian era. Also built before 1850 were Hill Street (originally named Queen Street), Swan Street, Cleveland Street (then called Longlands), Mamble Road and Hanbury Hill.

New service industries had become established by 1850.[7] Numerous architects, auctioneers, surveyors and land agents could now be consulted, although only one accountant was listed (James Smith of Love Lane) as this was still a very young profession. Fire Insurance Companies were well represented in the High Street with agents for the Norwich Union, Phoenix, Royal Exchange, Protestant Dissenters, Birmingham Clerical and Medical, and Independent West Middlesex organisations. Attorneys still dominated local life, as indeed they had done for several centuries, and included amongst their ranks were such well-known characters as William Blow Collis, George Grazebrook, John Harward, William Hunt, Rowland Price, Charles Roberts and Clement Wragge. The 20th-century partnership of Harward and Evers, which was formed in 1905, traced its roots in the High Street back to the early 19th century, as John Harward was articled to William Hunt who was born in 1779 and practised from that same site. (Harward and Evers eventually merged with Higgs & Sons of Hagley Road in November 1989.)[8] Two

46   *The Parkfield cattle market in 1910. This later became the site for the fire station.*

well-known printers and booksellers in the High Street were Joseph Heming and Thomas Mellard, who traded at the Athenaeum newsroom. Mellard was succeeded in 1861 by Thomas Mark who took as his apprentice George Moody; the Mark & Moody firm became well known in Stourbridge for over 100 years as printers, publishers, retailers and proprietors of the *County Express* newspaper. Coach builders and proprietors, catering for an ever more mobile society, included Richard Gibson of Hagley Road, who supplied 'all kinds of carriages on the most modern and improved principles'; over 50 men were employed there by 1894 and the premises extended back to Union Street. For inhabitants' final journey the specialised funeral agent had arrived on the scene in the person of Joseph Parkes of New Street. Barbers had become hairdressers and were well represented in the town centre by Samuel Hughes, Mary Mills, Henry Morgan and James Wilkins in High Street alone. Thomas Mills of Lower High Street had come from London and was advertising his 'celebrated vegetable extract for cleansing, beautifying and strengthening the hair ... imparting a glossy appearance and beautiful tendency to wave', all for 1s. 6d. a bottle.

There was a choice of eating houses for those dining out. These included Thomas Bowkett in the Rye Market, Edward Corser and John Baggott in Coventry Street and the Temperance Coffee House run by Sarah Worrall in Windmill Street. Stronger drink had to be obtained from the spirit dealers in the High Street, represented by John Ash, William Lakin, Joseph Corns, Montague Taylor, James Nickolls and William Perks. The business of Nickolls & Perks was established on the corner of Lower High Street and Coventry Street, the site of the 17th-century family home of John Baker at 37 High Street. In 1797 the property was leased to William Nichless, and when George Richards later obtained the lease it became The Liquor Vaults. The *Board Inn* opened on the site in the 1860s and Francis Perks became licensee until 1928, when the Reading family took over the inn and adjoining grocery business. This ancient company still trades on the same site today.[9] There was also a cider mill in Farlands Road, Oldswinford owned by George Edward; the road was named after Farlands House that once stood on its south side. Clock and watch making seemed very popular, an occupation carried on in the town centre by Charles Beavington, John Blurton, James Edwards, Joseph Adams and John Hall. The greater spending power of the Victorians resulted in a multitude of small shop owners. There were basket, cabinet and chair makers, chemists, china and glass dealers, clothes dealers, confectioners, fishmongers and fruiterers, furniture brokers, grocers, hatters, drapers, locksmiths, milliners, provision dealers, saddlers, seedsmen, straw hat makers, tailors, tallow chandlers and a toy dealer (John Hall), to name but a few. Those who could not afford their products were tempted into the town's pawnbrokers residing in Coventry Street: John Compson, Hugh Sproat, Richard Webb and the renowned Edwin Stringer who later moved into the Market Hall House. The older way of life still survived as evidenced by Henry Round of Oldswinford who simply listed himself as a 'cow keeper'!

During the 70 years to 1850 the streets in Lye had mushroomed. They now included Hill Bank, Orchard Lane and Dock Lane (probably so named because it was to the warehouses there that hundreds of domestic nailmakers brought their nails to the middleman or 'fogger' for disposal). Also to be found were Connops Lane, Fanny's Lane, Green Lane, Back Street, Church Row and Spring Street besides the numerous yards that led off the main streets. Other parts of the ancient manor of Oldswinford did not change their character quite so quickly at that time, land there being reserved for the mass housing estates of the 20th century. In Oldswinford itself only New Street (now called Hall Street) had been added to the map, although it is interesting to note that Rectory Road was then called Crab Mill Road. The expansion of Wollaston was just beginning to get under way with the development of King Street, Cobden Street, Moore Street and New Street. King Street was probably named after Henry King, a local auctioneer and surveyor who lived there at that time, and Richard Cobden (1804-65) was a famous national Liberal politician. The population centre of Wollaston was beginning to shift at that time from the ancient *Barley Mow* district towards the streets mentioned above. This was a result of the turnpiking of the Stourbridge to Bridgnorth road in 1816 and a substantial sale of 386 acres of land from the Wollaston Hall estate in 1848.

The influence of the Foley family had waned by this time and in 1844 they sold the manor of Oldswinford to Lord Ward, Earl of Dudley. The most important industrialists on the early 19th-century Stourbridge scene were by now the Foster family. Henry Foster had come from Cheshire in the late 18th century with his two sons, William and James, and married Mary (née

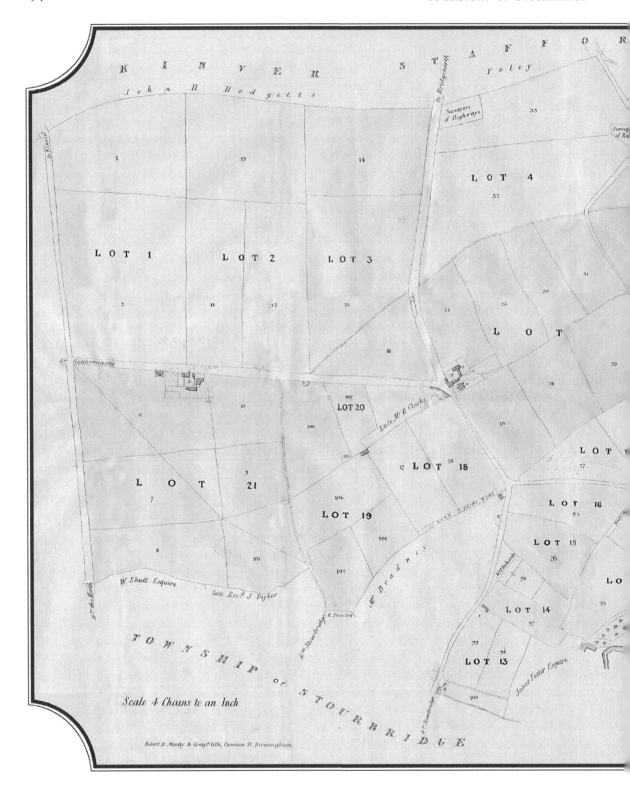

Scale 4 Chains to an Inch

Robert B. Moody & Compy lith, Cannon St Birmingham.

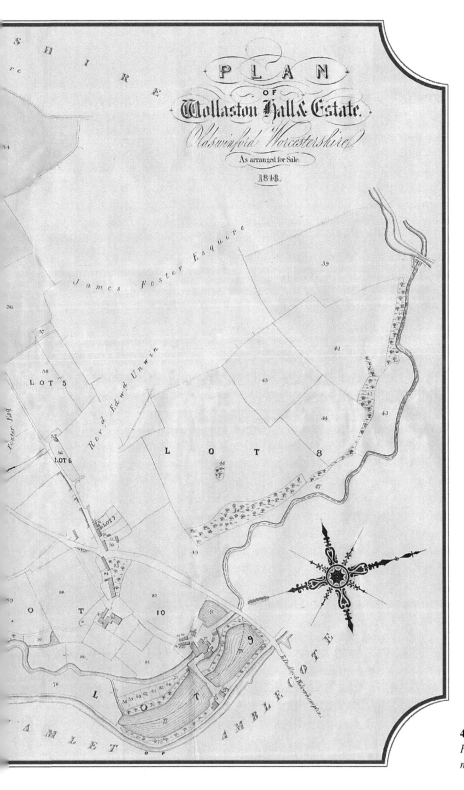

47 *A plan of the Wollaston Hall estate during the sale of a major part of the land in 1848.*

Haden), the widow of Gabriel Bradley. Henry's son James Foster (1786-1853) was a business genius. He started his career in the office of his half brother, John Bradley (1769-1816), and a number of his ventures were in partnership with the Bradley family. John Bradley had founded the Stourbridge Ironworks company bearing his name in about 1800 on a site to the west of the Royal Forge, and he built a second works in 1808 to the east of the Royal Forge. In 1814 James Foster also went into partnership with John Urpeth Rastrick (1780-1856), a brilliant engineer who had patented a steam engine, and the resulting firm of Foster, Rastrick & Co. made several famous steam locomotives at Stourbridge in 1828/9, including the *Stourbridge Lion* and the *Agenoria* (see below). James Foster eventually became sole proprietor of the Stourbridge Ironworks. For many years James Foster lived at Park House in Lower High Street, but in 1833 he moved to Stourton Castle. He was elected Member of Parliament for Bridgnorth and in 1840 became High Sheriff for Worcestershire. When he died in April 1853, leaving a massive estate of £700,000, such was the respect for him that 1,000 of his workmen, walking four abreast, marched through Stourbridge town to his funeral at St Mary's, Oldswinford. In the south chapel of that church a memorial tablet in the shape of a sarcophagus surmounted by a bust in white marble commemorates his life. His nephew and heir, William Orme Foster, endowed Wollaston church, school and vicarage. He also became a Member of Parliament, dying in 1899, and was succeeded by his son William Henry.

Journeys at that time were mainly made by horse and coach. In the 1840s the coaches serving Stourbridge had romantic names such as the *British Queen*, *Red Rover*, *Erin-go-Bragh*, *Rocket*, *Everlasting*, *Bang-Up* and *Greyhound*. Journeys could be made directly from Stourbridge to Birmingham, Brierley Hill and Dudley, Wolverhampton, Worcester and Kidderminster, and Bewdley, Tenbury, Leominster and Ludlow.[10] Coaches on Birmingham and Worcester routes were owned by Joseph Gardner of Windmill Street. Another carrier was Joseph Pemberton, who ran to Birmingham, Bristol, Dudley, Tipton and Worcester from the *Coach and Horses* Inn in the High Street. Richard Smallman of Oldswinford was a letter carrier. Benjamin Dovey and Crowley & Co. (both of Stourbridge wharf) transported goods and people by canal but the emergence of railways and problems with increased weight of traffic using their canal bridges started a decline in the canal company's fortunes which became very severe by the 1870s.

The days of coach transport were also numbered. The development of the railways was just beginning, and some eight years before Victoria came to the throne Stourbridge played a major role in that revolution with the production of two of the first steam locomotives ever to run on rails, the *Stourbridge Lion* and the *Agenoria.* The firm of Foster, Rastrick & Co. was building stationary steam engines in the early 1820s, but in 1828 it manufactured the famous Stourbridge Lion, to satisfy an order worth $2,915 from the Delaware and Hudson Canal Company. Its name derived from a workman painting a red lion on its boiler to cover up a bump or defect. The engine was shipped from Stourbridge to Liverpool in February 1829 and reached New York on 13 May. It was transported up the Hudson to Honesdale and made its trial trip on the following 8 August, the first steam locomotive ever to run in the Western Hemisphere. It soon proved to be rather too heavy for its rails and was put into storage until 1849, when it was dismantled and substantially lost; only the boiler and a few original parts still remain on show in the Smithsonian Institution, which also possesses a full-scale replica. In the early summer of 1829 the *Agenoria* was built and this did service locally on

48   *The Stourbridge to Birmingham mail coach in c.1850, outside the* Old Kings Head *(133 High Street), near the site of the present Lloyds Bank.*

49   *The* Coach and Horses *Inn in High Street in 1860. This later became the site of Sketchley's dry cleaning shop.*

50 *A full-sized working replica of the 1828* Stourbridge Lion *locomotive, made in 1932 by the Delaware and Hudson Railroad Company.*

51 *The* Agenoria *(built at Stourbridge in 1829) at Shutt End, Pensnett,* c.*1870.*

the Shutt End colliery line (opened on 2 June 1829) from Pensnett to the canal at Ashwood. The locomotive was a 0-4-0 tender engine with wheels 48¾ inches in diameter, and could be distinguished from the *Lion* by its amazing 14 ft. chimney. It was donated to the Kensington Science Museum by W.O. Foster in 1885 and was sent to the York Railway Museum for safe keeping during the Second World War, where it can still be seen, but minus its tender. Two further locomotives called the *Hudson* and *Delaware* were built by the same works and shipped to America, but all trace of those has been lost. The Foster and Rastrick partnership was dissolved on 20 June 1831 by mutual consent.[11]

The authorities were being forced to deal with more cases of industrial unrest than in former times, one of the reasons being the intense concentration of workers into very small buildings and confined areas. On 7 November 1831 a disturbance had taken place in Stourbridge that was caused by striking colliers, furnacemen and other workers and the Yeomanry Cavalry were called out to quell the riot. In 1842 a vast mob of over 1,000 people gathered in the streets of Lye. When Captain Richard Hickman (affectionately nicknamed 'Tommy Trot') and his cavalry arrived, they were forced to retreat by locally made iron balls with multiple spikes (variously called 'crows feet' and 'tis-as-it-was') being scattered across the road, thus preventing horses from advancing. Persons arrested included John Chance of Oldswinford (a local leader of the Chartist movement) and Benjamin Bache, an unemployed nailer of Careless Green. Bache was given four months' hard labour for assault, but next year he was in even more trouble for stealing a ewe from Samuel Grove and was sentenced to 15 years' transportation at the Worcester Sessions. Another Stourbridge person suffering that fate was Joe Moreton, sentenced to transportation by the Worcester Midsummer Sessions in 1843 for the comparatively minor crime of stealing a book. Many minor crimes such as riotous conduct, being drunk and incapable, assault, neglect of work and damaging gardens and property were dealt with by the local magistrates, but the death penalty for serious crimes such as murder was still frequently passed. When in 1839 a permanent police force replaced night watchmen, however, and the rate of crime detection increased dramatically, magistrates could no longer cope with their increased workload and the severity of sentencing lessened with penal servitude replacing transportation for the majority of crimes.

Life between 1850 and 1880

During the 50 years to 1901 the population of the township of Stourbridge grew from 8,332 to 10,372, a lower rate of growth than in the first half of the century. But in the same years the population of the remainder of the parish of Oldswinford (i.e. Upper Swinford, Lye, Wollescote and Wollaston) showed a massive increase from 9,861 to 20,054, partly due to people preferring to move to the more salubrious outskirts of the town. The number of people living within the area covered by the Stourbridge Urban District Council (the Town, Upper Swinford, Norton and Wollaston) increased from 14,891 in 1891 to 16,302 in 1901.

In about 1850 the town's main street was divided into Higher and Lower High Street;[12] the shops in both sections had become very modern for their day. Even so there were at least 20 private dwelling houses remaining in the street, in addition to the people who lived over their business premises. Musicians played in the street, dogs lay in the middle of the road and water carts sprinkled the surface in hot weather to lay the dust. Various yards led off High Street;

52 *The Stourbridge town clock and Lower High Street in the early years of the 20th century.*

53 *High Street c.1860, looking north from Hagley Road, reproduced from a daguerreotype photographic plate.*

on the east side were Bury's, Barlow's, Star, Simm's and Pope's yards and on the opposite side yards named Ball's, Webb's and Trueman's. In 1854 it was proposed that the street be lit by gas, and in 1857 the town clock was installed on its present site in the town centre, being built at John Bradley's ironworks and designed by their works engineer, William Millward. It was wound twice a week from a loft in the Market Hall (until its electrification in 1972) and is still a familiar sight to Stourbridge residents. In 1860 the grammar school buildings were enlarged to a design of Thomas Smith, following the purchase of the ancient *Old Horse Inn.*

A temporary setback to the town's economic growth occurred in July 1851 when the Rufford and Wragge Bank collapsed with a deficit of £225,000 at the Stourbridge branch and £227,000 in Bromsgrove. The winding up was a complicated and distressing affair costing £17,412 in expenses alone, and resulting in Stourbridge customers receiving only 2s. 7d. for every pound invested. This caused considerable hardship to some local people and destroyed the public's confidence in the private banking system.

In 1852 the first railway reached Stourbridge, revolutionising travel opportunities for all its inhabitants. This was the line of the Oxford, Worcester and Wolverhampton Company; its building had caused much annoyance to local landowners as large gangs of unruly work-men camped nearby. The onward line to Dudley opened on 16 November for freight and on 20 December 1852 for passengers. The original Stourbridge Junction station was sited at the convergence of Junction Road and Rufford Road. The initials OWWR became synonymous with the words 'old worse and worse railway' because a series of costly disasters hit the owners of the line. The engineer Isambard Kingdom Brunel seriously underestimated the cost, resulting in the shareholders not receiving any dividends. When the Rufford and Wragge Bank went into liquidation the bank's chairman Francis Rufford was personally made bankrupt; because he was a major local shareholder and chairman of the OWWR the company was deprived of £24,000. There was serious rioting amongst the workforce and frequent breakdowns of locomotives when they did eventually run. Even the width of the line had to be changed from the originally planned broad gauge after squabbles with the Great Western Railway Company. Soon after the line opened a major accident occurred when some 17 packed carriages of a Worcester to Wolverhampton excursion train became detached at Round Oak, and rolled backwards into the following train at Moor Lane bridge in Brierley Hill. That resulted in 14 persons being killed and 220 injured.

In 1854 a long-awaited Act was passed authorising a scheme to supply the town and neighbourhood with piped water; it was completed in 1857. The new waterworks were constructed under the supervision of Edward Bindon Marten (who also managed the undertaking in later years). A pumping station in Mill Meadow on the Amblecote side of the Stour was used to pump water from natural springs up to a covered reservoir on Amblecote Bank. A

54   *The original Stourbridge Junction railway station in Junction Road at the end of the 19th century.*

bar attached to a float in the reservoir protruded above the cover so that the pumping station attendant could see it through binoculars and keep the level of water correct. Sewage continued to be dealt with by the 'night soil men', who had the unpleasant job of emptying the middens or closets from the gardens of houses. These middens had an ashpit alongside; at night the dung and the ash were mixed together, wheeled away in barrows and often dumped in the roadway. Later an iron dungcart would collect it and deliver it to local farmers. Such dreadful conditions resulted in a mortality rate of 2.4 per cent in Stourbridge, which was much higher than in similar towns. It was not until 1881 that a Main Drainage Board was instituted for the area and sewage pumped to a farm at Whittington in Kinver parish. Lye High Street had to wait until about 1900 to be connected to that disposal service.

By the 1850s brick houses were rapidly replacing the haphazard mud dwellings on Lye Waste (but the last mud house, situated on Cross Walks, was not demolished until the 1960s). In 1866 the vicar of Lye, the Reverend David Robertson, described how there were no fewer than 53 beer shops for a population of 7,000 in the hamlet of Lye. The wealthier industrialists there were beginning to move into high-class residential properties in Oldswinford, Pedmore, Wollaston and Norton. Oldswinford Castle was typical of an upmarket Stourbridge property at that time and when it was sold in 1855 the house had the following accommodation: On the ground floor an entrance hall, dining room, drawing room, library, butler's pantry, servants' hall, kitchen and cookery kitchen, dairy and yard; On the first floor four chambers, three dressing rooms, water closet and bathroom; On the second floor four chambers and two storerooms; Outbuildings consisted of boathouse, cornhouse, double coachhouse, pig furnace, potting shed and cowhouse.

James Evers-Swindell bought the castle estate in that year for £2,350. When he sold it in 1897 to the Great Western Railway company, he was already an old man and was therefore allowed to live there for the rest of his life, after which it was intended to convert the property into a hotel. Unfortunately for the company he did not die until 1910 when aged 93, and it was decided that a hotel near the Junction station was no longer needed.

The 1850s witnessed the Crimean War (1854-6) and Indian Mutiny (1857). When in 1859 there was panic over the possible invasion by Napoleon III, the spirit of voluntary service was revived in Stourbridge resulting in the birth of the volunteer movement and the formation of the First Stourbridge Rifle Corps with 110 members. W.O. Foster was captain and M.P. Grazebrook lieutenant. The uniform consisted of a dark grey cloth tunic and trousers (officers were in black), and the chacos (head dress) was adorned with plumes of cocks' feathers. The uniform was provided locally, the cloth by Mr. Doody, the chacos by Mr. Dykes and the belts by Mr. Richards, a saddler in Stourbridge. (The Territorial Army succeeded the old volunteer movement in 1908.)

In 1860 the OWWR changed its name to the West Midlands Railway Company. In the same year the Stourbridge Railway Act enabled a branch line to be commenced which eventually linked up with the Great Western Line from Smethwick to Snow Hill Birmingham, thus giving the local population easy access to this rapidly growing city. The service as far as Cradley Heath was opened on 1 April 1863 and the extension to Old Hill on 1 January 1866, the full link to Birmingham being completed by April 1867. The railway viaduct over the river Stour at Stambermill was originally a wooden structure (the old stone supports can still be seen),

55 *The former wooden viaduct at Stambermill, demolished in 1882.*

and it was here that another mishap occurred on 15 October 1876, when some eight wagons became derailed and crashed 70 feet into the river valley below, having become separated from the rest of the train further up the line. Kellett and Bentley constructed the present brick-built viaduct at a cost of £13,835 in 1881; this impressive structure is 98 feet tall at its highest point, while its foundations reach a maximum depth of 56 feet. Meanwhile, in 1879, a branch line was built to serve Stourbridge town centre, together with an extension to the Amblecote goods depot and canal basin just below Lower High Street (the depot was closed in 1965).

Local government saw further significant changes in the 1860s. The lack of purposeful activity by the town commissioners encouraged a Stourbridge solicitor named Rowland Price to lead a group of influential people to apply to Parliament in 1866 to obtain an Act for the better running of the town's affairs. The legislation that followed at a cost of £2,000 reconstituted the town into three wards, each having nine commissioners as representatives. The first were elected on 4 October 1866, with William Akroyd taking the chair. The new commissioners had greater powers than their predecessors to make improvements to local services. Qualification for the office was reduced to property worth £500, thus enabling a greater section of the population to put themselves forward for election. In 1868 parish rates were finally abolished, resulting in the duties of the rector's and people's wardens at St Mary's, Oldswinford becoming less onerous.

56 *Stourbridge fire brigade and fire engine at their Market Street site, c.1920.*

A fire-fighting service for the area began to be formed by the major insurance companies, who would issue firemarks to their clients for display on the outside walls of their houses. The Phoenix Fire Office kept an engine in Stourbridge, depositing the keys with a blacksmith named Jones in Enville Street and a second set at the *Talbot Hotel*. In 1869 the District Fire Office and the Alliance Assurance Company gave a fire engine to the Improvement Commissioners for the inhabitants of the town. John Sanders took charge of the machine, which was kept near the Bell in Market Street; he had six assistants to help him, each being paid 2s. 6d. a night (the fireman himself earned 7s. 6d.). Following a series of serious fires in the area a new Volunteer Fire Brigade was formed on 30 December 1878, with Henry Turney as captain, making use of premises in Market Street. The two insurance companies offered their equipment to the new and greatly improved service, which won several national competitions over the following years. In April 1879 an alarm bell was installed and in the following year the fire engine moved to purpose-built premises at Smithfield. In December 1880 a new 32 cwt. steam-propelled engine was tried out but this proved to be too heavy, and in December 1882 a 15 cwt. steam engine was purchased for £69 2s. 6d. A new station was constructed in 1892, opposite the existing building. (By 1911/12 the Volunteer Fire Brigade had 21 members and remained in its red brick premises until 1968, when a more conveniently situated station was built off St John's Road.)

Winter continued to cause hardship for the poor. In January 1867 a soup kitchen was opened in Lye to feed distressed families, in January 1871 committees were formed to raise money to provide coal and bread for the poor, and during 1885-6 the exceptionally hard winter caused extensive distress amongst the needy of the district, especially in Lye; 22,000 pounds of bread and 150 tons of coal costing £128 were distributed in a three-month period in Stourbridge. Serious health problems still existed. There had been another epidemic of cholera in the late 1850s and in 1867 an outbreak of typhus fever raged for several months in Lye. Stourbridge surgeons in the mid-19th century included Thomas Bancks, Henry Betts, Thomas Cooper, Richard Leacroft Freer, Henry Giles, Thomas Massey Harding and Henry Wilson.[13] In July 1876 the town's first medical officer of health, Robert Eager, was appointed at a salary of £50 per annum.

57 *High Street in 1872, showing the castle decoration for the County Agricultural Show held at Amblecote.*

Stourbridge was increasingly turning into a business and social centre for a large part of North Worcestershire and South Staffordshire at that time. During the last week of March the annual Stourbridge Fair was held in Foster Street, resulting in a great number of visitors coming from surrounding areas to enjoy the shows, whirligigs, shooting galleries and swings. It was described as 'one of the most celebrated horse fairs in the kingdom, which is well supplied and attended by dealers from the continent and all parts' and ran for about ten days.[14] One special event held in Stourbridge at the end of August 1872 was the great show of the Worcestershire Agricultural Society; people from far afield invaded the town to see the fine display of animals, farm implements, horticultural show and horse jumping. Stourbridge was decorated with flags and banners and a large castle-like arch was erected across the High Street near the town clock.

The Final 20 Years of Victoria's Reign

The last 20 years of the century saw a marked increase in the construction of new roads. By the 1880s Vauxhall Road, Victoria Street, Cecil Street, West Street, Albert Street, Parkfield Road (or Street), Brook Street (the Wollaston end only), Prospect Hill, Pargeter Street (named after Joseph Pargeter, a nail ironmonger of Careless Green House) and Baylie Street had all been developed near the town centre to meet the rapidly growing need for housing. Ten years later Western Road (or Lower Hill Street), Beale Street, Cross Street and Greenfield Avenue (at that time a cul-de-sac) had also appeared on the map. Activity increased in Oldswinford with the construction of Swinford Road (previously a field track), Stanley Road (quaintly named Bogs Road at that time), Craufurd Street, Corser Street, Farlands Road and The Furlongs. Craufurd Street was named after Charles Henry Craufurd, the church's rector who held the living in Oldswinford from 1835 to 1876; originally it had been called School Street. Grange Road was still a footpath. Roads built in Wollaston included the lower part of Park Road, Duncombe Street (Thomas Duncombe, who died in 1861, was a radical politician), Wood Street, Laburnam Street, Ridge Street and Firmstone Street. Henry Onions Firmstone (1815-99) was an iron and coal master who lived at Wollaston Hall. By the end of the century Gladstone and

---

Stourbridge through Time: 1880 to 1901

1881   Main Drainage Board is formed and sewage farm built
1882   Closure of the town's only glassworks at The Heath
1884   First steam trams run
1885   New post office is built in the High Street
1887   New town hall is built in Market Street
1889   First supply of electricity in the town
1890   First telephone exchange at Lye
1893   Corbett Hospital is opened
1895   Formation of Stourbridge Urban District Council
1899   First electric trams run
1901   Queen Victoria dies

Bridle Roads had been constructed, but were then known as Bridle and Upper Bridle Road, part of an ancient pathway which previously ran from Bowling Green Road through to the New Wood Farm area. After the consecration of the new Stourbridge Cemetery in 1879 part of South Road was renamed Cemetery Road, and by 1890 Cherry Street and Witton Street had been developed at Norton.

Some local through-routes had been disturnpiked in 1877, including the ones from Stourbridge to Wordsley Green and from Amblecote to Wollaston and Churchill.[15] It was left to the 1888 Local Government Act finally to wind up the remaining turnpike trusts and make the newly created county councils responsible for all main roads. The changeover from parish council administration was completed in 1894 when local councils became responsible for the remaining local highway network. The increasing number of roads and dwellings meant that more local maps and directories were produced. The first large-scale Ordnance Survey map for Stourbridge was published in 1888 having been surveyed in 1882. A delightful late 19th-century trade map was issued by Stephens and Mackintosh of Leicester, entitled the Business Street Map of Stourbridge; the scrolled map was surrounded by the adverts of local traders. But the greater number and improved surfaces of roads did result in an increase in the number of traffic accidents at that time, causing some fatalities.

A local tram network became available in the 1880s. Horse-drawn omnibuses had been running since at least the 1860s, but in 1880 the Dudley and Stourbridge Steam Tramway Company was formed. After several years of negotiation the laying of track commenced, the town's High Street being much disturbed for that purpose. The first trial on the line from Stourbridge market place to Dudley took place on 15 May 1884. The tramcars, which carried 30 persons inside and 32 outside, were 30 feet long, 5 feet 6 inches wide and 13 feet 10 inches high, running on a gauge of 3 feet 6 inches. The fare charged was twopence to Brierley Hill and fourpence all the way to Dudley. The first electric tram ran along the line on 25 July 1899. Two years later, in April 1901, the romantically named Kinver Light Railway made its debut for the British Electric Traction Company. The track was set into the road, running from the tram shed near the *Fish Inn*, Amblecote (now Mr. Driscoll's warehouse) to High Street Wollaston and on to the Ridge Top, from where it followed the verge of the road as far as the *Stewponey* and *Foley Arms*. From there it went across private land to the Hyde Meadows at Kinver.[16] On 7 December 1900, the Stourbridge to Kingswinford tramline was opened. That was followed in 1902 by three new lines, one from Wollaston Crescent to Stourbridge High Street (via Enville Street), another from the market place to the top of Stourbridge High Street, and the third from Foster Street to The Hayes at Lye. In 1904 Birmingham and Midland Tramways acquired the Kinver Light Railway from the British Electric Traction Co.

The 1880s also saw many important changes affecting administration and living conditions in Stourbridge. In 1883 a strenuous effort was made to obtain a Charter of Incorporation for the town and parish (also to include Pedmore and Wordsley). That scheme was put forward by W.J. Turney but was strongly opposed by several factions of local society and eventually collapsed. In the same year the authorities decided to hold court sittings at the County Court in Hagley Road rather than in the old rambling police and magistrates' court building with its three cells (which stood in Court Passage). The old building had fallen into a very dilapidated condition, but the new arrangement still produced criticism from

58 *Stourbridge town hall in the 1920s.*

people who objected to prisoners being escorted from the cells through the streets in full public view. In 1885 a new red-brick post office was built, having been previously situated in Lower High Street and before that in Crown Lane for many years. To celebrate Queen Victoria's Golden Jubilee in 1887, an impressive new red-brick town hall was erected in Market Street, Stourbridge, at a cost of £5,000, financed by public subscriptions that included £1,000 each from W.J. Turney and C.E. Swindell. Earl Beauchamp, the Lord Lieutenant of the county, opened that building on 14 November. The following year saw a new corn exchange, fire station, council chamber and municipal offices incorporated into the scheme at the Smithfield end of the building; a further £2,500 was found to finance those additions, which were opened on 18 October 1888 by W.J. Turney. A carnival on ice was held at the Heath Pool on 17 January 1887 in aid of relief of the poor but unfortunately only 100 spectators turned up because of the heavy fall of snow on the day.[17]

For the Diamond Jubilee of Queen Victoria ten years later the town was again *en fête* with flags and bunting adorning public buildings, shops and houses in every street. On that occasion celebrations were also arranged at the Heath Pool, a location which gave as much pleasure to local people then as it does today. An 1837 map of Stourbridge clearly showed the small island within its lake, and by the 1880s the pool had acquired many attractions including a good stock of fish and a small boathouse on its banks.[18]

The first supply of electric current arrived in the area in 1889 and this certainly brightened the lives of the town's inhabitants. Two or three manufacturers promptly made arrangements to have electric lighting installed in their works, and the commissioners discussed whether to have the streets electrically lit but eventually decided to retain their gas lighting. In May 1890 telephone communications with Birmingham were formally established. A small telephone exchange was installed at Lye by the National Telephone Company through the efforts of Edward Bindon Marten, a local director of the company. At the time of the opening of the line there were only three subscribers. The first to join was Thomas Rhodes & Sons at their Providential Works with a telephone number of 1. Early in 1894 the National Telephone Company opened an exchange in Stourbridge. Previously there had been a call box in High Street for which subscribers paid nothing and non-subscribers a minimum of threepence a call. The earliest Stourbridge subscribers were Timmis and Co. (brick manufacturers), Jones and Attwood (heating engineers), E. Baylie and Co. (chain manufacturers), Stourbridge Fire Station, the Corbett Hospital, the *County Express* newspaper, Stourbridge Police Station, Bernard, King & Co. (solicitors), Mark and Moody and Edward Marten. Towards the end of 1898 a larger telephone exchange was fitted out in Stourbridge, but it was impossible to operate it properly for some time as many people objected to the wires passing over their property. This problem was eventually overcome by the erection of telegraph poles.

In 1891 the town commissioners had their numbers cut from 27 to 18, contributing to the speedier and more efficient management of the town's affairs. More important changes took place in the administration of the area following the 1894 Local Government Act, which transferred the civic functions of the vestries to new parish councils. The final meeting of Stourbridge commissioners took place on 30 December 1894 when Stourbridge, Wollaston and the parish of Upper Swinford joined forces as an Urban District Council. Its first meeting took place on 1 January 1895 under the chairmanship of Walter Jones (the head of Jones

59 *A Lye public telephone with a winding handle, photographed in 1955.*

60 *Market Street in the 1890s, looking from the corner of New Road and Worcester Street.*

61   *The Amblecote mansion called The Hill in 1885, some eight years before it became the Corbett Hospital.*

and Attwood). Lye and Wollescote formed local parish councils in 1894, but three years later combined as an Urban District Council.

In 1893 the town commissioners decided to purchase the gas undertaking on behalf of the town for just under £100,000. Then, on 19 June, Viscountess Cobham laid the foundation stone for a new dispensary costing £1,700, situated on the corner of Worcester Street and Greenfield Avenue. Initially the building had two in-patient beds. If a sick person were considered a deserving cause for charity, he or she would be issued with a 'ticket' by a subscriber, which had to be presented to the dispensary within 14 days. Amongst instructions for patients printed on the ticket in 1900 were: patients neglecting to attend for one week without giving information of their inability would be discharged; a suitable single truss or other surgical instrument would be supplied to any patient requiring the same, in return for tickets to a corresponding value; patients were expected to provide bottles and gallipots.

On 31 July 1893 the town's first hospital (the Corbett Hospital) was opened in a recently converted mansion called The Hill at Amblecote, initially having 18 beds. This was thanks to the generosity of 'Salt King' John Corbett of Droitwich (a Brierley Hill man by birth), who in 1892 had bought The Hill Estate for £6,500 and spent a further £4,500 converting and endowing it. In 1896 a children's ward was opened and at the turn of the century John Corbett built Hill House in the grounds as a residence for the surgeon.

A number of important benefactors donated time and money to the well-being of the town. An outstanding figure contributing to all the improvements was William J. Turney, who for many years was chairman of the town commissioners. His skin works, W.J. Turney & Co., were famous for their bull or hooter, always used to announce major national events. William had a brother named Henry, who was founder and captain of the Stourbridge Volunteer Fire Brigade. In 1903 William's widow gave the pulpit in Oldswinford church in his memory. Another benefactor was Walter Jones, the first chairman of the Stourbridge Urban District Council, who donated the bandstand and fountains in Greenfield Gardens in 1903. John Harward, a well-to-do Stourbridge solicitor, guaranteed £200 in 1861 for the minister's stipend at the newly built St John's church. A well-known local solicitor was William Blow Collis, who acquired Wollaston Hall in 1848 for £3,500. During his lifetime he held many local offices including

62 *A portrait of the Stourbridge benefactor and businessman, W.J. Turney (1841-95) who was born in Boston, Lincs.*

63   *Frederick Ray's removal cart at The Heath towards the end of the 19th century.*

clerk to the Magistrates and Board of Guardians, superintendent registrar of the Stourbridge Union, treasurer of the County Court and director of the Stourbridge Water Company for 42 years (including being chairman of that concern for 27 years). William Akroyd was another Stourbridge character of great energy, foresight and ability whose daughter Annette was the mother of Lord Beveridge. Frank Short, who was born in Wollaston, became one of the town's most distinguished sons. He was a pupil at the School of Art and began his career as a constructional engineer in Stourbridge. Later he became a renowned artist, full Member (1911) and Treasurer (1919-32) of the Royal Academy and President of the Royal Society of Painter-Etchers. When he was knighted in 1911 a memorable exhibition of his pictures was arranged in the Music Rooms. In 1922 he presented the mayoral badge to the town.

An air of solemn melancholy settled on the district when news was received on 22 January 1901 of the death of Queen Victoria. Muffled peals were rung on the bells of the churches, and many inhabitants went into mourning. With the death of the Queen, a new age dawned.

VII

The Growth of Trade and Industry

Throughout its history Stourbridge has been a town with important interests both in agriculture and in manufacturing. The granting of a royal charter in 1482 increased its importance as a market town, enabling it to hold a flourishing weekly market. A thriving woollen industry grew up, only to decline in the mid-17th century. Although in earlier times most people made their living primarily from the land, residents of Stourbridge were always greatly blessed with a unique combination of natural resources which lay below them on the north-eastern side of the town, particularly in the Stambermill and Lye areas. To this was added the powerful source of energy provided by the Stour itself. As the centuries progressed these natural benefits provided more and more employment, trade and prosperity. The immigrant glassworkers chose Stourbridge as their preferred manufacturing centre in about 1610, the town obtaining a world-wide reputation for the fine quality of its products. Following successive innovation in the iron industry, production mushroomed in the mills along the river, which resulted in the manufacture of a multitude of nails and other metal goods. The area's clay also attracted the brickmakers. But all of these traditional industries were in decline by the 20th century, being replaced by a rich variety of service and other light industries.

Regulation of Trade in Earlier Times

In medieval times traders were regulated by their own craft gilds, although records of any such gilds for Stourbridge have long since disappeared. Further restrictions were decreed by the lord of the manor and carried out by his various officials. In Tudor Stourbridge a variety of regulations existed to protect poorer members of society from the scheming ways of the richer merchants. It was an offence to: forestall the market by selling any provisions before the market bell; buy more than one week's supply of provisions before 12 o'clock on market day; sell provisions in places other than in the open market; sell unwholesome food, stinking fish or mixed wines; sell light weight or short measures, or at prices excessive to those fixed by the assize.

A butter cross (a stone cross rising from a stepped base) stood near the old town hall from as early as 1549.[1] Besides being a reminder to traders to deal honestly, it had the more down to earth use of displaying goods on its base. From time to time the cross was obviously misused for in 1583 it was ordered that 'no artificer called a pedlar or petichapman should sell his wares next the somerpole or the butter cross on three legged stands or other contrivances on market days'. In 1639 it was decreed that 'no butcher shall henceforth at any time place any skins over the cross of the butter cross or around the cross' and that 'no butter seller shall stand to sell any butter betwixt Richard Cox, his house, and the butter crosse, to hinder the passage of the markett, but shall stand where is fitt by the appoyntment of the lordes bayliefs'. The bailiff of the manor tested and assized the various measures in a corner under the old town hall building, and had custody of the standard weights. He also had to keep account of the fines collected. The bellman would ring the bell to announce the start of the market and collect the rents from the traders' (called stallage). Three other officials appointed by the manor court assisted the bailiff and bellman. The Clerk of the Market accounted for the market tolls, the Inspector and Sealer of Leather checked the quality of shoes and similar articles, and the Victual Taster tested to see if the food and drink on sale were fit for human consumption. It was obviously difficult in a close knit society for any of these officials to accuse a close friend or neighbour. It was the duty of the assistant constables to bring the guilty to account at the three-weekly court, and if they failed to do this they were liable to pay any fines from their own pockets!

Many of the fines levied by the manor court were considered as licences which allowed merchants to carry on trade without further hindrance. In September 1615 some 50 Oldswinford inhabitants were fined 10d. each by the manor court for selling ale in short measure or at prices that were greater than laid down by statute. Eight bakers were fined 4d. at the same court for selling sub-standard bread and 20 butchers were fined one shilling each for slaughtering their cattle in a manner that broke the local bye-laws. Similar fines were imposed at each autumn court in that decade. The actual amount of the fines was set by the steward, who had to be extremely careful not to price the traders out of their jobs altogether.[2]

Traders were encouraged to take pauper children as apprentices from 1597 onwards. The first mention of this happening in Stourbridge occurs on 6 September 1624 when the church-wardens' accounts record an indenture apprenticing John Haden to John Hill, a mason. Over 600 apprenticeship indentures covering the period between 1670 and 1794 survive for the parish of Oldswinford, each document signed by the churchwardens, overseers of the poor and two justices of the peace. Pauper children were forced into apprenticeship at the tender age of seven. Apprentices could not commit fornication or contract matrimony, play cards or dice, haunt taverns, drink alcohol or absent themselves during day or night. The master had to provide two suits of wearing apparel for holy days and working days.

Tradesmen employing children received a payment from the parish of approximately £1 10s. on commencement of the apprenticeship, but even so parishioners needed much persuasion by magistrates to take them. Many of these children were maltreated, and on rare occasions the indenture had to be terminated by a document called a discharge of apprenticeship. Examples occurred in Stourbridge in 1722 when John Rochhill was forced to release Sarah Penn from their contract because he had beaten and otherwise abused her, and again in June 1813 when it was ordered that the overseers prosecute Benjamin Spittle for abuse of his apprentice.[3] Nearly all girls were apprenticed into housewifery and by far the most popular occupation for the parish's boys was nailmaking, but other trades included locksmiths, ironmongers, blacksmiths, weavers, scythesmiths, colliers, masons and glassmakers. From 1692 children automatically obtained a right of settlement once they had served an apprenticeship in the parish.

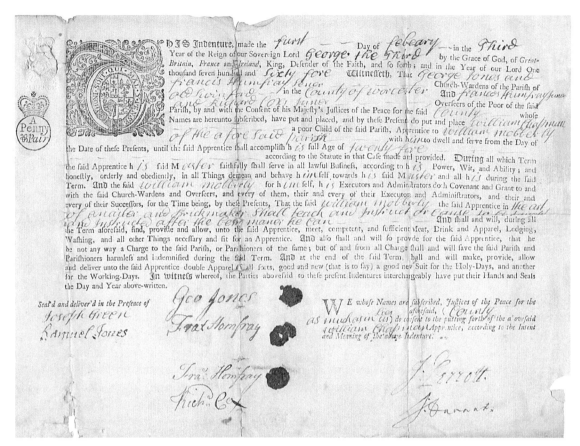

64   *A 1764 indenture apprenticing a poor child named William Chapman to brickmaker, William Mobberley.*

By the 18th century other types of protective societies were appearing. In May 1768 there was mention of a Friendly Society of Tradesmen meeting at the *Talbot*, the entrance fee being 2s. 6d.[4] To be eligible to join, one had to earn at least nine shillings a week and not be over 40 years of age. Thieves, bumbailiffs, women and miners were banned from its doors and members were actually fined for playing cards, gambling or getting drunk. In 1776 an Act was passed to enable the easier and speedy recovery of small debts within the parish of Old-swinford. Sixty-seven commissioners were appointed, any three of whom could form a Court of Requests to try cases and in 1840 this met on every other Tuesday. Any protection against the miserable conditions endured by the mass of women and children employed in the period known as the Industrial Revolution came about very slowly indeed, and then only as a result of national legislation and the gradual growth of trade union power in the 19th century. Later still various Stourbridge traders began to form their own associations: in 1863 the Licensed Victuallers, in 1895 the Master Builders, in 1910 the Stourbridge Chamber of Trade and in 1911 the Master Butchers Association.

Farming and Problems with Animals

The oldest occupation in Stourbridge was naturally agriculture, be it cultivating land for crops, rearing animals for food and clothing or using rivers and ponds for fishery. Many crops were grown in the town's common fields in medieval times, but it was the breeding of animals that caused most problems for the population, and not least amongst these were the terrible smells. Pigs were the most useful to past generations because all parts of the animal could be eaten; besides bacon, delicacies included chawl, pig's head, trotters, tail, pig's pudding, bony pie and faggots. On normal weekdays pigs were allowed to wander through the streets of Stourbridge scavenging for all kinds of rubbish and leaving behind large quantities of foul-smelling droppings. They had always to be ringed. On market day it was the bellman's duty to expel pigs from the town centre and in the 16th century their owners had to pay 1s. 1d. to recover each animal; one shilling went to the lord and one penny to the bellman (by 1600 that had risen to the large amount of one pound for every pig). Stray animals were put into the lord's pound (which at one time was situated on the corner of Heath Lane and Worcester Street). It often happened that the animals were illegally rescued, resulting in further heavy fines and repair costs provided that the culprit could be brought to justice. The cattle market was held at one time in Smithfield just off the present Market Street and the pig market in Coventry Street. It was a strict rule that butchers had to slaughter their sheep and calves in their own doorway in the open street, and they could be fined 3s. 4d. if they carried out the act in secret at the rear of their premises. Tanners tended to throw the animals' bowels and offal into the street and inhabitants were often fined for disposing of dead dogs, cats and pigs in the country lanes. An ordinance of October 1618 required that dogs called 'mastyves' had to be muzzled. Horses were not allowed to be tied up on the public highways on market day; if the rule was contravened the bellman led them away to the pound and the owner was fined. The right to fish in the river Stour was reserved for the lord of the manor and in 1593 it was ordered that no one from Stourbridge should bathe, fish or set a trap in the Stour between the Stepping Stones and Wollaston Mill.

Service Trades in the 16th to 18th Centuries

As in any local community, service trades gave employment to large numbers of Stourbridge people. In medieval times inhabitants were employed in providing food, drink, clothes, small wares, woodworking and building. Stourbridge traders providing food and drink (the year of the reference is given in brackets) included:

> Innkeepers: Thomas Harrison (1595); Paul Hawkes (1610); William Walderne and William Wall (1612); Humphrey Cole (1620); Humphrey Sutton (1670); Thomas Price (1681); John Fellowes (1684); William Norton and William Thomas (1703); William Howard (1704); William Rose (1718); Samuel Smith (1720) and Ralph Nickson (1730) amongst a host of others.

> Butchers: William Gaunt, Paul Hawkes and Richard Smart (1595); John Bullas (1602); Humphrey Cole (1605); John Wylie (1619) and Richard Wylie (1620) to mention just a few. There were numerous instances of butchers selling meat that was in an unfit state.

Baking was another occupation carried on by a large number of people, resulting in regular court fines.

The following traders provided clothes and other household necessities:

Barbers and wigmakers (who often doubled as surgeons): Henry Walker (1607); James Lloyd (1623); John Smith (1630); Thomas York (1720); William Fownes (1728); Henry Wakeman (1769); James Tyler (1779).

Bookseller: Jeremiah Taylor (1703).

Bucklemaker: Thomas Palmer (1703).

Chairmakers: James Blunt (1717); Richard Fisher (1729).

Chandlers (who supplied such essentials as candles and soap): Anthony Weatherhill (1607); Ezekiell Partridge (1673); Thomas Pearce (1692); Walter Bradley (1703).

Chapmen (dealers in small wares) and tinkers: John Jones (1619); Christopher Bell (1628).

Cutlers (dealers in knives): John Bell (1619); Samuel Parkes (1729).

Glovers and skinners: John Pennall and Richard Smith (1595); David Taylor (1615); John Smith (1710); John Dowler (1714); Joseph Walloxall (1747).

Grocer: Thomas Nott (1657).

Hatter: Samuel Burton (1712 and 1734).

Mercers (dealers in costly materials such as silk): Thomas Madstard (1587); Richard Madstard (1595); Jonathan Butler (1665); Thomas Slater (1681); Richard Baker, Thomas Moss and John Roe (1703).

Pipemakers: William Farmer (1687); William Bellamy (1784); Harry Bellamy (1790).

Potters: Ralph Shaw (1755); Edward Brocksop & John Blakeley, who was apprenticed to Aaron Wedgwood at Burslem (1769); Benjamin Cox (1784); Benjamin Brocksop (1786).

Shoemakers: Richard Cox (1587); John Rock (1595); Richard Dun (1602); William Coxe (1608); William Hall and Humphrey Brisko (1619) and many others.

Tailors: Thomas Lea (1597); Denis Silvester (1605); Henry Pearson (1619); Robert and Edward Millard (1623), to mention but a few.

Toymaker: John Bird (1729).

Upholsterers: Ralph Bell (1610); John Cheltenham (1623); Richard Gearing (1676); Joseph Thorpe (1686).

Watchmakers: William Stokes senior and junior (1723).

Other craftsmen looked after citizens' needs by building their houses, arranging their travel and transporting their goods:

Blacksmiths: Thomas Potter (1583); Lawrence Owen (1594); John Wildsmith (1619); John Malpas (1623); Francis Cowper (1627 & 1721); Benjamin Richards (1729 & 1730); Samuel Raybould (1741); William Darby (1750); Thomas Morgen (1758).

Bricklayers: William Parker (1713); Richard Doddell and Samuel Parker (1720); John Ellis (1736); John Hill (1787).

Carriers: John Pemberton (1634); Samuel Holt (1728); Elizabeth Tomson (a clay carrier in 1733); John Edgley (1764); William Egginton (1769).

Coopers: Thomas Northall (1541); Thomas Stafford (1728); Robert Bradley (1771).

Gunsmiths: John Malpas (1632); John Spittle (1728).

Saddlers: Richard Smith (1640); Zachary Haywood and Paul White (1692).

Wheelwrights: John Raby (1602); William Marson (1685); William Best (1689); Isaac Taylor (1727).

In addition there were masons, carpenters and sawyers too numerous to mention.

The Woollen Trade

The woollen trade was an important Stourbridge industry before the mid-17th century, although it certainly did not create as much employment here as in the neighbouring town of Kidderminster. Much of the spinning was performed in individual homes, which is evidenced by an inventory of John Hill of The Lye who died in 1558. He possessed 'a spynning whelle, a peyre of cardes, a hachell, a peyre of combes, a peyre of sheres and a peyre of balandes', the sum of which were valued at 2s. 8d.[5] In 1550 John Harte was a weaver who owned a hempyard and Roger Bryttell possessed 'two tenements all under one rooffe with two hempeyards on the west syde'.[6] Those individuals could have lived in the area known as The Hemplands, which led off Enville Street; this was once a courtyard frequented by weavers. In the 17th century the prominent families of Hickman, Jeston, Newbrough and Scott grew very wealthy through their association with the woollen trade. The district at Norton named Gigmill is a further reminder of the woollen trade; a gig was a machine to raise the nap on woollen cloth. A three-acre pool there called the Gigmill Pool originally served a cloth mill that later in 1782 had become a plating forge in the ownership of an ailing Benjamin Pratt, manufacturing spades, shovels and hoes.

After the Civil War a gradual decline set in and families in the trade moved their capital into the newer iron and clay based industries. It was to counter the decline in the woollen trade that an Act was passed in 1678 which stated that 'no corpse of any person (except those dying of the plague) shall be buried in any garment other than of pure sheep's wool' under penalty of £5. An affidavit had to be sworn and a fee paid for each burial, unless it was a pauper being interred. That Act remained in force until 1814 and a register was kept by Oldswinford parish for all the 'burials in woollen'.[7] The depression in their trade did not stop rich Stourbridge woollen merchants from building some very fine houses, particularly in Lower High Street. The erection of St Thomas's church in Market Street in the early 1730s was due to the generosity of a cloth worker, John Biggs.

The Mining Industry

Within Stambermill and Lye could be found large deposits of coal, clay, marl, iron and sand. At nearby Dudley and Sedgley good quality lime could also be obtained. Coal was mined in Stourbridge from at least as early as the 13th century, albeit on a small scale, and in 1322 there were two coal mines worth 20 shillings a year in the manor.[8] Those mines were probably in an area close to the present viaduct at Stambermill. The main coal seam began in a field named Round Hill and ran south in the direction of Hungary Hill through land called Glasshouse Piece and Colepit Leasow, ending just below the old Stourbridge Junction Station (at the end of Junction Road) near the Pot and Kettle Pools. Much of the coal lay at a depth of some 75 feet and the lord of the manor had the legal right to enter copyholders' land for the purpose of mining under it, but later landowners received a royalty for each ton of coal extracted from their ground. As the scale of mining increased in the first half of the 16th century manor courts limited the amount that was taken out of the ground and imposed fines for any infringements, but these had ceased by the 1570s. The Estate Book of Grafton Manor (near Bromsgrove) mentioned coal being purchased from William Hodson of Stourbridge in May 1569.

From the late 16th century onwards coal began to take over from wood as the main source of fuel for the local iron and glassmaking industries and its transport by packhorse must have

65   *Oldnall Colliery at Wollescote, c.1900.*

been problematical. In March 1630 William Tyrer of Oldswinford was presented for selling trees called 'birches and ollers' for use as coal pit posts from land at Colliers Fields. Mining became prevalent over all the eastern part of the manor and the name Colepit Leasow could be found in three separate places in 1699; those locations were between Bott Lane and the Stour, on the eastern side of Rufford Road (near New Farm Road) and on the eastern boundary of the parish (near Hayes Lane). By the 18th century coal had become subsidiary to clay mining, but there were still 20 pits to the east of Stourbridge in the 1780s. During the 19th century the mining industry continued to employ more than 100 persons in the Lye area, but it became an insignificant employer in the 20th century and local mines were excluded from nationalisation. One of the largest mines in the parish at that time was the Oldnall colliery, which was taken over by the firm of Mobberley and Perry in 1901 after being unworked for some 25 years; it finally closed in 1944. Opencast mining continued for a time but most of the ancient mines were then built over. Their legacy remains today, however, in the form of disused shafts; it is said that at least half a dozen of these are sited under Lye's sports ground alone.

The Glass Industry

To the outside world Stourbridge is renowned for its glass industry, which owes its development to the fine quality of clay found in the area. In 1568 foreign glassmakers who were being persecuted in Flanders were tempted to England by a lucrative contract, and spent much of the next 40 years putting down roots in different parts of the country. The party included Annanias de Hennezel, who came with his brother Israel and mother Moingeon Massey (widow of George Hennezel) from Granges in Lorraine, where the family owned a glassworks called Houdrichapelle. Another family called Tyzack came from nearby Darney in Lorraine. Settling initially in the Weald of Surrey and Sussex, the glassmaking immigrants moved north to the Forest of Dean, to Bishops Wood near Eccleshall (brought there by Bishop Overton of Southampton after he had been appointed to the Lichfield diocese in about 1580) and to Newcastle upon Tyne. Early sites were all shared with the iron industry because the glassmakers were competing for the diminishing supply of timber to fire their furnaces. By 1610 experiments into alternative fuels were being conducted in the Stourbridge area. Dud Dudley stated in 1665 that in 1611 there was a new invention to make glass with sea coal, and that the discovery was made in the Stourbridge area.[9] Stourbridge had many of the ingredients needed for the manufacture of glass, including clay, coal and sand (although sand was obtained from Lynn at a later period). Potash was initially made by burning the green bracken from the local wastes, and that caused the Oldswinford manor court to issue an ordinance on 6 October

1611 forbidding anyone to burn bracken under threat of the maximum court penalty of 40s. Seaweed called kelp was obtained from the north of Scotland and the west of Ireland, and some potash was imported from Spain. Lead was first obtained from Derbyshire, but later in the 18th century manufactured locally. The final event giving Stourbridge the edge over previous locations was a royal proclamation of 1615 which forbade the glassmakers to use timber for production (because it was in such short supply), but at the same time forbade the importation of foreign glass, giving the glassmakers a virtual monopoly.

Annanias de Hennezel and his son Joshua commenced production on a site (which has never been identified) across the town boundary at Brettell in Amblecote. Paul Tyzack from Bishops Wood settled within the manor of Bedcote, in a field by the Stour called Colemans. The land was leased from the Addenbrookes and lay between Bott Lane and the Stourbridge to Lye road at Stambermill. It had the advantage of lying directly over both coal and clay. From

66 *A 19th-century portrait of glassmaker Annanias de Hennezell, who was born* c. *1580 in Lorraine, France*

the site a bridge crossed the Stour to Ravensitch Coppice in the neighbouring Amblecote manor. The Tyzacks erected a simple wooden shed in which there was a small square furnace; the cone shapes that dominated the skyline in the early 1900s did not appear until the first half of the 18th century. The first working team was Paul Tyzack (the gaffer), his brother Zacharius and probably James Legre. They soon became organised into shifts of six hours each, working for about forty weeks each year. The preparation of materials was done by a founder and the process of burning out organic impurities was called fritting. Only window glass was supplied to the market in the first instance (a product called broad glass), but later crown glass was also made (with its familiar circular crown in the centre giving a thinner and brighter appearance) together with bottles for the cider trade. In 1655 Paul Tyzack senior retired and went to live in Ravensitch Coppice, having handed over to his second son Paul, who paid his father an annuity of £40 for the remaining 10 years of his life. His place in the Colemans' team was taken by Abraham Bigo. In 1658 Paul Foley offered a contract to Paul and Zacharius Tyzack to make broad glass at Chelwood in Somerset, but in that same year tragedy struck when Colemans was burnt to the ground. Meanwhile ownership of the land had passed to the Lyddiate family, and when the Tyzack lease was renewed in 1664 a stipulation was that the ruined glasshouse had to be rebuilt, which cost the family £200. The business continued to prosper, especially when in 1664 a new contract was obtained from the Foleys to supply 1,600 cases of glass annually for three years at 20 shillings a case. The year in which the Colemans site ceased production is not certain, but later documents refer to a pottery mughouse there. Some remains of the site were still apparent at the start of the 20th century.[10]

Most of the major Stourbridge glassworks were not within the town's boundaries but in Amblecote and Wordsley in Staffordshire. The Heath Glassworks was the one major exception and this consisted of a building close to Heath House in the present Mary Stevens Park. In 1681 the Jeston family established their connection with the glass industry by marrying into the Henzey family (formerly de Hennezels) and it was on the Jeston's land at The Heath that the works were built late in the 17th century. In 1691 Humphrey Jeston, an upholsterer by trade, and his son William mortgaged 'all that newly erected messuage and also that glasshouse' to Thomas Dalton, apothecary of London. This was indeed a difficult period to set up in the industry, as the monopoly granted to the trade had disappeared during the Protectorate, and to add to its woes the government decided to impose a tax of 20 per cent on flint glass and one shilling on every dozen bottles. Levied for the first time in 1695, this tax resulted in many petitions from the Stourbridge district and the duty was withdrawn after a short time in 1699. In that same year Mrs. Hunt was assessed for land tax on the Heath Glasshouse, indicating that she still owned the land on which it was built, but it was apparently still Thomas Dalton who occupied the premises in 1705. In 1709 the works were leased back to John Jeston, who by now was making bottles and white glass there, but the Jestons mortgaged the works again in 1727, suggesting that the trade was in some difficulty. In November 1734 Humphrey Jeston, glassmaker of The Heath, went into bankruptcy. According to the *London Gazette*, the business was worked by the Commissioners in Bankruptcy until 1736, when on 31 August an advertisement stated that Heath's New Glass-House was to be let by the year, or any term of years. In 1745 government imposed a further excise duty on the industry that was to last for 100 years. An annual licence had to be bought by each glassmaker, and duty paid on every

67 *A 19th-century engraving of the Glassworks at The Heath.*

pound of batch melted down, and on every pound in weight produced which was above 40 per cent of the weight of the original batch. To oversee this, three government officers were allocated to each glasshouse to maintain unbroken supervision, and six hours' notice had to be given before each process in the production could take place. Payments of duty were made after every round of six or seven weeks. By 1752 Edward Russell the younger had taken over at The Heath and when he died in 1778 he was reputedly quite wealthy, leaving his property to his three Witton nephews who continued to run the business. There was a problem with the works in 1782, because a number of local glassmakers (some of whom had been apprenticed to Edward Russell) applied for parish relief. In 1796 the firm was described as a nine-pot glassworks, but in 1801 Serjeant Witton became bankrupt resulting in the sale of the works. The Rufford family soon took over its operation and a William Walker joined the firm in the 1830s, the glassworks becoming known as Rufford and Walker. The Rufford interests were caught up in the collapse of the Rufford and Wragge Bank in 1851, but the Walker family continued in charge until final closure in 1882. The glassworks had only one cone in Victorian times. Its crowning glory was to make a chandelier for the sultan of Turkey priced at £10,000. The Heath was the only major glassworks in the area that was not served by the late 18th-century canal system, a fact that would have had some bearing on its eventual fate.

Scant records exist of other old glassworks within Stourbridge. The name Glasshouse Hill to the east of Oldswinford crossroads is one surviving clue. In common with The Heath, the land at Glasshouse Hill belonged to the Hunts in the late 17th century, and a small glasshouse there could have been a forerunner of The Heath Glassworks. In 1686 Dr. Plot wrote that there was a glassworks to the east of Oldswinford Cross by tradition. It was claimed early in the 1900s, by an old resident of the Field Cottage area (Edward Wright), that a firing chamber had been found on the hill, and a 19th-century excavation there revealed some glasshouse pots and the skeleton of a young boy. Hungary Hill was the site of another old works, on its eastern side and opposite the present Junction Road. An article in the *County Express* newspaper on 11 November 1899 stated that 'a Mr. B. Wooldridge informs us that he once saw the foundations of Hungary Hill Glasshouse ... the works of Rufford & Co. swallowed up the foundations'. The same site was marked in 1699 as a glasshouse lying on land owned by Mr. Wheeler, and could well have been worked by the Tyzack family. Yet another Glasshouse Close is marked in that year on the edge of Lye Waste, which in 1782 was owned by a Mr. Grove. The Groves were successors to the Henzeys, and it was from the bricks of an old glasshouse there that the first school at Lye Waste was built. This in turn was the result of a legacy of a Mr. Batchelor who was a glass-manufacturing ancestor of Thomas Hill. To complete the list of former glass manufacturing sites, a glasshouse once existed in Gladstone Road, Wollaston that was owned by a Mr. Duffield, but few details are known about that enterprise.[11]

To mark the town's long association with the glass industry, the Borough Council made a decision following the success of the 1951 Festival of Britain Exhibition to form a collection of about ninety locally-made products at the Council House in Mary Stevens Park. It was opened in May 1952 by Councillor E.R.R. Tooby, and was augmented a few months later by some 300 items from the antique collection of Benjamin Richardson, a glass manufacturer of Wordsley Hall who had recently died. In 1956 John Northwood, a well-known local glass expert, donated another 140 pieces. This valuable display was seen by Queen Elizabeth II in April 1957 when she visited the town. After Dudley took over the administration of Stourbridge in 1974, the collection was eventually transferred to the Broadfield House Glass Museum at Kingswinford. Many of the ancient glassmaking firms in the district ceased production towards the end of the 20th century and all those that still survive now operate outside the boundaries of Stourbridge.

Growth of the Iron Industry
The early mills mentioned in Domesday Book were powered by the river Stour and would only have been used for grinding corn. In the following years watermills were also utilised for fulling cloth, sawing timber and as blade mills. In 1338 Joan Botetourt, lady of the manor of Oldswinford, granted a watermill called Rotherford Mill to her tenants at an annual rent of 14s.; by that time the usefulness of watermills in the process of making iron had been established. In the following centuries watermills were supplemented by windmills, which could once be found on the summit of Church Street, Stourbridge opposite its junction with the present Junction Road, and in Vicarage Road, Wollaston close to where the old vicarage stood. Church Street windmill was still there in 1837 (when Church Street was called Windmill Street), but a large Victorian house called Redholme was built in front of it (which eventually

became a private school named Queen's College). The ancient Wollaston windmill was marked on a 1699 map and it was still marked on the first O.S. map dated *c*. 1834, although the site was still called Windmill Piece.

The practice of digging for iron ore in parts of Stourbridge continued from earliest times to the 19th century. The early wrought iron was corrosive resistant and made by itinerant bloom-smiths who used horses to supplement water power. The bloomery consisted of a charcoal fire on which the iron ore was agitated by primitive bellows, the resulting spongy mass being taken out and beaten with a hammer to produce the bloom. At the beginning of the 16th century the first blast furnaces were introduced into Surrey and Sussex from Europe; the first one in the Midlands was at West Bromwich in about 1561 and the process had become common in the area by the last quarter of the 16th century. Fineries and chaferies were the next stages in production, collectively termed the forge. When cast iron from the blast furnace was cold, it was reheated in a finery and stirred with an iron bar whilst a blast of air was directed at it in order to burn out the carbon. The resulting lump of iron was then hammered to expel the surplus slag. The iron was next moved into the chafery where it was reheated to be drawn or forged under a tilt hammer. The period from 1575 to 1625 saw a massive development in the use of water power along the Stour for working the hammers in the many forges mush-rooming along its banks. The 17th century saw the introduction of the slitting mill, imported from Flanders and patented in England by Bevis Bulmer in 1588; it was first used locally in 1628 by Richard Foley at the Hyde Mill near Kinver. Strips of iron were passed through the slitting rolls and made into various sized nail rods; these had previously been chiselled by hand from bars heated in charcoal fires. Another development at that time was the introduction of coal, rather than the decreasing supplies of timber, as a fuel for the furnaces. A local person-ality called Dud Dudley (1599-1684) did many experiments at his ironworks (which included Cradley and Lye Mills), roughly coking the coal on a hearth and producing a charcoal called smithy char. He published his ideas in 1665 in a book called *Metallum Martis*, but it was not until 1709 that Abraham Darby brought his ideas into commercial use at Coalbrookdale. The harnessing of steam power in the 19th century, following the invention of the steam hammer in 1856 by James Nasmyth, enabled some of the local forges to continue in use long after the general decline of water power.

Mills along the Stour

On both sides of the river Stour on its course westwards from Salt Brook End to Wollaston were to be found many mills. The first mill of note was the ancient Lye Forge (situated to the east of Dudley Road, Lye). This enterprise was worked through nearly all the different ages of iron production, only ceasing trade in the second half of the 20th century. The early owners were the Addenbrookes, who worked the neighbouring Cradley Water Mill from as early as 1535. With the setting up of a major blast furnace at Cradley in the last quarter of the 16th century, Lye Mill later became the chafery which reheated the bloom of iron produced at Cradley. A survey of the Lyttelton lands in 1602 described how Henry Addenbrooke owned 'the Milhouse in Le Lee' including two water mills with an adjoining watercourse.[12] In 1620 'Addenbroke Myll' was mentioned at the manor court when widow Addenbrooke was fined for not clearing her ditches between the mill and Hay Green, and a further reference was made in 1622 in a description of the Bedcote manor boundaries. In March 1697 Zachary Downing acquired from John and Dorcas Addenbrooke a 99-year lease on Lye Mill, which at that time was operating as two corn mills. It included dwelling houses and two closes called Mill Leasowes and Jenk Ridding. Downing used the mill as a forge, and in 1699 it was described as Downing's Forge, sited in the corner of a field owned by the Addenbrooke family called Mill Leasow.

Zachary Downing became bankrupt in 1710 (by which time John Addenbrooke was already dead). The businesses of Lye and Cradley Forges were sold to the executors of John Wheeler and a new lease in 1713 mentioned land called Mears Coppice; there is still a lane on the site bearing that name. In June 1724 Lye Forge was conveyed to Edward Kendall (who had probably been managing the works for the Wheelers) by Richard and Edward Wheeler, and an inventory of stock in the documentation confirmed its use as a chafery.[13] From 1725 to 1727 William Rea of Monmouth was partner in Lye and Cradley Forges with Edward Kendall. The widow of Edward Kendall later offered the lease to Lord Ward who sublet it to Richard Croft; he still managed the business in 1782. In 1788 the lease was taken over by Thomas, Richard and Benjamin Gibbons of Kingswinford, who had other mills and forges in the area. In 1808 the Gibbons left Lye and sold out soon afterwards. A set of floodgates was installed in 1836 but Lye Forge at that time passed through a number of hands and probably became run-down. In the first half of the 19th century the whole area around the forge became known as Lye Forge and Dudley Road was called Lye Forge Road.

In 1853 Constantine and William Folkes (the sons of James Folkes, who had moved from Abinger Hammer in Surrey in the late 18th century to continue his occupation in the forging industry) took over the lease of Lye Forge at an annual rental of £76. In the winter of 1858 the mill pool gave way, causing a stop to work at the forge for some time. This was probably the reason why William Folkes left the partnership in January 1859, but with the help of a steam hammer the business survived the trade depressions of the late Victorian era. At that time the forge was producing anvil butts, building irons, vice moulds and brick irons.[14] The First World War resulted in the production of a much wider range of products to cope with the massive demand for all types of machine, ship and engine forgings and a new forge was constructed on a nearby site in 1931. In 1934 new technology saw the introduction of a 1,000-ton steam press. Production was transferred to Kidderminster from 1961 to 2000 when the forge was eventually closed. The name is continued as an industrial trading estate in Dudley Road which is still owned by the Folkes Group of companies.

The next mill encountered along the Stour was Stambermill, lying several hundred yards south of the river. In the 19th century it was situated to the north of the main Stourbridge to Lye road, near where the Birmingham railway line now crosses. To the south of that road were two large artificial pools (fed by Shepherds Brook) which produced power for the mill, and earlier mills had probably been sited on that side of the road. A mill at 'Stanburn' was mentioned in 1573 when John Wakelambe of Hibernia (whose heir was Thomas Wakelambe) died owning one watermill called 'Stamermyll in Le Lye',[15] but it was probably considerably older than 16th century. One of its artificial pools was created by damming the stream short-ly before 1713, in which year the mill was bought by Gregory Hickman and let to Francis Witton at £4 12s. per annum; it was then used as a blade mill for scythes. By 1759 the mill had a set of floodgates and around 1820 its use was changed to grinding corn. In 1828 it was owned by Littlewood & Co. and later worked as a plating forge by Joseph Fellows, who had taken it over from Francis Hill. It ceased production in the second half of the 19th century.

Further west, its floodgates straddling the Stour to the west of Bagley Street, lay a mill that in 1699 was called Mr. Gray's Fulling Mill. It was built on land called Atcham Meadow, probably in the 17th century. Robert Richards converted it into a corn mill in 1719 and it was known as Walk Mills and worked by the Richards family as tenants until 1785. In that year it was let to Dudley Bagley (hence its one-time name of Bagley's Mill) who ran it as a corn and blade mill until 1822. In following years it was taken over by various clay merchants, and in the 1870s used by the Silvester family for brewing before becoming disused. To the west of Bagley Mill was Bedcote Mill, lying south of the Stour close to where the present Stamford Road joins Birmingham Street. Little has been written about this building, but it was probably the mill owned in 1317 by Sir William Stafford, Lord of Amblecote.[16] When Bedcote manor was sold to Richard Jervois in 1538, there were two mills in the manor, Bedcote Mill and Stambermill. In 1837 a Mr. Aldred owned Bedcote Mill and the building was still standing in 1882.

On the north bank of the Stour and just to the east of the town bridge stood the Town Mill. This was originally the ancient Amblecote manorial mill to which all inhabitants had to bring their corn for grinding. It gave its name to Mill Street in Stourbridge. In 1518 the lease of the mill was granted to the Clare family with tenants' multure (the right to receive the tolls from the mill). Leonard Clare was granted a lease for three lives on two watermills in 1530.[17] By 1730 it had become known as the Town Mill, having been converted into a forge and slitting mill, but in 1734 the Scott family took it over as a fulling mill for the cloth trade. The Scotts also resumed the grinding of corn there, but the mill gradually became less used because of scarcity of water. In 1811 the Pitman family acquired the mill for dressing leather, but it ceased operations around the year 1837. Near that site in about 1830 William Orme, brother-in-law of James Foster, built a new ironworks and this became part of the firm of Foster and Orme in 1848.

To the west of the Town Bridge (and also in Amblecote) lay the grand sounding Royal Forge, which was also called the Town Forge at certain times in its history. This ironworks, which had floodgates situated in Spring Meadow, was set up in the 17th century by the Newbrough family, who had close trade connections with the Foleys. In 1680 the works passed to Joshua Bradley,[18] but three years later they were again sold to Ambrose Crowley (1657-1720), whose grandson (also named Ambrose) established an ironworks at Smallwell in County Durham.[19] This sale also included a 'steelhouse' on the Stourbridge side of the Stour. In the 18th century the forge was worked by Francis Homfray who died in 1737, and by 1784 Thomas Hill was manufacturing from the site; his products included small quantities of steel. From 1837 to 1847 the site was a plating forge leased to Thomas and John Sidaway. In 1847 James Foster bought the Royal Forge from J.A. Addenbrooke of Hagley and it became another part of the Foster and Orme ironworks, being merged with the other works to the east of the bridge in the following year.

John Bradley & Co. built their first works to the west of the Royal Forge in 1800 and a second works to the east of it in 1808.[20] They were situated on a narrow strip of land between the river and the canal to the north. By the early 1800s the works already had an annual production of 26,000 tons of iron, cast into cannon, mortars, shot and shell, and in 1813 John

68 *An 1860 engraving of Stourbridge Ironworks, taken from a guide to the Great Western Railway.*

69 *A portrait of Stourbridge industrialist, James Foster (1786-1853).*

Bradley and James Foster bought out the other partners. James Foster became the head of the firm on John Bradley's death in 1816 and was quick to realise the growing importance of the emerging railway industry at that time. Foster went into partnership with John Urpeth Rastrick (1780-1856), a brilliant engineer who had patented a steam engine in 1814. Foster, Rastrick & Co. was situated south of the Stour near the present Lowndes Road on the eastern boundary of Wollaston and slightly to the west of the original Bradley company. It became part of the Foster conglomerate, then known as the Stourbridge Ironworks, which at that time employed at least 600 people in Stourbridge alone and had a major influence on employment in the area. In 1821 the works were described as the largest and most complete of any in this part of the country and perhaps of any in England. When Henry Bradley left the company in 1837 James Foster became the sole owner of John Bradley & Co., but the company name was retained. At its height, the Foster family controlled at least ten large iron companies, including the Royal Forge and Orme's Ironworks mentioned above. By 1869 the company had 95 puddling furnaces but after that the business began to decline because of the introduction of cheap steel, and in 1882 only 29 furnaces were still being operated. The company remained unprofitable for the rest of the century and the Foster family sold their interests in 1919 to a company owned by Edward Taylor. The company was finally closed in 1982.

At the north-east end of Wollaston High Street could be found the ancient Wollaston Mill with its associated pools. The residence called Wollaston Hall and its attached mill appear always to have been under common ownership. When William Perrott died in 1573, he owned a watermill in Wollaston, and in 1577 and 1581 further references were made to 'Peretes Mille'.[21] In 1592 the establishment was referred to as 'two water mills built under one roof' and was probably producing scythes at that time. Two centuries later, in 1772, James Dovey of Brettell Lane was using Wollaston iron mills for cutting glass; in about 1790 he was said to be the first person in the area to introduce a steam-driven plant into a mill. Wollaston Mill, together with the hall, changed hands several times in the 19th century. In the 20th century the mill became the town's largest producer of edge tools run by Isaac Nash, but was taken over in mid-century by the Birmingham Sound Recorders group of companies and became a factory for producing record players, until fierce competition brought production to an end in 1983. In March 1998 the Sunrise Medical Group opened a new eight million pound complex on the site covering 370,000 square feet. This specialised in supplying wheelchairs and other equipment for disabled people.

Nail, Chain, Lock and other Metal Industries

The end products of the iron mills included chain, spades and shovels, edge tools, vices, anvils and ironmongery. But the one occupation that employed most Stourbridge people over the centuries was nailmaking. Nails had been made in the district since at least the beginning of the 14th century, as there is a reference to them in the household expenses of Edward III (1327-77). At that time it was mainly husbandmen who turned their hand to nailmaking in their spare time. The tools they needed were very simple (a hearth, bellows for blowing the fire, an anvil and a hand-held hammer) and the set-up was still much the same in the 16th century. Nicholas Ratclyffe of Stourbridge, who died in 1542, besides leaving 50 sheep and many other animals, had a smythie with 'one payre of beloes, one ondfeld [anvil] and hamis [hammers]' valued at

20 shillings. Richard Warner, who died in 1557, seemed to spend most of his time at the anvil; amongst his possessions were 'an anvyle valued at 26s. 8d., a peyr of ballys (20s. 0d.), 6 viles, a fyre showle, 2 bowysters and a nayling toole (3s. 0d.)', besides various hammers including one for making nails (valued at 5s. 4d.). The Civil War meant a vastly increased demand for nails, and the poorer classes were attracted into the industry at that time, many of them settling locally on Lye Waste. In 1665 Dud Dudley claimed that 'within 10 miles of Dudley there be nearly 20,000 smiths of all sorts'.[22] The nailing industry reached its peak in the years 1775 to 1830.

A typical later nailers' settlement could be found at The Dock at Lye Waste. Men, women and children worked as many hours as daylight would permit within the confines of a small shop with square barred windows. These purpose-built premises were to be found at the rear of the nailers' cottages, and served the purpose of outdoor toilets in the 20th century, before they were demolished in the 1960s for a road-widening scheme that has still not taken place. In the shops could be found an open hearth fuelled by coke (called breeze by the nailers)

70   *Number 48 and the rears of numbers 38 to 43, The Dock at Lye,* c. *1930. The nailmakers' cottages had no back doors.*

and brought to life by hand-operated bellows made of a leather-clad wooden case with brass fittings. A hammer (called an oliver after the name of a local hammer maker) was operated by a foot treadle and suspended under a timber-sprung pole and this struck an anvil that was usually an iron slab; nearby was a tool rack. Children were constantly being burnt and even killed by the sparks that flew from the red-hot rod iron when it was removed from the hearth (colloquially called a flash of lightning). Three workers usually sat around one fire and it was not unknown for 3,000 nails to be made by one person in the course of a day (representing 60,000 blows of the hammer). The rod iron would be supplied from a warehouse owned by one of the many local nailmasters (called foggers) who would also buy back the finished nails for resale. Many foggers were unscrupulous cheats, not averse to using false weights and paying in tokens that could only be exchanged in the shops that they themselves owned (so-called 'tommy shops'); nailers were often so poor they were unable to fight back. In 1827 the main nail warehouses in Lye were owned by Joseph Brookes, Thomas Pargeter, Thomas Eveson, Thomas Perrins, Thomas Attwood, John Perry, Edward Robins, John and

71   *Mr. Tom Cartwright, one of the last of the nailmakers, inside a typical nailshop at Pargeter Street, Lye in 1952.*

Joseph Walters and William Hart, all members of well-known local families.[23] Many of those same families expanded into other local industries during the course of the 19th century. In about 1833 Tommy Ewbank invented a machine that could make 57,500 nails in one hour, and soon nails began to be mass-produced in Birmingham and Wolverhampton, and the demand for hand-made nails declined very rapidly. This in turn led to a drastic cut in the wages paid to workers for making nails in their own homes (the local name was a bate, short for abatement), and caused five general strikes and several partial stoppages between 1838 and 1863. The most serious was in 1842 when riots took place. By 1851 several larger companies were producing nails in Lye, including John Brookes & Co., Thomas Eveson & Sons, Edward Robins and Benjamin & Philip Round.

By the end of the 19th century the hand-made nail had all but disappeared, but a brief success was scored in one particular speciality called the frost cog. This was made from mild steel and had a sharp chisel head that would bite into the road surface. Four cogs were pre-inserted into a square hole in each shoe of a horse and these prevented the animal from slipping in frost or snow. Originating as frost nails and screws developed by Eli

72   *The staff of Henry Wooldridge's frost cog works at Lye,* c.*1900.*

Wooldridge of Attwood Street, Lye, they were manufactured by Henry Wooldridge (born 1840 at Careless Green) who erected 13 houses in Bromley Street for his outworkers. An improved method of manufacture was invented in 1884 by Wooldridge's employee, Benjamin Baker, that brought him considerable trade until the motor car reduced the number of working horses.[24] Baker himself established a factory in King Street, Lye in 1887, which transferred its production to The Hayes in 1893. By the turn of the century some 300 men were employed in the trade, mainly in small workshops, and frost cog manufacture provided jobs for in excess of 1,000 people during the first decades of the 20th century. Swinnerton & Co. of Oldswinford sent many thousands of frost cogs to the Western Front in the First World War and was still making them in the 1950s. Wesley Perrins was taught the trade by his father and became leader of the trade union until 1935.

For a short time some nailers turned to making chain (a 19th-century Cradley Heath speciality) because the equipment was very similar, but chainmaking never became a major industry in the town. The oldest chainmaking concern was probably Thomas Perrins of Careless Green, which was established in about 1770. The trade was carried on in the 1800s by Eli Baylie & Co. in New Street, Stourbridge and by George Wood & Brothers, Thomas Eveson & Sons and Edward Robins in Lye.

Locksmiths and scythemakers carried on other early metal trades in Stourbridge and both occupations were quite common from at least the 16th to the 18th centuries. In 1595 John Lane gave his occupation as locksmith. During the 17th century Richard Gascoyne, Richard Wildsmith, John Huntbach, Robert and Edward Millard, Robert Bradley of Lye, Thomas Cox, Gilbert Bullas junior and John Perkes were all carrying on the trade locally. The Perkes family of Careless Green had a long association with lockmaking, and it was a Mr. Perkes who was asked by the parish in June 1740 to set up the first locksmith's shop in the newly opened parish workhouse. In 1852 three Stourbridge locksmiths were listed in directories, namely Robert Grant and Francis Tandy working in the High Street (they were also in the trade of hanging bells) and Thomas Richards of Beauty Bank.[25] Making scythes was an even more ancient trade. When Richard Cole died in 1552 his inventory included 16 dozen scythes valued at £12, three anvils (£4), a pair of bellows with hammers and tongs (£2) and unwrought iron and steel (30s.). He was owed money from clients as far away as Oxfordshire. Amongst those

following the trade in 17th- and 18th-century Stourbridge were the families of Hornblower, Westwood, Smith, Witton, Raybold, Badger, Hancox and Wheeler. In common with certain other metal trades in the area, the manufacture of scythes appeared to have virtually died out by the end of the 19th century.

Much of the metal industry employment lost in Victorian times was replaced by jobs in the iron plate trade. Its typical products (buckets, dustbins, baths and all kinds of kitchen-ware) were hollow in the middle, and their production was collectively termed 'holloware'. Although some articles were tinned or enamelled, most were galvanised (the sheet iron was dipped into acid, washed, dried and then coated with zinc that gave a bright silvery appearance and prevented rust). The local pioneers of the trade were George Hill (of The Hayes Galvanised Iron Works founded in 1864 when he was 18), Phillip Round (founded as a nail factory in 1849) and Thomas Rhodes, who founded the Providential Works in Lye in 1856 before handing over to his son Robert on his retirement

73 *A chain maker at the works of Eli Baylie in New Street just before its closure in 1961.*

in 1886. The Providential Works covered an area of seven acres and by 1894 employed over 150 people, producing buckets, baths, bowls, basins, watering cans, colliery baskets and beer and milk cans. There were many other smaller firms in the trade, bearing family names such as Boaler, Croft, Eveson, Tayler, Turner and Sutton. It provided more work for local families in the early 1900s than any other industry at that time and Lye became the 'bucket capital of the world'. Machines inevitably began to take over from hand production, especially after the First World War, and the trade became insignificant by the 1950s.

Brickmaking

The clay needed for brickmaking was found on the banks of the Stour and was claimed to be the best in the country. It had been dug from medieval times, when it was a strict rule that holes had to be filled in within 10 days. Stourbridge clay was used for brickmaking, earthenware and pottery from the 18th century onwards. By the end of the 18th century the major sites mining clay were at Hungary Hill (some 70 acres owned by the Milwards and Unwins), The Grange (22 acres worked by the Ruffords), Hay Green (21 acres of the Hickman family) and Mill Field, Lye where the Waldron family had 23 acres.[26] A huge increase in demand for refractories in the 19th century caused the clay industry to expand. Red clay was used for house bricks and white clay (which could withstand great heat) for firebricks. It is said that the bricks for the building of Christ Church, Lye, were baked in kilns on the site made from fire clay dug up in the churchyard. In 1860 E.J. & J. Pearson Ltd. was founded, working mines at Lye and Brierley Hill. A mixture of clay and lime called marl (although the words clay and marl are often used synonymously) was to be found near the present York Crescent (to the north of Vicarage Road in Wollaston). In 1699 those marlpits were owned by the Compson family and in 1782 Lord Foley was shown as owning Marlpit Inhedge and Upper and Lower Marlpit Field in the same location. Sand was also locally available from The Ridge area of Wollaston, a deposit that ran through Norton to Iverley.

As early as 1573 Christopher Francis was described as a brickmaker, but the industry was only conducted on a small scale before 1750, often being combined with nailmaking. Examples of persons employed in both trades include John Hill in 1720, Thomas Perkes in 1750 and William Mobberley in 1758 (many of the Mobberley family specialised in brickmaking throughout the 19th century). In 1782 there were six fields in the Stambermill / Hay Green area with 'brick kiln' in their names, on land owned by William Waldron, Thomas Brettell, Francis Unwin, Lord Foley, Francis Witton and Hungerford Oliver. When Lye Unitarian Chapel was built in 1806 half the bricks were supplied by John Yardley and the remainder by Serjeant Witton and Francis Rufford. In 1827 Stourbridge had six brick kiln yards of which Francis Rufford junior occupied two. These consisted of a three-acre site at the foot of the eastern side of Chawn Hill (approximately where Chawn Hill Close now stands) and a three-acre site north of New Farm Road (almost opposite the end of Junction Road on land that was owned by Francis Unwin). On the southern side of New Farm Road, opposite the second Rufford kiln, was a brickyard owned by Littlewood & Co. which covered one and a half acres. The fourth brick kiln was a two-and-a-half-acre site to the east of Pedmore Road, Lye (near the present Morvale Street), which was owned and occupied by James and John Brookes. The other two sites were of a minor nature.

The largest mid-19th-century firebrick manufacturer in Stourbridge was Rufford & Co. at the Stepping Stone Works in Stamber-mill, employing about one thousand employees and making 60,000 firebricks a week by 1840. Other brickmakers operating in that year in the Lye district were Davis & Hickman, Benjamin Hill, Joseph & William King and Brettell & Rufford.[27] By 1852 some 14 million bricks a year were being made in the area by firms such as George King Harrison, King & Co., Richard Hickman & Co., George Attwood & Sons, and particularly Francis Rufford, whose porcelain baths were also famous. Trade began to decline at the beginning of the 20th century, although well-known firms still included Hadcrofts in Grange Lane, Hickmans in Pedmore Road (near its junction with Cemetery Road), Lunts in Bott Lane, Ruffords at Stambermill and George King Harrison. The George King Harrison works in Dudley Road, Lye covered an area of 35 acres. By 1948 only 500 workers were still employed in the local trade. The last two surviving firms of note were Mobberley & Perry (trading at The Hayes at Lye and founded in the 1850s as The Hurst Brickworks) and Timmis & Co. (who were working an old site near St Mark's church, Stambermill). The Price-Pearson Group later acquired both these companies.

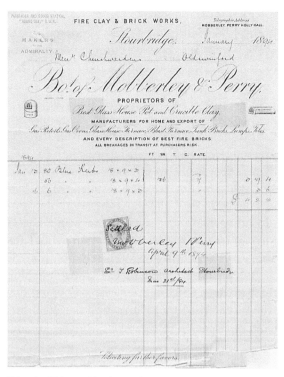

74 *An 1894 Mobberley and Perry invoice, supplying kerb bricks for the pathway to St Mary's Church, Oldswinford. These bricks are still in place today.*

Working conditions in the brickmaking industry in the 19th century were extremely gruelling, especially for the large numbers of women employed in nearly every process. Female workers could be found working on the clay banks, sorting the clay and shovelling it into the mill used for grinding the clay down. They danced on the watered-down material with bare feet to soften it up and carried the clay in baskets on their backs, sometimes taking over a hundredweight at a time up to the moulders in the works, who could also be female. It became the norm for a moulder to produce a standard 1,025 bricks during each day's work, which meant each worker would be handling at least 28 tons of material. After drying, the bricks were wheeled to a round kiln to be fired, a process that usually took a full 14 days for the six to ten thousand bricks involved. Women then took 12 bricks at a time (each weighing some 10 pounds) to the dispatch point, and tossed the bricks two at a time into wagons. The brickmaking industry did not suffer anything like the same amount of industrial unrest as found in the nailmaking trade, the other major employer of female workers in the 19th century, because the impact of new machinery was not nearly so great.

Local Banks

In the 17th century the Royal Mint produced silver and gold coins, but the right to manufacture everyday copper coins was granted as a monopoly to enterprising aristocrats who often cheated by issuing unpopular underweight coins. Those monopolies were suppressed by Parliament in 1644, causing an acute shortage of the smaller popular coins. After the execution of Charles I in 1649 local traders took matters into their own hands by issuing their own tokens. Patent halfpenny and farthing patterns for Stourbridge were issued between 1656 and 1669 by Jonathan Butler, Andrew Muchall, Ezekiel Partridge, John Pratt, Edward Sparry, Humphrey Sutton, Thomas Nott and John Richardson.[28] In 1672 the government of the day began to issue its own copper coins to alleviate the situation.

By the end of the 18th century the emergence of local banks and banknotes made it easier to borrow money and gave the wealthier Stourbridge iron, clay and glass merchants a means of putting their surplus funds to work. The first bank in Birmingham was opened in 1765 by Samuel Lloyd and John Taylor, and about fifteen years later Hill, Waldron and Hill opened their doors to the public in Stourbridge, on the corner of Coventry Street and High Street opposite the town's market hall. In 1797 local inhabitants agreed to accept their banknotes, and in 1800 the bank lent £250 to the parish to build a new workhouse. By 1820 Thomas Bate and William Robins had become partners and the Waldron family had relinquished their interest in the firm. The confidence of the depositors always tended to be a little on the nervous side (rightly so, as it turned out later) but, in 1825, 200 people signed a petition affirming their confidence in Hill, Bate and Robins. Known as the Old Bank, by 1852 it had been taken over by the Birmingham and Midland Bank and was opening its doors at that time from 10 a.m. to 4 p.m. daily. The bank was rebuilt on the same site in 1917, by then a branch of the London & Midland Bank. It still stands on the same site today and is now owned by the Yorkshire Bank.

75 *The original site of the 18th-century Rufford & Wragge Bank at 118 High Street (which later became offices for solicitors Harward & Evers), photographed in 1958.*

The second bank to appear in Stourbridge (termed the New Bank) was opened in about 1796 by Rufford, Willan and Biggs in premises halfway along Upper High Street on its west side. By 1802 Mr. Willan had dropped out, and in 1832 the firm was known as Rufford, Biggs and Rufford. Ten years later a solicitor named Charles John Wragge of Red Hill House and another partner, Stephen Griffiths of The Heath, had joined the company, now called Rufford & Wragge. Disaster struck the undertaking in 1851 when the bank collapsed. One local industrialist who was not caught up in the affair was James Foster. When asked without

76 *A local banknote issued by the Stourbridge & Kidderminster Bank, founded in 1834.*

77 *The Birmingham and Midland Bank in High Street in 1880.*

warning in 1834 by Stourbridge Old Bank to repay his overdraft, his immediate reaction was to push a wheelbarrow full of gold sovereigns through the main street of the town, tip them onto the floor of the bank in front of the manager, and close his account on the spot. He then retaliated by forming the Stourbridge and Kidderminster Bank on 29 January of the same year, occupying premises in Bank Street (off Lower High Street). The bank had an initial capital of £250,000. Eventually it became part of the Metropolitan Bank of England and Wales. After further mergers it ironically became a branch of the London and Midland Bank, reuniting Foster's capital with the ownership of the Stourbridge Old Bank. Two other savings banks were opened in 19th-century Stourbridge to attract smaller investors. On 21 January 1836 a branch of the Kingswinford Savings Bank (founded two years earlier in Kingswinford) was established in Waterloo Place, Hagley Road, but that only opened for one hour each week on a Friday; it still boasted some 1,000 depositors by 1840. In July 1853 Stourbridge Institute started a Penny Bank, which managed to attract about 370 depositors by the end of its first year, a sign that confidence in the town's banking system was beginning to return.

78 *Dipping skins at Mark Palfrey & Co. in 1956.*

79 *The chimney of Turney's works, a well-known landmark in Mill Street, at the time of the firm's closure in 1957.*

The Leather Trade

Firms involved in the leather trade in Stourbridge in the 19th and 20th centuries included Joseph Pitman, W.J. Turney and Mark Palfrey and Co. Mark Palfrey co-founded his firm in 1871 with John Ick (who died in 1884). At their Forward Works they were the first firm to introduce the manufacture of sheepskin hearth rugs, carriage mats and door mats into Worcestershire. The sheepskin workers of Stourbridge, clattering their way to work wearing clogs on their feet, were a common sight. In 1957 Turney's old skin works in Mill Street were closed, the land being redeveloped in the 1970s as an industrial trading estate for Lunt, Comley & Pitt.

VIII

Religion and Education

The Mother Church

The mother church of St Mary's, Oldswinford was most probably founded in the early 10th century, many years before any other church appeared on the local scene. From earliest times the ancient parish covered the manor of Amblecote in addition to that of Oldswinford. Domesday Book confirmed that one priest was living in Oldswinford in the 11th century. When the church was extensively rebuilt in 1843, it was said that the old church was of great antiquity, one arch being either Saxon or early Norman. The oldest surviving part of the present church is the square tower, reputed to be late 14th-century.

The earliest known incumbent was simply called John; he held the office from 1199 to 1216. In 1304 John, the newly appointed rector of Oldswinford, was granted a licence to study within England and to farm out his church to any other priest in order to relieve his debts, provided that church services and the care of souls in his parish did not suffer. In 1313 a rector also named John was cited by the Prior of Worcester for some minor matter concerning the Will of John de Simplingford; the executors won their case against him and the rector was distrained in order to meet his obligations.[1] In 1342 Edward III needed to finance his wars against France and his *Nonarum Inquisitiones* imposed a tax of 18 marks on Oldswinford church for that part of the parish that lay within Worcestershire, and 'one ninth of sheaves, fleeces and lambs, worth four and a half marks and no more' for that part lying in Staffordshire. In 1553 an inventory 'of all the bells, plate, juells and ornaments' in the church was made by the parson, John Mungary, and churchwardens John Bradley, and John Crofts. That document listed three bells in the steeple, one silver chalice, three pairs of vestments ('one of Bruges and the other of white fuseyan'), one cope of 'olde damaske', one satin cope, four altar cloths and 11 old towels. The 1588 Sheldon tapestry map confirmed that the 16th-century church had a spire; a sundial carved with the same date, the year in which great rejoicing took place when the Spanish were defeated by the Armada, is said to have once stood on the old rectory lawn. The tower and spire had always been expensive to maintain: in 1609/10 John Brookes was paid £4 10s. to mend the steeple and in 1698 the parishioners sent a petition to the bishop which read, 'There is an ashtree growing upon our steeple and in danger of throwing great part of it down to the hazard of many peoples lives. But may be prevented if a few stones are taken down and the root destroyed.'

Bellringing played an important role in announcing local and national events. Maintaining the church bells was certainly not inexpensive; in just one year (1605/6) entries in the churchwardens' accounts showed expenditure of 15s. 8d. on the bells. The three bells of 1553 were replaced in 1658 by another set of three, weighing 10 cwt., 8 cwt. and 7¾ cwt. respectively. A note in the church registers stated that those bells were weighed at Worcester for the bellfounder (John Martin), the churchwarden (Adam Read) and the parish clerk (Edward Raby) on 10 August 1658. In 1698 a parishioner sent a petition to the bishop stating that 'We have but one of our three bells usefull. But a clapper in one. I desire some gentle admonition be sent to the churchwarden to take speedy law about it.' Five of the eight bells presently in the tower date from 1686 and 1687, and were made by Matthew and Henry Bagly of Chacombe in Northamptonshire. Charles Carr later recast one of those in 1891 and John Taylor & Co. of Loughborough again recast it in 1902. In 1740 Abel Rudhall of Gloucester cast the tenor bell. It bore the inscription 'to the church the living call, and to the grave do summon all' and was restored in 1965 by D.K. Penn. Two more of the present bells were cast to commemorate the wedding of William Cochrane to Eliza Collis in May 1895. On 6 December 1913 members of the local Worcestershire District Association of Changeringers, conducted by Joseph Smith, rang 5,056 changes on the bells lasting three hours and three minutes.

In 1696 Thomas and Robert Foley, together with Samuel Hunt, paid for a new south aisle to be built onto the nave which included a gallery called Slater's Gallery. According to a plan drawn up in the 1820s by a local architect, Mr. R. Robinson, it probably lay at a slightly higher level than the main building as steps are shown between the two sections. The rectory next to the church was rebuilt in the style of Wren (but probably designed by his pupil Nicholas Hawksmoor) in 1700, replacing a 'low and mean' Tudor parsonage. Later additions to the

80 *The elegant Oldswinford Rectory, photographed in 1970, and dating from 1700.*

81 *St Mary's Church, Oldswinford and part of a Georgian mansion called The Laurels from an 1817 engraving.*

rectory were the west front and the north wing stables, the kitchen and other rooms. Mention was made in 1712 of repairs being carried out to the lychgate and to the path leading to the north door of the church. The churchyard was extended southwards towards White Hall in about 1750 and in 1780 a brick wall replaced the wooden pales between the rectory and the church. During December 1784 6s. 6d. was spent extinguishing a fire in the church roof and in 1800 iron rails had to be fixed to the windows to prevent them from being smashed. In 1807 yet more land for burials, situated to the west of the then churchyard and to the south of the rectory, had to be consecrated to cater for the rapidly rising population in the parish. (The eventual consecration of the town cemetery in South Road on 31 March 1879, followed by the opening of the Lye and Wollescote Cemetery on 19 May of the same year, overcame the burial problem.) On 25 March 1810 the church was packed to hear the new organ in-stalled at the west end of the church being played by a Mr. Simms. That position appears to have been a family monopoly for many years as Henry Simms was organist at the church in 1883 at a salary of £40. Towards the end of the 18th century the ancient fabric in the church was proving very costly to maintain. The spire was found to be in a dangerous condition and was rebuilt in 1810 at a cost of £443 3s. This was followed in 1826 by the rebuilding of the south-east corner of the church, including a new gallery situated above it for the use of the

82 *A print of St Mary's Church in 1832.*

Sunday School children; the total cost of that project was over £600. In 1828 the roof on the southern side of the church cost in excess of £180 to repair. The print of the church shown in Scott's 1832 book on the history of Stourbridge shows the south aisle with a flat roof and a tall narrow porch on the northern side, whereas an engraving from 1817 shows a sloping roof and more ancient porch. During 1838 the steeple was again repaired at a cost of £47 14s.

A proposal at the vestry meeting on 4 July 1840 to rebuild the church completely was opposed, but the idea gained favour when it was guaranteed that none of the cost would be paid out of the rates. The old church was duly demolished, but some of its stone blocks can still be seen in certain older streets of Oldswinford such as Hall Street. The ancient lychgate was demolished at about the same time. The new church was erected during 1843 using approximately the same floor area as the former building, although the new nave was longer and not so wide. £3,500 of the total cost of over £4,500 came from public subscriptions. Amounts of £50 or over were donated by Mr. Badger, the Rev. C.H. Craufurd, the trustees of the Earl of Dudley, the feoffees of Old Swinford Hospital, the Earl of Stamford and Warrington, and Messrs. Foster, Harris, Hickman, Pitman, Perry, Rufford, Robins and Walker. The whole cost of the windows was donated by William Hunt, a solicitor who was killed by a fall from his horse in April 1843, just prior to the opening of the new building by the Bishop of Worcester on 29 October of that year. The new church was designed in Decorated style, but unfortunately constructed from an inferior local sandstone that soon began to crumble. It had no separate chancel, the altar railing and communion table being in a small recess at the east end. John Nicholson of Worcester built a new organ at that time in the west gallery; the instrument had two manuals and a pedalboard. During 1863 Mr. Rufford paid for gas fittings to be installed in the church and five years later 160 persons subscribed to the new clock in the tower; Mr. Frodsham supplied it at a cost of £353. During 1876 stalls for clergy and choir were provided at the east end (the organ still remaining at the west end), and the position of the pulpit was also altered. John and Mary Blew donated the present altar table in 1894.

Thanks mainly to the efforts of the Rev. Alfred Bell Timbrell, a new chancel, vestry, south chapel and organ loft were constructed in 1898 to complete the east end of the church and Edward Webb, a seed merchant, gave the new east window. The extension was officially opened on 21 May of that year at a cost of £3,769. A brand new three-manual organ was constructed at the east end in 1901 by Messrs. Norman & Beard of Norwich, the bellows being operated by a Tangye gas engine. Hedley Glanville Satchell, organist at the church for 50 years to 1922, provided the specifications for the instrument; he had succeeded the long-serving Simms family and was himself followed by Donald Frederick Lambert who occupied the seat for a further 47 years to 1969. The choir had traditionally been paid for their services from Victorian times until the 1950s, and even the organ blower, Mr. E. Chance, received three pounds a year for his services in late Victorian times. The present pulpit was given in June 1903 in memory of W.J. Turney. The steeple was again repaired in 1913 for the sum of £48, and in 1926 electric lights were put into the south chancel in memory of Francis Warr. In 1930 Ernest Stevens provided a new gateway, wall and approach path to the church on the north side in addition to land for a further extension of the churchyard. During 1939 the organ was renovated and enlarged, thanks to the generosity of Arthur Webb and his friends. The Victorian galleries over the north and south aisles were removed in 1955. In December 1982 the steeple was found to be in a most dangerous condition and had to be dismantled, thus removing a landmark that had been familiar to local people for some 500 years. During 1995 the Norman & Beard organ had a £50,000 major overhaul by Trevor Tipple, supervised by the church organist Richard Hall. Improvements included a new solid-state piston capture system and replacement of the noisy pneumatic stop machines by silent solenoid slider units. New ranks of pipes were added and the pitch lowered to enable orchestral accompaniment. The old rectory coach house was renovated in the 1990s to be used for teachers' and artists' courses. Dr. Carey, Archbishop of Canterbury, officially opened the building in October 1995.

83 *A group of stallholders at an Olde Worlde Fayre held at the St Mary's parish rooms in Oldswinford in June 1912.*

Rectors of St Mary's

There have been many colourful characters amongst the clergy at St Mary's. A succession of learned rectors from the 17th to 19th centuries included Simon Ford from 1676 to 1699. He was born in East Ogwell in Devon in 1619, a descendant of the founder of Wadham College. As a chaplain to the king and to the lord mayor of London in later life, he became a friend to many distinguished men of his day, including Sir Christopher Wren. With Puritan leanings, he earned a reputation as a great scholar and fiery preacher, which often landed him in trouble in his younger days. Oldswinford was his last living, which he accepted at the age of 57 because of ill health. He lived on to the age of 80, however, and whilst here his writings included an exposition and enlargement on the New Catechism, a new version of the Psalms of David in metre, and translations for an English version of Plutarch's *Morals*. Many of Simon Ford's sermons were published, especially those preached at times of large state occasions. In 1696 the subject centred on the criminals brought into church to do public penance at Lent. One sermon, famous in its day, concerned the judgement of God on a Kingswinford man, John Duncalfe, who had first denied stealing a bible, and predicted that his hands would rot if the accusation were true. His hands and feet did actually begin to rot away and that strange happening was witnessed by hundreds of people before Duncalfe died in June 1677, after eventually confessing his sin. Ford died on 7 April 1699 and his remains lie buried in Oldswinford beside his wife, Martha Stamp, who originally came from Reading and died on 17 November 1684.

Rectors of Oldswinford in the 18th century included William Hallifax DD, a well-travelled Lincolnshire man who held the Oldswinford living from 1699 to 1722. He too was a scholar and fellow of Corpus Christi College, Oxford. As a pluralist he preferred to be buried at his other church, St Michael's, Salwarpe. He was succeeded by an eminent preacher, George Wigan DD, who held the living for 55 years. Wigan had been a fellow of Christ Church and principal of New Inn Hall, Oxford. The clergymen of the 19th century also played memorable roles in the life of the district, and the church still managed to attract the occasional controversial rector. Thomas Philip Foley, who held the living from 1797 to 1835, was an eccentric man who in his younger days claimed to be the best-dressed undergraduate at Cambridge. In London in the 1790s he met the famous prophetess Joanna Southcott, and became her most important supporter. For a few months in the summer of 1803 she came to live in the rectory at Oldswinford, and it was here that her famous sealed box was deposited between June 1825 and Foley's death in 1835. The box contained predictions that she made on the last day of every year; controversy still rages today over who should be present at the opening of her box. In the spring of 1814, at the age of 64, Joanna believed herself to be with child when her body began to swell, but this inevitably proved to be a phantom pregnancy and she died in the following January. Thomas Foley, however, is reputed to have kept a white horse ready in the rectory stables to ride to the New Jerusalem once a new Messiah had been born to Joanna.

Charles Henry Craufurd, who was rector of the mother church for 41 years to 1876, was the eldest son of the gallant Major General C. Craufurd who was killed during the Peninsular War. He was also a descendant of landscape gardener 'Capability' Brown. In 1865 he defied no less a person than the Archbishop of Canterbury as well as his own diocesan bishop by refusing to have a 'day of humiliation'. Two years later, by now a gouty old widower, he set local tongues wagging by marrying his 27-year-old cook, Mary. On 29 March 1867 he

84 *A visit by a later archbishop of Canterbury, Arthur Michael Ramsey, to St Mary's, Oldswinford in 1962. Also pictured are the bishop of Worcester, Lewis Mervyn Charles-Edwards and the rector of Oldswinford, Alfred Vincent Hurley. On the far left is the Rev. John Andrew, archbishop's chaplain, who subsequently became minister at St Thomas, Fifth Avenue, New York.*

imprudently decided to devote a sermon to defending his action, and on that day it is said that every seat in the church was filled at least one hour before the service commenced. He told his congregation that he preferred the company of a lady who dropped her aitches to that of a mushroom nobility. The local and the national press duly rebuked him.

A Chapel for the Town

By the 15th century the town was sufficiently large to need its own separate place of worship. A chantry foundation, called the Service of the Trinity, was created in Stourbridge on 21 May 1430 by the Haley family. Philip Haley and his wife Joan gave a piece of land to build and endow the chapel in Lower High Street (where Stourbridge Sixth Form College now stands) and to support a priest called William Smith. The priest would say prayers for their souls in perpetuity and was removable at the will of the parishioners. Amongst other duties he 'taught a gramer scole, taking nothing thereof of poore mens children accordyng to the foundacon of the same chauntery' and 'hath also in tymes of necessitye to ayde and assyste the curate there'.[2] Twenty pence a year was to be given to the poor of the town of Stourbridge out of a total chantry income of about 113s. 6d. The original deed of gift for the chantry refers to a piece of land in Stourbridge 'as it is newly marked out', indicating that it was a parcel of a larger piece of ground. Despite the efforts of the Haley family to find immortality, one knows almost nothing about them today. The only clue to their past can be found in the seal of the later grammar school which had the legend 'S : Officii : Stapule : Civitat : Lincoln.'; this has been identified as that of the wool staple of the city of Lincoln that went out of existence in 1369. As the chantry was founded 61 years afterwards, the inference is that the Haley forbears came from Lincoln and brought the seal with them.[3]

The utilisation of that chapel as a place of worship ceased when Edward VI abolished chantry foundations in 1547. Nicholas Rocke, who was chantry priest and schoolmaster in Stourbridge at that time, was described as 'lernde and of honest conversacion, but for certen empedymentes not able to keep a cure'.[4] The foundation still had its own rental two years after it had been abolished, showing there were eight tenants by indenture and three at the will of the lord.[5] How the lord of the manor came to own the dozen messuages and cottages in the foundation is an interesting story. In the 1430 foundation deed, 22 trustees were appointed to hold the property and normally, as each one of those trustees died, their own executor would have legally taken over the duty. Owing to faulty drafting, when the last of the original trustees finally died all the property escheated or reverted to the lord of the manor of Bedcote, because there remained no legal heir. Natural justice was partly restored in 1627 when Nicholas Sparry, the then lord of the manor of Bedcote, transferred some of the property back into the hands of Stourbridge Grammar School.

Religious Dissenters

The first religious dissenters to appear on the local scene were the Quakers, whose registers of birth date back as far as 1651. Thanks to the labours of George Fox, they erected their Meeting House in about the year 1666 on a small track leading out of Queen Street (the building is still standing today in Scotts Road on the west side of the town's ring road). In 1688 Ambrose Crowley, a wealthy local ironmaster, leased the building and its small burial ground at a peppercorn rent to members for a term of 1,000 years; during 1698 the burial ground was enlarged. At the end of the Commonwealth period many nonconformist ministers had lost their benefices, and quite a few of these were attracted to the Stourbridge area because of the patronage of wealthy industrial local families such as the Foleys. Because nonconformists were prevented at the time from building their own places of worship, some were meeting in the

85   *The Quaker Meeting House in Stourbridge in 1983.*

chapel of Prestwood Hall in the adjoining parish of Kingswinford (a building then owned by Philip Foley, the son of the founder of Old Swinford Hospital, Thomas Foley); others met in a room at the *Talbot* in Stourbridge, also Foley property. From 1672 nonconformist ministers could legally conduct their own services if licensed, and in 1689 protestant dissenters were exempted from some of the more severe penalties they had previously suffered, provided that their places of worship were certified by a justice of the peace at the quarter sessions. In 1697 the house of James Scott, the leading independent minister in Stourbridge, was so certified.

In 1698, thanks to the mercer Richard Baker, the Independents built their first chapel on the corner of Coventry Street and Lower High Street (behind the present wine shop of Nickolls & Perks). Even as late as 1715 the dissenters were still very unpopular in Stourbridge, their minister George Flower having to creep into his chapel by back alleyways. One dark night on 18 July of that year a riotous gathering of people, chanting 'down with the roundheads', attacked the building. In the words of inhabitants of the time, it was 'pulled down and demolished by divers riotous tumultuous and rebellious people, and the doores, windowes, pulpitt seates, galleryes and timberwork therein by them carryed of and greate parte thereof burned'. Not to be defeated, the chapel was rebuilt almost immediately and continued in use for the rest of the century.

During 1788, at the end of Benjamin Carpenter's ministry, there was a serious split in the ranks of the Independents. Many of the congregation transferred their allegiance to William Scott, who in that year erected the Presbyterian chapel on the western side of the Lower High Street at a cost of £1,205. Attached to the new chapel was a burial ground, and a parsonage was built in New Street. The building became the fashionable place for the wealthy to worship in early 19th-century Stourbridge. Two years later James Scott, who was Unitarian minister in Netherend, held his first meeting of the Religious Discussion Group on Lye Waste, which then met on the first Monday of every month at Richard Pardoe's club room. Meetings were

86 *The Presbyterian Chapel in Lower High Street in 1983.*

often violently interrupted and those attending were always in danger of physical abuse. After 15 years of meeting on private premises, the society saw their Unitarian chapel opened
on Lye Waste in January 1806; it had seats for 100 people and cost £245 14s. 9d. Of that
amount James Scott's aunt, Mrs. Ann Scott of Birmingham, donated £200 and the land was
purchased from John Brookes senior; by 1827 the building was called the Socinian Chapel.
James Scott died in 1827 and was buried in the sister Presbyterian chapel at Stourbridge.[6]
Due to the rapidly increasing population, a new chapel was erected in 1861, designed by the
Stourbridge architect Francis Smallman Smith, and a Unitarian parsonage was built in Belmont
Road in 1888. One very well respected Lye Unitarian minister was Isaac Wrigley, who during
the years of his ministry (1891-1924) supported many good causes. The Lye Unitarian chapel
finally closed in July 1991, due to diminishing support.

   Meanwhile the remaining section of the Independents (who later became Congregationalists)
worshipped in Coventry Street until 1810, when, through the efforts of their minister, John
Richards, they too built a new chapel in Lower High Street, sited on the eastern side opposite
their old rivals. The building had 400 seats and cost £3,100. A new organ was built there in
1839 and a proper front was added to the building during 1841 and 1842. There could be
found the grave of six-year-old Milton Melancthon Jerome, elder brother of the famous author

87 *The Unitarian Chapel at Lye Waste, built in 1861.*

88 *Enville Street Methodist Church shortly before its demolition in 1965. It was erected in 1857.*

Jerome Klapta Jerome whose family lived in Worcester Street, Stourbridge (on the corner of Hill Street) between 1860 and 1862. Old rivalries were put to one side in 1972 when the Congregationalists united with the Presbyterians to form the United Reformed church. The last service in the building was held on 17 September 1978, after which the congregation of the United Reformed church removed to the then redundant St John's church. The Lower High Street building was demolished following a major fire and redevelopment of the site started in 2000. A Society of Independents chapel was also erected at Lye Waste and opened on 1 January 1821. That was replaced by a finer building (known as Mount Zion) in 1827 which provided 340 seats for its congregation. The earlier building was converted into a vestry and schoolroom, and George Wood later provided a parsonage.

The Baptists were the next religious sect to appear on the Stourbridge scene. First mentioned in the area in the 1770s at Brettell Lane, Amblecote, by the 1780s they were meeting in a house in Mill Street that was described as having a garden running down to the Stour. They also met in a Mrs. Young's house in Stourbridge High Street. In 1801 the Baptists were evicted from their rooms for arrears of rent and their then minister, William Snow, departed for Cradley. During 1823 they started again to meet in Stourbridge at The Hemplands. A small chapel measuring 31 feet by 17 feet was built in Duke Street in 1828. On 8 June 1836, thanks to the exertions of their minister John Savage, a fine new chapel with seating for 270 persons was opened in Upper Park Street at the foot of Hanbury Hill at a cost of £900. An organ was later installed.[7]

Methodism also appeared in Stourbridge in the late 18th century. John Wesley first visited the West Midlands in 1743, but without leaving any great impression on the area. When he visited Stourbridge on 19 March 1770 he commented that 'many of the hearers were wild as colts untamed, but the bridle was in their mouths'. His final visit to Stourbridge took place in 1774. It was not until about 1790 that the first Methodist community began to worship in Stourbridge, probably in Mill Lane. Their numbers began to grow far more quickly than those of the Baptists, forcing them to use Stourbridge Theatre in Theatre Road. In 1805 the Wesleyan Methodists raised £1,600 by the issue of shares and built a chapel in New Road that had an organ and galleries on three sides, seating a massive 868 people. Registers date from 1809, and the chapel was further enlarged in 1826 and 1829. It was not until 1828 that a separate Stourbridge circuit was formed out of the older Dudley circuit. Further Wesleyan chapels were built at Lye Waste (1837), Enville Street (1857, the foundation stone being laid by Rowland Hill of postage stamp fame) and Gigmill (1884). There were also Primitive Methodist chapels at Duke Street, Stourbridge with 120 seats, at Lye Waste (built in 1830) with seating for 170 people and at Bright Street, Wollaston. In addition New Connexion chapels were erected at Lye Waste (1822 and reported to be attended by a numerous audience), New Road, Stourbridge (1836) and Hay Green (1839), serving the needs of an industrial population that was increasing at a rampant rate. New Road church was built in 1928 to mark the centenary of the first Stourbridge circuit.

An influx of Irish families into Stourbridge in the early 19th century created the need for a permanent Roman Catholic place of worship. A tiny chapel existed in the town in 1820, but in 1823/4 another chapel was erected in New Road, Stourbridge at a cost of £1,200; it seated 236 persons and contained a gallery and an organ and next door was the priest's house. The present fine Gothic-style church, designed by E.W. Pugin, replaced that chapel in 1864; its 130 ft. spire and 14 cwt. tenor bell were added in 1889.

William Booth founded the Salvation Army in London in 1865, but earlier in 1863 he had conducted a six-week mission in Lye. When the Army appeared for the first time in 1881 it made a very big impact on the people, although some viewed the movement with great suspicion. The Army's barracks were originally in Church Street on Lye Waste, but in September 1888 an agent of General Booth acquired the Victoria Hall and Rink in Bell Street, Stourbridge for £650. In November 1889 the new building was opened as a Salvation Army barracks with seating accommodation for some 600 people. On 18 August 1904 General Booth again passed through the town conducting a campaign by motor car. A large crowd was gathered near the town clock to greet him.

89 *The Salvation Army Citadel at Church Street, Lye in 1967.*

New Anglican Parishes

Following the cessation of their chantry chapel in 1547, townspeople of Stourbridge had to wait another 200 years to have their own place of worship again. St Thomas's Chapel was erected in Rye Market (now Market Street) during the years 1728 to 1735, and this eventually met the needs of the town's inhabitants, especially as the poor did not have to pay for the use of pews as at St Mary's. The building was financed mainly by public subscription, although a clothier named John Biggs left £300 in his Will dated March 1736 to encourage the project. Terrible problems arose when the rector of Oldswinford, George Wigan, tried to put his own curate into the chapel and to enclose part of a local common to provide a regular income. That resulted in an outcry and petition from the town's inhabitants, who had donated almost £2,000 of their own money and consequently felt that the living should be nothing to do with the church in Oldswinford. The result was that the new chapel remained vested in the inhabitants of the town, as did the presentation of the incumbent. The election of ministers in the 19th century was akin to a political contest; all the town's inhabitants could vote, including non-Anglicans. The elections were accompanied by music, bellringing, placards and much rowdy behaviour that was sometimes violent. The first curate was Walter Hickman, who was a son of one of

NO GO!

Mr. J. H. H. FOLEY has declared that he did not go to KINGSWINFORD WORKHOUSE and **PULL THE PLUGS OUT OF THE BEER BARRELS** to prevent the Poor from having the Beer.

HUMBUG!

If he did not Pull the Plugs out HIMSELF, **HE ORDERED** the Housekeeper to pull them out, and I solemnly declare he **DID GO** to the Workhouse and did,

Prevent the Poor from having the Beer.

and that he would not leave the Workhouse until **EVERY DROP WAS MADE-AWAY WITH.** ASK Mr. and Mrs. JEFCOATE IF THIS BE NOT TRUE, who were Governor and Matron of the Workhouse at the same time.

In the Barrel of Ale in the Cellar I sat,
When FOLEY came there with his Horsewhip and Hat;
With rage he was foaming, I can swear it is true,
He cried pull out the COCK—I cried *Doodle Doo !*

JACK SPIGOT.

Kingswinford Workhouse,
July 7th, 1837.

90 *A political poster issued in 1837, accusing Mr. J.H.H. Foley of stopping the supply of beer for the inmates of the workhouse.*

the trustees of the chapel, Gregory Hickman. Walter Hickman remained in office from 1736 until 1742, despite not having the other trustees' consent. He augmented his salary by letting out certain pews for amounts varying from 2s. 6d. to 4s. 0d. The Queen Anne-style building by the year 1759 was enhanced by the addition of a square tower with a peal of eight bells. An organ and gallery were added in 1809 and the chapel was further enlarged in 1837. By the time it became a parish in its own right on 3 April 1866, 339 of its 968 seats were free. In 1870 a Georgian house in Market Street was purchased as a vicarage, and eight years later Miss Hunt donated a clock. During 1890 a new chancel was added, and the site was completed when a new church hall was built on adjoining land in 1914.[8]

Growing population resulted in the parish of Oldswinford being further subdivided during the 19th century. It was in the highly industrialised district of Lye that the main pressure was felt, and in 1813 Lye Chapel of Ease was erected, thanks to an endowment from the manufacturer and banker Thomas Hill of Dennis Hall, Amblecote. The building cost about £9,000 and was opened on

91 *St Thomas's Church in Market Street, c.1900, before the church hall was built in 1914.*

5 December 1813. The first curate was Matthew Booker, who died in office on 2 June 1817. He was succeeded by John Hodgson, who served for the next 22 years. The congregation was quite small at that time, due partly to the competition from the many other chapels in the area and partly to the fact that the building was very cold inside. The church was consecrated and dedicated as Christ Church on 30 August 1839, and its registers commenced from that date. The first 'perpetual curate' of The Lye was Henry Thomas Hill, who according to one of his successors was a 'cultured and delightful man', and a grandson of the founder of the church. He was succeeded in about 1844 by his brother, Melsup Hill. The story goes that this unfortunate gentleman was 'stoned out of Lye' by the inhabitants, and only held office for just over one year. His successor from 1844 to 1865 was the much-loved James Bromley, who was born in 1811 into an old established Staffordshire family. During the earlier years of his ministry the church was greatly enlarged, providing a total of 1,000 seats of which 300

92 *A portrait of James Bromley, the much-loved minister of Christ Church, Lye, who died in 1865.*

were free. He took a tremendous interest in his flock, especially in the youth of the parish, attempting to civilise them by teaching new standards of cleanliness and godliness. One of his first acts was to go to the rescue of two drowning miners; it was a common sight to see him at four o'clock in the morning administering to the miners on their way to work. He was not averse to fearlessly entering a public house and physically dragging out some poor member of his congregation who had reverted to sinful ways. He died suddenly in office in December 1865 leaving a widow and 10 children; his sermon the previous Sunday was based on the text 'he being dead, yet speaketh'. He was so respected by his congregation that more than £3,000 was raised for his family; as the living was only worth £240 a year, this was an amazing amount. He was followed at Lye by David Robertson, who saw many changes in his nine years in the parish. A wall was built to enclose the dilapidated parsonage and the rather poor organ in the church was replaced by an instrument in a new chamber at the east end, built by Henry Jones of Fulham. Sir Arthur Sullivan personally revised the list of stops on the instrument for Robertson. Robertson married in 1871 and two daughters were born at the parsonage before he left for Market Deeping in Lincolnshire in May 1875.[9] One of the two curates who helped him during his ministry was F.W. Haines, who himself in 1879 became minister of Lye in succession to R. Fletcher. In 1885, the year when H.C.W. Phillips took over, a new spire was built by W.H. Jones (the design was by Owen Freeman). It replaced an earlier wooden structure, but this steeple itself was eventually demolished in 1985. The parish of Lye can claim fame in having produced an archbishop of Wales. Alfred Edwin Morris was born in 1894 to a jeweller in Stambermill, and was bishop of Monmouth from 1945 to 1957 before becoming archbishop from 1957 to 1971.

93 *Christ Church, Lye, c.1900.*

Further new parishes were soon carved out of the ancient mother parish. Amblecote church was built in Old English style with yellow bricks in 1841/2 on a site given by the Earl of Stamford and Warrington. With seating for 860 people, it catered for a separate parish from 1845. Thanks to the generosity of W.O. Foster, Wollaston also erected its own church in 1859/60 and a vicarage was built half a mile away in Vicarage Road in 1861. The church at that time was unusual in that it was heated by pipes running directly from the Foster iron-works. Wollaston also became a parish in its own right, having been part of Amblecote for the previous 15 years. George Gilbanks, who met the Foster family when he was chaplain at Himley Hall, was the first vicar of Wollaston church and he tended his flock in the hamlet for the remainder of the century, dying in office in January 1913 at the age of 86.

The year 1857 saw the Stourbridge solicitor, John Harward, purchase the former Primitive Methodist chapel in Duke Street and fit it out at his own expense as an Anglican church for the people of Stourbridge. It was duly dedicated to St Peter, but was only intended to be a temporary place of worship until a larger new building could be afforded for the increasing congregation that wished to worship there. The Earl of Dudley came to the town's rescue when in 1860 he provided one quarter of the £4,000 involved in building the church of St John the Evangelist on the site of the former Warehouse Field in Stourbridge. The great Victorian architect G.E. Street, who was also responsible for the Strand Law Courts in London, designed it. The church was opened on 13 January 1861 and yet another separate parish was established. The chancel roof was badly damaged by fire in 1908, but was subsequently restored.

The last of the 19th-century churches to be built was St Mark's, Stambermill, which was dedicated at a service on 6 December 1870 at which Henry Hill preached; Lye curates had previously held services in the schoolrooms there. Francis Tongue Rufford gave the site, but because of the danger of mining subsidence, the pillars were constructed of cast iron and the wooden arches reinforced by ribs of iron. In 1987 the decision was taken to demolish the church.

The size of the ancient parish of Oldswinford was further reduced in the 20th century with the consecration of St Andrew's church in Wollescote by the Bishop of Worcester on 5 June 1939. For some time the Church of England authorities had recognised the need to provide a church at Wollescote which had seen great growth as a residential area. The old Belmont Mission was considered to have served its purpose, and in 1939 work on erecting the new church was begun. Finally, in 1951 Norton became a separate ecclesiastical district, carved out of parts of St Mary's and St Thomas's parishes. This was based on the church of St Michael and All Angels, which had been opened earlier in October 1929, at a cost of £2,350, replacing a corrugated iron structure known as St Thomas's Mission church. The Venerable A.V. Hurley dedicated a £10,000 church hall there in September 1956.

Stourbridge Grammar School
After the Haley Chantry had been closed in 1547 part of its income was used to re-establish a school on the site of its chapel in Lower High Street on 17 June 1552. The new Stourbridge Grammar School was further endowed with property that had previously belonged to Evesham Abbey and the College of Fotheringay. The early emphasis was on the classical subjects of Latin and Greek, together with religious studies (all the headmasters up to the early 20th

century had taken holy orders). Life for the scholars must have been somewhat harsh, for amongst the list of rules in 1578 was the prohibition of speaking any language other than Latin at school or in the streets. Monitors had to take the names of those who offended that rule, or of any boy who swore, absented himself or arrived late. Another requirement was for the mandatory attendance at church on Sundays and Holy Days of any boys remaining in the town or parish. Lessons began at 6 a.m. (an hour earlier in summer) and ended at 5 p.m., with only one half-hour break for dinner. The headmasters themselves had their failings. Richard Allchurch, appointed in about 1575, was a loveable rascal who was reputed to practise magic and cast horoscopes, but he also sold ale in the schoolmaster's house and was discharged in 1590, becoming a master at Wombourne in 1594.[10] He died in January 1609/10 at Oldswinford.

At the beginning of the 18th century, additional rules governing the life of the school included: no boys to be admitted who were under the age of five years; no boys to be admitted for the sole purpose of learning to write or to cast accounts; no stranger to be admitted without the consent of one or more governors; no money to be paid by the scholars' parents; masters could be dismissed if the scholars did not gain any benefit from them.

As a 15-year-old boy, the renowned Samuel Johnson experienced the rigours of the school for over six months in 1724 when staying with his cousin, Cornelius Ford, in Pedmore. When alterations were later being made to the school, the initials 'SJ' were found carved on wooden panelling from the old A1 schoolroom; popular tradition has it that it was Samuel Johnson himself who embellished the panelling. Towards the end of the Napoleonic wars in 1813, the school had no scholars at all for several years, but the headmaster Joseph Taylor continued to draw his salary of £200 a year. Following a meeting of the inhabitants of the town and parish on 3 March 1832, it was resolved that the school should be revitalised. New rules were drawn up which encouraged the teaching of mathematics, geography and English composition, and the age of entry was raised to seven. Numbers attending the school rose from eight in 1832 to 17 in 1840 and 41 in 1849, but by 1859 the attendance had diminished again to 38. Expansion in late Victorian times brought the numbers up to 111 in 1900 and 143 in 1905. Fees were imposed in 1909, although 12 free places were given to boys living in the ancient parish of Oldswinford. Soon afterwards a preparatory

94 *A portrait of lexicographer Dr. Samuel Johnson (1709-84), who attended Stourbridge Grammar School in 1724.*

department was opened and by 1934 there were 600 boys in the school. In 1950 the school ceased to be fee-paying and voluntary aided status was granted. A further reorganisation in 1976 turned this ancient institution into Stourbridge Sixth Form College.

For several hundred years the grammar school buildings consisted of the headmaster's house (which grew out of the original chantry priest's house), the second master's house and a schoolroom. The latter consisted of one long and narrow room, which had desks for the boys running the length of its two longer sides, and was reached from the High Street by a very dark passageway. The school also had a tower with a cupola on the top; this was badly damaged by a fire on Whit Tuesday 1812, which brought an old bell crashing to the ground. The tower had to be rebuilt and the bell replaced. In 1859 the *Old Horse Inn* on the northern

95   *Stourbridge Grammar School, c.1900, before the extension into the adjoining Green Close.*

96 *Stourbridge Grammar School charter day luncheon in June 1932. Standing at the top table are C.F. Leeson, H.E. Halliday, T. Clare, J.E. Boyt (headmaster), H.E. Palfrey, H.P. Jones, V.J. Wilkes and P.D. Folkes.*

boundary of the school was purchased and the two masters' houses were enlarged. That was followed in 1907 by the purchase of more adjoining property called Green Close, enabling the school to be further enlarged with a longer hall and an extra bay. During 1926 Longlands House was acquired to house the headmaster away from the school, and in 1931 the two masters' houses were demolished to make way for a new hall, the old hall being turned into a library. Many specialised buildings were subsequently constructed on land between High Street and the eastern boundary of the school in Duke Street.

Old Swinford Hospital

One hundred years after the foundation of the town's grammar school, a new school building appeared on the Oldswinford horizon. Old Swinford Hospital, standing on a slight rise overlooking the Hagley Road, was founded in 1667 by industrialist Thomas Foley (1617-77). The founder's father, Richard Foley (1580-1657) had acquired the manor of Bedcote from Nicholas Sparry in 1630. In 1634 he bought from Edward Smith two cottages and a parcel of land called Catherwell lying within the manor of Bedcote and originally part of the common fields of both Bedcote and Oldswinford manors. It was on those fields that the school was later built. Richard Foley was buried at Oldswinford in July 1657 and his son Thomas continued to amass the family fortune. Within the space of a few years in the 1660s and 1670s he purchased the further manors of Oldswinford, Wollaston, Pedmore and Great and Little Witley, making his home at Witley Court and becoming High Sheriff of Worcestershire and ironmaster to the navy in 1660. His annual income was reputed to have been some £5,000 a year, a vast amount for those days. In 1671 a coat of arms was confirmed to him emblazoned 'argent, a fesse engrailed between three cinquefoils' and he was buried at Oldswinford in 1677. One of Thomas's sons, Robert Foley (1624-76) also lived in Stourbridge and married Anne, second daughter of Dudley, Lord North.

A sermon by Thomas Foley's puritan friend, Richard Baxter, had inspired him to build the school, which was modelled on Christ's Hospital (then in London). It was magnificently endowed on Foley's death with some 1,500 acres of land, most of which lay within the manor of Pedmore. The original trustees were Thomas, Paul and Philip Foley (the founder's sons), Robert Foley, Thomas Jolliff, William Talbot, Leonard Simpson, Richard Amphlett, Nicholas Addenbrooke, Joshua Newbrough, William Winchurst, John Davis and Edward Paston, augmented by clergymen Thomas Wright, Robert Pierson, Ambrose Sparry and John Taylor. Foley instructed his trustees that 'no boys be chosen into it but such as are real objects of charity, and that they may be taught by such masters as may bring them up in the fear of God, and that when they shall be fit to be apprenticed, care may be taken to place them with such masters as may answer my great end, being the glory of God and their real good'.

In due course 60 boys were admitted, including three from Oldswinford, four from Stourbridge and a fixed number from surrounding parishes. The first eight boys took up their places in 1670, on completion of the original Founders Building. It remained a strict rule that scholars were to be selected from the parents of the industrious poor, and parents who were claiming parish relief were excluded from sending their sons. The purpose of the education given was directed more to fitting the boys for their future employment, in contrast to the purely academic character of the subjects taught at Stourbridge Grammar School. The dress included long cloth breeches, which were abandoned in the mid-19th century in favour of drab corduroy trousers. The long blue coats that gave the school its familiar name of the Blue Coat School ceased to be worn in 1928, except as Sunday best. Boys were normally admitted at the age of seven or eight and were apprenticed out to suitable masters when they attained 14 years. Conditions were reputed to have been extremely harsh; on at least one occasion in the 19th century there was a mass rebellion and walkout by the scholars. In 1836 the boys were awoken at 6 a.m. in the morning (half an hour later in winter), and were sent to bed at 8 p.m. in the evening. Their breakfast consisted of bread and milk, dinner of bread and cheese on Thursdays and

97   *Old Swinford Hospital from the Hagley Road gates, before the building of the College of Further Education.*

Saturdays (meat on the other days), and supper of bread and milk (except that broth was served on Tuesdays and Fridays with puddings as an occasional treat). By 1832 the number of scholars was still only 70, but in 1852 that had risen to 100 with a further increase to 160 in 1882. In that year a large matching building, now known as Maybury House, was constructed at a cost of some £500, which increased the limited accommodation originally provided in the ancient Founders and Barn Block edifices. Four years earlier a spacious sanatorium had been built overlooking Love Lane to further the medical interests of the boys, but the building proved to be rather larger than necessary and is now used as Foster boarding house.

The 20th century saw many new buildings on the site, mainly to provide further boarding houses. A fine new school hall with 300 seats, headmaster's study and feoffees' room was built in 1905, followed 20 years later by a new house for the headmaster and administration. In September 1946 Worcestershire County Council began to contribute towards the costs of some boarders. A Lyttelton wing was added adjacent to Barn Block in 1950, and in that year voluntary aided status was granted. In 1951 a sixth form was established. Unfortunately the outstanding prospect of the school from Hagley Road was ruined in the 1950s when land was sold to the local education authority for use as a College of Further Education. During the 1980s four new boarding houses were built, one of which (Witley House) was opened by the Duchess of Gloucester in 1983; she made a return visit to the school in January 1994. In 1986 the ancient granary in the centre of the school was demolished; it was originally built in 1682 and had been used as a swimming pool since 1887. The new buildings enabled the number of pupils to reach 500 and in 1989 the school was one of the first to become grant maintained. A fine new sports hall was built in 2000 and today the school is still a flourishing institution.

Charity, Church and Private Schools

In the 17th century several other wealthy Stourbridge citizens attempted to make education available to local children, although these foundations were smaller in size than the two principal schools. Henry Glover of Oldswinford, who was Thomas Foley's brother-in-law and chief business associate, died in 1689. Under the terms of his Will a sum of £400 was put on trust, to be administered by the Rev. Philip Foley and other governors of Stourbridge Grammar School. This was in order that a further six poor boys (being children of honest and industrious poor inhabitants of Oldswinford and Stourbridge) could be educated in English, writing and arithmetic. Every year one of those boys was to be apprenticed at a premium of five pounds. Whether due to legal snags or apathy, it was not until 1711 that his charity was finally effected. At the same time John Wheeler executed an indenture dated 26 October 1708 which endowed a trust fund with properties at Beauty Bank and Birds Bank in Stourbridge; one of those houses was to be turned into a school for the instruction in reading, writing, arithmetic and religion of 20 poor boys living in Oldswinford and Stourbridge. The two charities were used to run a combined schoolroom attached to a dwelling house halfway along Red Hill, called Red Hill School, the master living on the premises. In later years the house was called Wheelergate. By 1832 the Glover and Wheeler School had 32 pupils, of whom 26 were paid for by the Wheeler Trust, the remainder by Glover.[11] In 1883 the trustees successfully applied to have the funds transferred to help poor boys enter Stourbridge Grammar School; the school premises were sold and the proceeds added to the fund.

Another small charity school was founded on the death of Presbyterian William Scott on 21 December 1792. The first building was erected in 1816 in Wollaston Road, Stourbridge (close to the Quaker Meeting House) on land given by his nephew, John Scott. This was initially used for public worship and two years later a further room was added. The premises were utilised jointly by Scott's Charity and the Presbyterian schools and by 1832 they had

98   *A sketch of Scott's charity school in the 19th century.*

Government School of Design, Stourbridge

(DEPARTMENT OF PRACTICAL ART.)

President.

THE RIGHT HON. LORD WARD.

Vice-Presidents.

THE RIGHT HON. THE EARL OF STAMFORD AND WARRINGTON.
THE RIGHT HON. LORD LYTTELTON.
J. H. H. FOLEY, ESQ., M. P.

Council.

HON. & REV. W. H. LYTTELTON   JOSEPH PITMAN, ESQ.   MR. JOSEPH WEBB
ROBERT SCOTT, ESQ.   MR. AKROYD   MR. B. RICHARDSON
W. O. FOSTER, ESQ.   MR. JOHN COOKE   MR. E. BLURTON
JOHN HARWARD, ESQ.

Treasurer.

JOHN AMERY, ESQ.

Master.

MR. ANDREW M'CALLUM.

Porter.

MR. HENRY BIRD.

LIST OF ANNUAL SUBSCRIBERS.

	£	s.	d.
Right Hon. Lord Lyttelton	2	2	0
J. H. H. Foley, Esq., M. P.	2	2	0
Wm. Orme Foster, Esq.	2	2	0
Robert Scott, Esq.	2	2	0
Hon. and Rev. W. H. Lyttelton	1	1	0
S. H. Blackwell, Esq.	1	1	0
Henry Wentworth Foley, Esq.	1	1	0
W. B. Collis, Esq.	1	1	0
J. Amery, Esq.	1	1	0
J. Harward, Esq.	1	1	0
Henry Corser, Esq.	1	1	0
E. W. Bernard, Esq.	1	1	0
Henry Bradley, Esq.	1	1	0
Henry Giles, Esq.	1	1	0
Mr. Akroyd	1	1	0
Mr. Joseph Webb	1	1	0
Messrs. Davis, Greathead & Green	1	1	0
James Evers Swindell, Esq.	1	1	0
Charles Evers Swindell, Esq.	1	1	0
Joseph King, Esq.	1	1	0
Joseph Purser, Esq.	1	1	0
B. Parham, Esq.	1	1	0
Miss Pargeter	1	1	0

	£	s.	d.
Messrs. Wood, Brothers	1	1	0
R. L. Freer, Esq.	1	1	0
Joseph Pitman, Esq.	1	1	0
B. Pargeter, Esq.	1	1	0
Mr. W. J. Hodgetts,	1	1	0
Messrs. Keep & Watkin	1	1	0
Mr. B. Richardson	1	1	0
Mr. Mellard	1	1	0
Mr. B. Brooks	1	1	0
Mr. Vernon	1	0	0
Rev. A. W. Worthington	0	10	6
Mr. Charles Webb	0	10	6
Mr. T. Wilkes Webb	0	10	6
Mr. W. Hutchings	0	10	0
Mr. A. Green	0	5	0
Mr. A. P. Morris	0	5	0
Mr. Adams	0	5	0
Mr. Heming	0	5	0
Mr. Alcock	0	5	0
Mr. Stringer	0	5	0
Mr. Nicholls	0	5	0
Mr. Pritchard	0	5	0

99 *An 1852 list of annual subscribers to the Stourbridge School of Design.*

as many as 60 pupils.[12] In 1841 the master was listed as Thomas Haslock Richards,[13] and a bequest in 1848 enabled a girls' school to be started. When the local council eventually took over the running of the school, the charity fund was used to provide scholarships to Stourbridge Grammar School. At Lye Waste Thomas Hill made a bequest of £130 in 1830 to set up his Lye Batchelor School, which in 1832 professed to have 120 pupils,[14] and in 1841 the master was listed as Richard Fiddian.[15] Because so many young girls were acting as nursemaids for the babies of older women working in the nailmaking industry, in the 1830s it was decided to start a school for girls in a shed on Lye Waste. The teacher there in 1841 was Catherine Everitt.[16]

In 1848, due mainly to the interest of members of the Mechanics Institute, a School of Art was opened in Stourbridge 'to promote a taste in the fine arts especially in their application to manufacture and design'. In 1851 a building in Theatre Road which, until a short time earlier, had been a theatre, was purchased and the School of Art installed. It continued there until 1905 when the present building incorporating the Public Library was opened. The first master at the school was named Bowler, but in 1852 he was succeeded by Andrew MacCallum (1821-1902) who excelled in the art world, having many pictures hung in Royal Academy exhibitions and some work included in the Tate Gallery and the Victoria and Albert Museum collections.

By the late 18th century the social climate in Stourbridge was ready for the setting up of schools by the local churches, which were becoming increasingly interested in providing some education for their younger members. The Oldswinford parish workhouse appointed Fanny Pardoe in 1770 to teach the children of the inmates, but tuition in such an institution must have been very basic. Sunday schools became popular following the success of Robert Raikes in Gloucester during 1780. Oldswinford parish instituted a number of such classes in November 1785, but these were temporarily discontinued in 1795. The classes were restarted in 1825 following the erection of a large elevated building on the northern side of Glasshouse Hill which accommodated two parochial Sunday schools; by 1832, 400 children were study-ing there.[17] Further Sunday schools were run at that time by the Presbyterians, Independents, Methodists, Baptists and Roman Catholics, and some of those institutions were turning their attention to teaching on other days as well. In 1832 there were 133 scholars in Stourbridge attending the Independents' school (founded in 1800) with a further 180 boys at their Mount Zion school at Lye. The Roman Catholics founded a school in New Road, Stourbridge, in 1827, supported by voluntary contributions and children's pence, and by 1832 it had 36 pupils. When Thomas Kemble was master there in 1852, the number attending had increased to 60 girls and 40 boys. The vicar of Lye, Henry Hill, was instrumental in having a school erected just to the east of his church, which was opened on 10 February 1840; the previous school (which his uncle Thomas Hill had set up) was closed and the income transferred. Ten boys and ten girls were given free education whilst the remaining 150 pupils each paid one penny per week (or twopence if they could already write), although nothing was paid for books. Teachers' salaries were paid from Thomas Hill's charity fund. In James Bromley's time there followed a number of new educational buildings, including an infants' school, a school at Stambermill, a girls' school and a wooden building at Belmont for the children of Lye Waste and Careless Green.[18] A more permanent Belmont Mission was built on Hill Bank in 1878, acting as a 'chapel of ease' to Lye church and replacing the wooden structure.

By 1841 Mary Jackson was already heading a Church of England infants' school in Old-swinford parish supported by subscriptions.[19] During 1859 a new blue brick school was built in Craufurd Street, Oldswinford at a cost of about £3,000. St Thomas's church built their school in Enville Street in 1844 and Wollaston school was built soon after their church in the 1860s; it had accommodation for 270 children and a house for the schoolmaster was built on adjoining land. The first headmaster was Edward Hackwood and the first headmistress Miss Elizabeth Evers. The headmaster from 1919 to 1946 was Joseph Pearson, who played for As-ton Villa Football Club and later took an active part in the public life of Stourbridge, serving as mayor from 1941 to 1943. Wollaston School was eventually closed in 1985. Many of the schools were supported by the National Society for the Education of the Poor, established in 1811 when it took over from the earlier Society for the Propagation of Christian Knowledge. Those establishments became known as 'national schools', their principles being to impress

100 *Craufurd Street Church of England junior school in Oldswinford in 1958, some 20 years before its demolition.*

subordination, frugality and gratitude upon the 19th-century population. A national school was built in 1865 next to St John's church in Foster Street, Stourbridge, at a cost of £1,400.

Existing alongside the national and church schools in the 19th century were a growing number of small private schools affectionately known as 'dame schools' (although gentlemen tended to run them as well). In 1841 the following were listed in the Stourbridge area: Eliza Baylie (ladies boarding), Church Row; Jane Gill Coltman (ladies boarding), High Street (she was still there in 1852); Charlotte Green, Hagley Terrace; E. & E. Loverock (ladies boarding), Hagley Terrace (in 1852 a Miss S. Loverock was running a boarding school in Church Row); Mary Pemberton, High Street; Elizabeth, Mary and Ann Stinson (ladies boarding), Park Row; William Wright, Windmill Street, and John Compson at a school named Nodland (in 1852 he was teaching in Church Row).

101   *Wollaston Church of England junior school in Bridgnorth Road.*

In 1852 additional private schools included Elijah Cartwright's boys' day school in Duke Street, Baptist minister John Hossack's boarding and day school in Oldswinford, Maria Grove's day school in Union Street, Sarah Trewin's day school at The Heath and the Misses Sugden's ladies' boarding school at Greenhill House. Greenhill House had become Miss Kingsbury's school by the time of Queen Victoria's 1887 Jubilee; its girls had the audacity to write to the Queen and ask her to grant an extra week's holiday! Her Majesty actually agreed to this, provided that it did not interfere with the school's activities.

Education Acts

A series of Education Acts, commencing in 1870, began to pull together all the different strands of the education system that had grown up over the centuries; for the first time they gave every single person the chance to be literate. The 1870 Act set up undenominational Boards of Education for each district (Stourbridge was a separate district), with powers to build new elementary schools if there should be a need. The new local authority buildings became known as Board Schools, the first such school in the Stourbridge area being built in Hill Street. One result of the Act was a rapid diminution in the number of small independent schools. The next Education Act in 1880 made attendance at school compulsory for all children until the age of 10 (or 13 if the child had registered too few attendances by the age of 10). Cemetery Road School opened in 1882, becoming known as 'the little school'. In 1891 elementary education was made free for every child. In that year the Stourbridge and District Technical Education Board was set up, holding classes in the Stourbridge Institute and at Orchard Lane School in Lye (opened in a new building in 1882 but in existence as a school since 1870). Balfour's Education Act in 1902 transferred Board Schools into the hands of the County Council. In 1905 a new girls' secondary school was started in the basement of the recently opened Stourbridge library in Church Street. This was transferred in 1928 to a site at Junction Road, where it has remained and was converted into the Red Hill Comprehensive School in the 1970s. On 25 September 1911 Lye Valley Road Council School was opened under the headmastership of Frank Taylor (taking the older pupils from Orchard Lane). In 1918 the school leaving age was raised to 14, and further liberation of the education system came with the 1944 Education Act, which abolished fee-paying in state secondary schools and again raised the school leaving age, this time to fifteen. In 1946 Elmfield School was established in Love Lane, Oldswinford, working on the principles of Rudolf Steiner. The Foley College of Further Education opened on its new site in Hagley Road, Oldswinford in September 1956 to teach technical, vocational and recreational subjects. The old Art School is now attached to that college, using the former library building in Church Street, Stourbridge.

102   *Elmfield School in Love Lane, Oldswinford in 1956, at which time it was called Park Hill.*

IX

Recreation and Leisure

Early Pursuits

From earliest times the people of Stourbridge have found many and varied ways to enjoy their leisure. In the medieval and Tudor period several of those activities involved animals in ways which would be considered cruel today. One sport common in the 16th century was bull and bear baiting. In the 1570s Richard Harte was the town's 'bere-ward'; it was he who kept control of the animals with his staff. Dogs such as Staffordshire Bull Terriers, specially bred for their courage and endurance, were used to fight the bears (and indeed fights between the dogs themselves were by no means uncommon). The 1791 Stourbridge Act forbade any kind of bull or bear baiting under threat of a five-pound fine, and ordered that fierce mastiffs or bulldogs should not be allowed to roam the streets. Legislation had little effect on some local people, especially those living in Lye. In 1832 bull baiting was still practised there[1] and bull rings could be found at The Cross, Lye Forge, Cross Walks, Stambermill and in a field now covered by Spring Street.[2] Large crowds would gather, vying for the highest seats, and several pounds could be earned by the owner of any dog that defeated the bull; any losing dog was quite often tossed high into the air by the bull. It is reputed that the last bullfight ever to be staged in this country took place on Lye Waste.

Cockfighting as a sport dates back to at least the 12th century. In the late 17th century Jonathan Pyrke, the first landlord of the *Talbot* in Stourbridge, set up the cock pens and 'all the bricks which made the seats about the cockpit' at his inn. The cocks were artificially armed with long spurs made of silver, and many bets were waged on the outcome of those fights. The rings were often in the back yards of people's houses, but purpose-built arenas were occasionally constructed. Although cockfighting was made illegal in 1849, it continued to take place locally. On 29 June 1874 the police interrupted a cockfighting match on the Ridge Top at Wollaston; the spectators, who numbered about one hundred and fifty persons, began to stone the local law officers, who had to retreat from the scene.

In early times the local alehouses (or 'tippling houses') sold both the traditional ales and the beers introduced from Flanders in the 14th century. The price of ale was controlled by law from as early as 1266 and magistrates also had powers to suppress the local ale sellers under a 1495 Act; from 1552 they were required to license all alehouses. Wine could only be sold in taverns, and from 1553 each town of the size of Stourbridge was allowed only one such outlet. In Stourbridge ale was tested and assized by the bailiff under the town hall and sold by measures called 'pewter potts of the potted quart' or 'legitimate pint'. Each of those

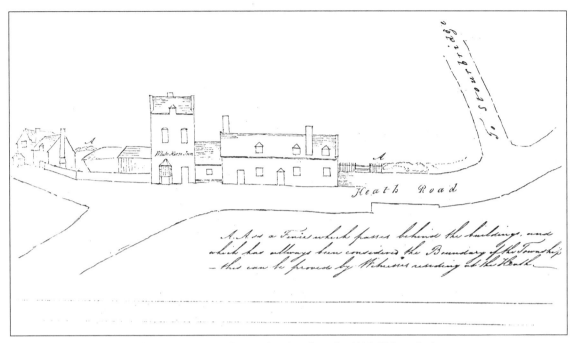

103 *A sketch of the* Old White Horse Inn *at The Heath, taken from the 1821 Oldswinford vestry minutes in connection with a dispute regarding manor boundaries.*

had to be marked with the official manor seal and a fine of 3s. 4d. was levied on anyone who abused the system.

An inn had to provide food, accommodation and stables as well as drink, and it is known that at least four such establishments existed in the Stourbridge area in Tudor times. The *Crown Inn*, squatting between Crown Lane (now Enville Street) and New Street, was owned in the 1590s by Mary Madstard and kept by Thomas Harrison, surviving under that name until the 20th century. The *George Inn* was also situated in the town on the east side of High Street just below Foster Street and was first mentioned in 1549 when it was owned by John Bradley (and before that time by Kenelm Smythe).[3] It then passed to Bradley's stepson, Roger Allchurch, who was a governor of Stourbridge Grammar School. It changed ownership in 1776 and had disappeared by 1837. The *Angel Inn*, situated at the junction of Coventry Street and Angel Street, also dated back to at least Tudor times but was demolished when the ring road was built in 1968. In 17th-century Stourbridge an inn called *The Roundabout* stood in the High Street to the north of the old town hall, having on one side the town's animal pound and on the other side the stocks. In 1680 it was rented by George Hickman, but eventually became a private house and was demolished in the 18th century. In the 17th century an inn called *The Cock* was also much favoured by town residents. In 1594 Thomas Goppe sold a messuage called *Le Whyte Hearte* in Oldswinford[4] and that establishment was mentioned again in October 1638 when Elias Hukin sold it to Thomas Deffell.[5] The *White Horse Inn* at The Heath dated back to at least 1782, when it was in the occupation of John Blakemore.

Sport and Culture in 18th-Century Stourbridge

Sport and leisure were becoming much more sophisticated. From as early as the end of the 17th century the annual horse-racing week had become an exciting sporting and social event for the people of Stourbridge. The ancient racecourse was situated on Stourbridge Common between Gibbet Lane, Dunsley and the Wollaston to Stewponey Road.[6] The races were discontinued from about 1742, but revived on Pedmore Common in 1821. The 19th-century racecourse was situated within Pedmore manor on the northern side of the road now called Racecourse Lane (towards the Norton Road end). Races were run for a whole week in August, and a ball and other amusements took place during the earlier part of the week.[7]

More and more Stourbridge residents were finding the time and money to meet socially on a greater scale. The establishment that began to play the major role in that social life was the *Talbot Inn* on the High Street's western side. The present front dates from the 18th century, but the building itself is much older. In the mid-17th century it was the private home of Richard Foley, and on his death in 1657 his fourth son Robert inherited it. It then passed to the Rev. Samuel Foley, who leased it in December 1685 to Jonathan Pyrke; he is said to have erected a 'signe and signepost next the street ... and at the back gate'. Jonathan Pyrke

104 *The Talbot Hotel in High Street, Stourbridge in 1950; this has been an inn since 1685.*

later moved to Exeter and on 20 June 1695 assigned the lease to Daniel Clarke of Newport, Shropshire. The building then had 13 rooms, including the blue room, a gatehouse chamber, a tapestry room and a brewhouse. Clarke died in 1707, and his inventory indicated that the building at that time had 22 rooms and three cellars (including the cock chamber). His widow, Mary Clarke, briefly took on the lease, and in 1710 bought the freehold from Samuel Foley (she also kept the local post office handling some five to eight hundred letters a month, for which she was paid a salary of £2 10s. 0d. a quarter). By her Will dated June 1733 she left the building to her son George, who added another storey and increased the number of rooms to thirty. George leased the inn to Thomas Savage of Bridgnorth in 1755. George's brother, Daniel Clarke, became an attorney in Bewdley and finally sold the inn in September 1776 to William Savage (the son of Thomas). After William's death, his widow eventually parted with the building in 1784, and John Wiley of Bristol became the new landlord. At that time the *Talbot* had a walled garden and a modern assembly room which later, in 1841, was fitted out as the New Theatre. The *Talbot* itself hosted many auctions of large local houses, as well as important meetings between Stourbridge inhabitants. Evenings of music and dance were often held there. It still survives today as a hotel and inn.

One of the oldest Stourbridge societies, the Freemasons, met at the *Talbot*. The earliest masonic lodge recorded in Worcestershire (Talbot Lodge no. 119) was warranted at the *Talbot Hotel*, Stourbridge on 21 August 1733. On 15 July 1773 the governors of Worcester Infirmary thanked 'the Honourable and Ancient Society of Free and Accepted Masons held at the *Talbot Inn* in Stourbridge' for their donation of five guineas. It is not known when that lodge ceased meeting, but the first gathering of the newly created Lodge of Stability no. 564 was held at the *Vine Inn* in Stourbridge on 16 July 1849, with Thomas Hassall, George Bate, Joseph Aston, John Weldon and James Evans as founding members. Many well-known local traders and personalities became members during the next 50 years.[8] Today the *Talbot Inn* is still host to a number of masonic lodges, including Stability.

A favourite cultural activity first enjoyed by Stourbridge people in the 18th century was a visit to the theatre. Exactly when a theatre was first erected in Stourbridge is uncertain, but there is mention in Aris's *Birmingham Gazette* of one being set up in the town in 1752. The first recorded performance was in 1766.[9] It was billed in the *Worcester Journal* on 14 January 1773 as simply The Theatre, Stourbridge and was held in a building at the rear of the *Bell Inn* where the famous Mrs. Siddons is reputed to have acted. Aris's *Birmingham Gazette* in March 1783 reported the following:

> We hear that the Company of Comedians that are now at Stourbridge have received much countenance and applause from the Nobility and Gentry that resort to Cheltenham in the season; this next summer will be the fourth of their attending there, and it is said that the new Theatre lately built by Mr. Watson in that Town is inferior to none for convenience and neatness.

On 8 June 1792 the first stone of a new Stourbridge theatre in Theatre Road was laid by John Halliday of The Leasows, Halesowen, accompanied by a musical band. It was substantial and lofty with dressing rooms and offices, including cellars and vaults below ground level. The new building was let on a 42-year lease to John Boles Watson (the Cheltenham comedian mentioned above) and William Miell (a Worcester comedian). Unsuccessful attempts were made to sell the theatre in 1797, and by 1813 a Mrs. Nunns had rented the theatre from a Mr. Crisp. When the assembly rooms at the *Talbot* were fitted out as the New Theatre in 1841 the amenities included gas lighting; it was often referred to as the Theatre Royal. The old theatre became the Music Rooms, and was dismantled and converted into a School of Design in 1852. At about the same time a wooden theatre known as the Alhambra was erected in Barlow's Yard (just behind the present post office in Stourbridge High Street). By 1869 the proprietors of that theatre were Bennett and Patch, and in January of that year they put on a pantomime entitled 'Conrad the Corsair'. A showman named William Patch had married a young Dudley-born actress named Eliza, whose family owned a travelling theatre. Eliza Patch became the proprietress of the Alhambra, and created a major reputation for herself on stage, becoming quite a celebrity. She gave her last performance there in January 1894 and passed away at the nearby *Coach and Horses Inn* on 27 November 1900 aged 76. In 1890 the Alhambra accommodated some 1,500 people who, in its heyday, were entertained by great actors such as the Hollywood star (Sir) Cedric Hardwicke and Bransby Williams. In later years it became more of a music hall and was finally demolished in 1932.[10]

From the early 18th century literate Stourbridge residents enjoyed the facility of a Reading Society. Their interests were further served when on 30 April 1790 a Subscription Library was established on the western side of Stourbridge High Street under the management of a committee of local residents. John Steventon was its first librarian and he was succeeded in 1796 by Peter Bird. By 1840 its members had daily access to 3,500 books in return for a subscription of one pound. It then became known as the Town Library. The Mechanics Institute library opened on 16 February 1835, being accommodated at first in Market Street but later in New Street. By 1840 it possessed 660 volumes and was complemented by a newsroom. Later the Institute opened a library and newsroom at the *Vine Inn* in Lower High Street. Inhabitants were further served by a Circulating Library, which in 1840 was based at Mr. Mellard's printing

105 *The Alhambra wooden theatre in High Street, Stourbridge, c.1885, with Mrs. Patch's carriage in the yard. The Alhambra closed in 1929 and was demolished in 1932.*

106 *Stourbridge Public Library and Technical School in the 1920s.*

and book shop in Stourbridge High Street.[11] Robert Broomhall later took over that business, and he merged the Town Library with his own Circulating Library in 1869. When he died, on 30 November 1894, he gave the whole library to the town, stipulating that it should be kept at the Stourbridge Institute. That central public library was consolidated when in 1902 Andrew Carnegie gave £3,000 towards a new purpose-designed building at the junction of Church Road and Hagley Road. The building was in continuous use until 1985, when the whole library was moved into the new Crown Centre complex.

A sport popular by the 18th century was bowls. A Bowling Green House existed at the rear of St Thomas's Chapel on the south side of Bell Lane, and gave its name to Bowling Green Road. It probably belonged to the *Bell Inn*. In 1791 an Act of Parliament exempted the green from paying any rates. In 1890 the *Bell Inn* was advertising 'the finest and best kept bowling green in the Midlands'. The main bowling green in the early 20th century was provided by the Stourbridge Institute, but that is now covered by the club's car park; it is fortunate that bowls can still be played in the town's parks.

107   *The Bell Hotel in Market Street, Stourbridge, c.1924.*

Recreation in the 19th Century

Early in the 19th century the town's inhabitants began to receive news of major happenings from around the world as well from elsewhere in their own country. The first local newspaper became available on 7 May 1813 with the publication of the *Stourbridge and Dudley Messenger.* It was produced in High Street at the offices of the printer J. Heming and was priced at six and a half pence per copy but only survived for a few years. When George Ford took over Heming's business in 1853 he started a newspaper called *The Advertiser* at Brierley Hill (although Stourbridge and Dudley also came within its scope). By now the price had been reduced to one penny and it appeared every Saturday. A rival newspaper called the *Stourbridge Gazette* was started by George Whitwell in 1857, but that soon went out of business. In 1864 another penny weekly appeared calling itself the *Observer* (later changing its name to the *Stourbridge Observer*). It was printed at the steam press of Joseph and Francis Heming in High Street, and was eventually incorporated into the *Stourbridge, Brierley Hill and County Express*, which had been founded by William Maddox Pritchard at Brierley Hill in 1867. That latter publication changed its name in July 1891 to the *County Express* after the paper was taken over by its printers on the initiative of George Moody. George Moody had been apprenticed to the printing trade under Thomas Mark and was eventually taken into the partnership, which had been founded in the first half of the century by Thomas Mellard. When Thomas Mark died, George Moody acquired his share of the business. In May 1972 the *County Express* was sold to the Berrows Organisation and in November 1979 it became a free newspaper called the *Stourbridge News and County Express*, competing with another free publication called the *Stourbridge Chronicle.*

An immense amount of beer was drunk in 19th-century Stourbridge, partly as a social activity and partly as a necessity during long hours spent working in very hot atmospheres. In 1830 the Beerhouse Act allowed any householder, provided that he was assessed for the poor rate, to retail beer from his own house on payment of two guineas. That legislation was intended to counteract the growing popularity of spirits, but led to a mushrooming of outlets selling beer, especially in the industrial area of Lye. The resulting increase in public drunkenness caused great concern to the local clergy and magistrates, and in February 1837 a Temperance Society was established, which held its meetings in the Mechanics Institute.[12] Included amongst the ranks of that society were many of the town's reformed drunkards. By 1854 there were at least 73 inns around Stourbridge, not counting the dozens of beer retailers. In 1874 a Temperance Hall was designed by J.M. Gething and constructed in Church Street, Lye, a handsome building with stone columns and stone balcony over the entrance. It was used as a concert hall and after 1910 as a cinema seating 460 people, before being finally demolished in the 1960s.

There are still a number of inns in the Stourbridge area which survive from the early 19th century (although nearly all have been rebuilt in the last 100 years). In Stourbridge town centre these include the *Woolpack*, *Mitre*, *Duke William*, *New Inn*, *Bell* (a Dutch-gabled building which in the 19th century had a walled garden), *Chequers*, *Crispin* and *Red Lion* (the latter two both now cut off by the ring road). Other inns from that time which have sadly been lost include:

108   *The old Temperance Hall in Church Street, Lye shortly before its demolition in 1967. Since its construction in 1874, it had been used both as a theatre and a cinema at different times. The projection box can be seen above the pavement.*

in Lower High Street the *Navigation, Saracens Head, Old Pipe, Bear, Vine Inn* (an old gabled building demolished in the mid-20th century but called *The Gatehouse* in 1687);

in High Street the *King's Head, Old King's Head, Three Crowns, Old Star, Hole in the Wall, Coach and Horses* (demolished as recently as 1970 to make way for a dry cleaning shop) and *Foley Arms*;

in Coventry Street the *Star, Pig, Anchor, Wheatsheaf* and *Britannic* (they were all within a stone's throw of each other);

in Market Street the *Falcon* (now the Stourbridge Institute building), *Seven Stars* (which belonged to Gregory Hickman in 1730) and *White Lion*;

in New Street the *Shakespeare Tavern* and *Nags Head* and

in Crown Lane the *Crown* and *New Inn*.

In Oldswinford the *Cross, Labour in Vain* (which was called the *Malt Shovel* before the 1830s) and *Seven Stars* (formerly the *Waterloo*) survive from before 1827. The *Crabmill*, which also dates from that period, was demolished in the latter part of the 20th century and turned into the *Oldswinford Lodge* in 1992 (now named *The Oldswinford*). The *Star* (situated on the north-west corner of Oldswinford crossroads) and *New Inn* (sited where the White House Flats now stand in Church Road) have also both been lost. At The Heath the former *White Horse* dates back to before the early 1800s (but was converted into a Harvester Steak Bar in 1985), as do the ancient *Barley Mow* and *Gate Hangs Well* in Wollaston. All of the many inns that the people of Lye would have known in the first half of the 19th century have now disappeared. On Lye Waste there were the *Swan, Anvil, Lord Dudley Arms, New Inn* and *Bush Inn*. Another *Bush Inn* and the *Cross Inn* stood in Lye High Street, the *Duke William* in Pedmore Road south of Lye Cross, and the *Brickmakers Arms* at the foot of Dudley Road opposite Lye Forge. In Hay Green could be found the *Duke of York* and the *Three Crowns*. Numerous other inns sprang up in Lye in the second half of the 19th century.

Victorian inhabitants used also to enjoy the exciting spectacle of bouts of prize fighting and wrestling. Quite often these bare-fisted fights were not for prizes at all, but merely to satisfy a man's pride after a personal quarrel. When prizes were offered they could be as small as a cock or, alternatively, a very large sum of money. Rounds could last up to 15 minutes and were decided by wrestling an opponent to the ground and pinning him down. The match could last for as many as 100 rounds and went on until one man collapsed from exhaustion, his knuckles shattered, fists swollen or forearms dislocated. A local fighting rink could be found in the vicinity of Wassell Grove and was named Hodge Hole; it was here that the big local names such as Adam 'Puffer' and Joe 'Smacker' settled the score. In one fight at the Cross Walks, Lye a pugilist suffered fatal injuries and his body was carried out of the arena in a big chair.[13]

As an alternative to spending time in the local hostelries, the people of Stourbridge began to join the many social and sports clubs that were founded in Victorian times. The Stourbridge Institute social club dates back to 1835, when it was founded in the Rye Market as the Mechanics Institute. From the start it aimed at improving the education and social habits of the working classes. It provided a library and a museum, and classes in writing, arithmetic, grammar, French, playing musical instruments and phonography (learning to write by listening to sound). The Institute moved home several times in its early days but in January 1839 new premises were opened next to the *Cross Keys Inn* in New Street, and a new tower was built housing a telescope (this was later the site of Baylie's Chain Works). In 1840 it became known

CAR AND HORSES INN,

Rye Market, Stourbridge.

CATALOGUE OF THE NEAT

HOUSEHOLD FURNITURE,

EXCELLENT CAR,

PAIR OF HORSES, IRON-BOUND CASKS,

AND OTHER EFFECTS,

Belonging to W. Yeates, of the Car & Horses Inn,

Rye Market, Stourbridge, which will be

Sold by Auction,

ON THE PREMISES, WITHOUT RESERVE, BY

MR. NEWBOLD,

On TUESDAY, March 13th, 1838,

(Under a Deed of Assignment for the benefit of Creditors.)

Kitchen.

1 SET of fire irons
2 Fender and stand
3 Ash grate
4 Copper tea-kettle
5 Two grid irons
6 Coffee pot and candlestick
7 Oblong drinking table
8 Do. do.
9 Two ash chairs
10 Two-arm chair
11 Nine spittoons
12 Clothes horse and stool
13 Two wire window guards
14 Tea and coffee pot
15 Sundries

Brewhouse.

17 Two vats
18 Mash-rule, sieve, and ladder
19 Two saucepans and coffee pot
20 Tub
21 Frying pan
22 Tram
23 Gawn and bench
24 Two shelves
25 Tin can and ale warmer
26 Child's chair
27 One and half doz. stone bottles
28 Lot of glass bottles
29 Sundries
30 Do.

Bar.

31 Sofa
32 Corner cupboard

33 Round table
34 Fender
35 Twenty-one forks and seven knives
36 Sundry tea ware
37 Quantity jugs and cups
38 Half gallon measure
39 Pewter quart, pint, and half pint measures
40 Two waiters
41 Lot of pipes
42 Dresser with 3 drawers
43 Shelf and hat rails
44 Window guard

Parlour.

45 Six ash chairs
46 Oak two-leaf table
47 Fender
48 Two flat irons and pair of tongs
49 Six chimney ornaments
50 Three pictures
51 Handsome mahogany card table
52 Basket
53 Eight jars
54 Eight plates and stone bottle
55 Lot of ware
56 Six ale glasses and butter cup
57 Decanter
58 Three jugs and 5 basins
59 Sundry glasses
60 Bird cage
61 Painted beaufet
62 Sundries

Cellar & Cellar Head.

63 Iron-bound hogshead, No. 1.
64 Do. half hogshead, 2
65 Do. do. 3

66 Iron-bound half hogshead, No. 4
67 Do. do. 5
68 Do. do. 6
69 Quarter barrel 7
70 Do. 8
71 Two trams
72 Two brass taps and tundish
73 Thirty-two bottles of porter
74 Safe
75 Two scoring boards
76 Shelf
77 Sundries
78 Plate rack

Chamber, No. 1.

79 Set of stump bedsteads
80 Mattress
81 Sheets and blankets
82 Quilt
83 Chair
84 Chamber ware
85 Sundries

Chamber, No. 2.

86 Set of tent bedsteads
87 Feather bed and bolster
88 Chair
89 Sundries

Chamber, No. 3.

90 Set of tent bedsteads and hangings
91 Feather bed and bolster
92 Pair of sheets
93 Pair of blankets
94 Coverlid
95 Three chamber chairs
96 Dressing table

97 Two carpets and looking-glass
98 Child's crib
99 Sundries

Yard.

100 Water tub
101 Spout and shelf
102 Tub and bucket
103 Clothes line and riddle
104 Wash tub
105 Sundries

Hay Loft.

106 Badger box
107 Large tub
108 Deal box
109 Sundries

Stable.

110 Malt mill
111 Cupboard
112 Set of car harness
113 Corn bin
114 Ladder
115 Collar and lantern
116 Spade and fork
117 Lot of odd harness
118 Two halters and two head stalls
119 Sundries

Coach House & Stable.

120 Handsome single bodied four-wheel car, painted yellow, with shafts and pole, either for single or pair of horses, (in excellent condition.)
121 Bay Horse, six years old, (perfectly steady in Harness)
122 Roan do. five years old, do.

The Sale to commence at Eleven o'Clock.

Accounts settled with Employers immediately on the close of every Sale.

☞ *The SALE advertised for WEDNESDAY next, the 14 inst. by R. MOSELEY, will not take place.*
STOURBRIDGE, MARCH 9, 1838. J. NEWBOLD, Auctioneer.

109 *The 1838 sale of contents from the* Car and Horses Inn*, which once stood in Rye Market.*

as the Institute for Popular Science and Literature and had 160 members, the majority paying a subscription of 10 shillings a year. Its annual general meetings and dinners were held at the *Vine Inn*. In 1845 it moved temporarily to the *Crown Inn*, and in 1848 to the corner of Foster Street (now Barclays Bank), by which time its membership had grown to 247. In the 1850s it faced competition from a Working Men's Institution that charged one penny a week and had 500 members, but the two clubs soon merged under the name of the Stourbridge Mechanics and Working Men's Associated Institute. Ten thousand people took part in a 'monster picnic' in Hagley Park in August 1857 to help raise funds for the society and on 2 November 1857 it reopened in new premises at the old *Falcon Inn* in Market Street, which it had purchased at a cost of £800. By the early 20th century the Stourbridge Institute had lost some of its working-class image. For that reason, in May 1903 another Stourbridge Working Men's Club was opened in an iron warehouse off Lower High Street. It was short lived, however, and closed on 25 February 1911 because of poor support. Stourbridge Institute set up a chess club and a camera club in 1903, and in 1911 land was purchased in Bell Street for a new bowling green. The Falcon Inn was demolished at Easter 1936 and on 8 May 1937 the present spacious building in Market Street was opened on that site, having been designed by G.F. Webb (who was also the architect of the assembly hall at Stourbridge Grammar School).[14]

Stourbridge enjoyed cricket from as early as 1842, at which time the game was played on a field adjoining Halfpenny Hall Lane (now Junction Road). In 1857 the club moved to its present Amblecote ground and 10 years later the team was known as Stourbridge United. At a meeting in February 1867 a new Stourbridge Cricket Club was proposed, which was to be completely independent of any previous club in the district. Ordinary members' subscriptions were 10 shillings a year, while honorary members paid a pound. This club has enjoyed a continuous existence ever since, and was admitted to the Birmingham League as long ago as 1894. In 1888 the cricket club began to share its ground with Stourbridge Football Club, which was founded as Stourbridge Standard in about 1876 and affectionately known as The Glassboys. Several county cricket matches were arranged on the Amblecote ground in 1892, but it was not until 1905 that the first official county championship fixture was played there. In 1928 the Amblecote ground was bought by the War Memorial Committee for combined use by the two clubs. Notable Stourbridge cricket players in the 20th century have included internationals Don Kenyon and Peter Richardson. Lye also had a cricket club, which was started in June 1858 and played at Hay Green for many years, where a fine pavilion and club rooms were built in 1958 to celebrate its centenary. Lye Town Football Club, founded in 1930, played at the same venue. In 1948 the Lye club turned professional and a new clubhouse was built in 1975. Rugby football was played in Stourbridge from the 1870s. A period when no rugby took place followed, but the Stourbridge Rugby Football Club was re-founded in 1922. At the beginning of the 1923 season a ground in Vicarage Road, Wollaston, was secured and a clubhouse costing over £3,000 was opened there in October 1956. After that ground had been redeveloped for housing, in September 1965 the club moved to an excellent site and clubhouse just outside the town's boundary at Stourton.

In 1867 it was decided to form a Conservative Association at 77 High Street, and at a meeting in May 1906 it was proposed that a Conservative and Unionist Club be established in the town. Premises in High Street were taken over and the club was officially opened in

110 *Stourbridge Cricket Club pavilion at the War Memorial athletics ground, Amblecote, in 1968.*

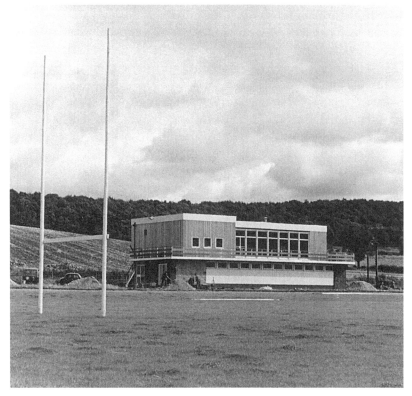

111 *The new Stourbridge rugby clubhouse at Stourton in 1965.*

December of that year; it soon had a membership of 400. In 1935 Stourbridge Conservative Club moved to new premises near the old War Memorial at the junction of Hagley Road and New Road and Anthony Eden spoke at the annual meeting that year. In October 1898 a Labour Party branch was formed at Lye; one of their early ideas was to municipalise the drink trade! By 1908 the Socialists in Stourbridge were becoming more active, having a membership of over 50, but had some difficulty in finding a room and meetings had to be held in the Alhambra Theatre; later meetings took place in the Music Rooms. In March 1909 the old club premises in Crown Buildings were taken over by the Independent Labour Party as a Labour Church and in 1928 the Labour Club acquired its present base, The Lawns in Hagley Road, which was previously home to Henry Wooldridge, inventor of the frost cog. In June 1902 a Liberal Club was opened in the Crown Buildings premises which stood at the junction of High Street and Enville Street, but it soon became evident that the accommodation was insufficient and in October 1904 a new club at Union Hall in Enville Street was brought into use. A Liberal Club was also opened in Church Street, Lye in July 1906.

The Victorian transport revolution meant that everyone could now travel further afield. On 9 June 1866 the *Advertiser* recommended the *Stamford Arms Hotel*, Enville, stating that 'pleasure parties visiting the Enville gardens (which are open to the public on Tuesdays and Fridays for the season) will find every accommodation at the above hotel, where tickets of admission to the gardens may be obtained'. The gardens were a great favourite with the public at that time. Another popular spot was Hagley Park. In June 1866 a great picnic was held there with a grand display of military bands, and the celebrated tenor, Mr. Cooper, sang favourite and popular songs. For an admission fee of sixpence members of the public were treated to foot races, a sack race of 100 yards, a comic singing contest and balloon ascents.

Roller skating became very popular in the second half of the 19th century. In November 1876 a new rink called the Victoria Hall was opened in Bell Street, its proprietor one Henry James Hainge. Admission to the rink cost one shilling, and skates were hired out for sixpence a session. Hainge was unable to balance his books, though, and disappeared suddenly, leaving a large deficit. New management took over in 1880, but in September 1888 the hall and rink were sold to the Salvation Army for £650. On 23 October 1909 a new hall, built in the garden of a house called Longcroft in New Road, was opened as a skating rink, but within a year this had been converted into the King's Hall Picture House.

The Victorians were very fond of their musical entertainment, some of which took place at the Alhambra Theatre. Before the building of the Victorian town hall in Stourbridge, many recitals were given in the rather drab Corn Exchange building, a memorable concert taking place there on 11 January 1876. Charles Halle (of later orchestra fame) and Madame Norman-Neruda gave a piano and violin recital, with seats expensively priced at between 1s. 6d. and 6s. 0d. In 1883 the Stourbridge Associated Institute Penny Singing Class was formed under Hedley Satchell and this soon grew into the Stourbridge People's Concert Society. In December 1883 the Stourbridge Philharmonic Society was founded to study choral music, with George W. Bates as conductor. The town received two brief visits at the Corn Exchange from the D'Oyly Carte Opera Company during 1884. In January *Iolanthe* was presented, and in November *Princess Ida* (soon after its first performance in London the previous January). Stourbridge had to wait until 1959 before it obtained its own Gilbert and Sullivan Club. The

People's Concert Society saw the 19th century out with their 70th concert on 27 December 1899. It consisted of a performance of Handel's *Messiah* conducted by George Halford, the principals being Maggie Jaques, Madge Robottom, Edward Kemp and H. Downing; Mr. L. Mancini led the orchestra and George Bates played the organ. The Stourbridge Institute Male Voice Choir was founded in November 1908 and Stourbridge Amateur Operatic Society in September 1909 by a local grammar school master, Dyson Williams. The year 1910 saw the formation of the Town Band under the conductorship of Harry Woodall. The Band made its first public appearance on 30 July when it marched through the town to the Greenfield Gardens, taking a collection on the way to help to pay for the smart scarlet uniforms with their gold braid trimmings.

Leisure in the Last 100 Years

During Victorian times small groups formed to play tennis and golf, enjoying the social life that the game also provided. Tennis clubs formed during the 20th century included the Upper Swinford Tennis Club in 1913, with its one hard and three grass courts at the rear of the Oldswinford parish rooms (now the location of Rectory Gardens). Wollaston Tennis Club was founded at the rear of Wollaston vicarage in 1930 and had two hard courts, but few other

112 *The programme for the last concert of the People's Concert Society in the 19th century.*

facilities. When the nearby rugby ground was developed for housing in the mid-1960s, the club moved to new courts and clubhouse at Prestwood Drive, Stourton, where it still flourishes. Public courts were also made available from the 1930s onwards in the town's parks. Two other well-established tennis clubs agreed to amalgamate in 1966. The North Worcestershire Club, which had its courts in Worcester Lane at Pedmore, and the Old Edwardian Club (in Job Lane at the southern end of Red Hill) developed a combined new £65,000 site at Sugar Loaf Lane, Iverley. With its eight grass, six hard and two squash courts it became the premier Stourbridge tennis club and is still expanding today. Stourbridge Golf Club was founded for lovers of the game in about 1892 on ground belonging to Racecourse Farm off Worcester Lane at Pedmore. After a dispute with a new tenant of the farm, it was forced to close in March 1897 until October 1903, when Mr. Yardley took over as the new tenant of the farm. In 1909 the club obtained a full complement of 18 holes at the course. The inter-war

113 *Lye Tennis Club members in the 1890s, during a match against Pensnett Tennis Club.*

years proved quite successful for its members, as during 1927 Dr. William Tweddell won the amateur championship and Miss Barbara Law won the Midlands ladies' championship, with Eric Fiddian winning the boys' open amateur championship. In 1932 Eric Fiddian won the English amateur championship, but was beaten in the final of the British amateur championship.

Another favourite Stourbridge attraction commenced in 1897, when on August bank holiday of that year the first two-day fête in aid of the Corbett Hospital was held, with balloon events, fireworks, band and fun fair. Half a century later in 1946 it was attracting a crowd of 35,000, made more popular by a horse show and gymkhana that had been initiated seven years earlier. By the beginning of the 20th century some 14,000 tourists in one day were being transported to Kinver by the Kinver Light Railway. This was an immensely popular destination for Stourbridge folk, especially at bank holiday times. Even more people turned out to see a famous visitor to Stourbridge in April 1904 when Buffalo Bill (Colonel W.F. Cody) visited the town with his Wild West show. He set up camp at Wollaston with 800 men and 500 horses and performed on a field between Bridgnorth Road and Meriden Avenue; the show included a representation of Custer's Last Stand and an act in which a cyclist came down a 90 ft. incline, leaping over a space of 45 feet onto another platform.

In the early 1900s a new use was found for the Alhambra Theatre, when a permanent home was sought for the bioscopes, or moving pictures, which from the 1890s had been presented by the travelling fairs. In 1910 Douglas Phelps presented his first Electric Pictures at the Alhambra, encouraged by a new law which stated that cinema shows had to take place in permanent buildings. In 1910 he also showed his pictures in the Temperance Hall, Lye, which was renamed the Lye Palace of Pictures and Varieties. On 3 October in that same year Douglas Phelps and a Mr. Wall opened Stourbridge's first picture house in Duke Street. It was called the Empire and could accommodate 450 persons, but was forced to close after a few months due to lack of support, despite the free cups of tea given at performances. Its closure could have been related to the fact that a competitor called the King's Hall opened its doors in New Road on 6 November 1910 (the building had been erected as a skating rink in the previous year, paid for by public subscription). Prices charged for seats here were twopence in the gallery, fourpence in the pit and sixpence in the stalls. The cinema was rebuilt in 1939 but eventually demolished in 1984, having been used as a furniture store for some years. In November 1988 a newly constructed B & Q store opened on the site. The people of Lye obtained their first purpose-built cinema when the Victoria Hall was opened on 5 January 1914; it was designed by Stourbridge architect Hugh Folkes, and was constructed in the remarkably short time of two weeks. An orchestra and vaudeville acts were laid on for the opening night. It was not until after the First World War that Stourbridge obtained its next cinema. The Scala in Lower High Street was designed to serve as a theatre as well as a cinema, but it proved to be too small for the former purpose. Opened on 11 October 1920, its name was later changed to the Savoy when the EMI Group took it over in 1944. Its circle was closed off in 1978 to save heating costs (but that still left 453 seats). It became the last of the town's cinemas to close, on 6 November 1982, and is now used as a fitness club. On 16 April 1926 the people of Stourbridge were treated to their first demonstration of a 'talkie' film at the King's Hall, but had to wait another three years before permanent equipment was installed. In May 1929 Ernest Stevens performed the

114 *The Victoria Kinema at Lye in 1912, shortly after it was built.*

ceremony to open the new Central Theatre in High Street, Stourbridge. It was renamed the Odeon after Oscar Deutsch, the founder of the chain of cinemas to which it belonged. On 8 February 1937 the Clifton cinema opened its doors at Lye, followed on Whit Monday 1940 by Stourbridge's fourth and last cinema, the Danilo, in Hagley Road; this building is still used as a night club. The 1950s witnessed the highpoint of cinema attendance, with most families going at least once a week. Since then all seven cinemas that once competed for the custom of Stourbridge and Lye people have closed; in recent years, however, a visit to the multi-screen cinema at Merry Hill has again become fashionable.

Throughout the 20th century other social clubs mushroomed in the borough, some also becoming popular for the bowls, snooker, billiards and dominoes facilities they provided. Old boys of Stourbridge Grammar School (later the Sixth Form College) decided to form their own social club: Stourbridge Old Edwardian Club was founded in 1898 in Alexandra Chambers. A fine new clubhouse was erected in 1931 on land in Victoria Street where Dane Tree House formerly stood. Stourbridge Rotary Club was formed in 1922 with Arthur Moody as first president and Hugh Folkes as secretary. In 1934 Mrs. Millward founded the Stourbridge Inner Wheel for the wives of Rotarians. After the Second World War many societies were formed by people with common interests; the year 1946 alone saw the Stourbridge Historical and Archaeological Society, the Theatre Society and the Soroptimist Club come into existence. Ballroom dancing also proved very popular at that time, including the Saturday evening dances at the Stourbridge Baths ballroom, music being provided by a local band led by trumpeter Brian Pearsall. The 1950s saw television sets appearing in the homes of many Stourbridge people, and competition from that medium killed off many earlier forms of entertainment. Mass car ownership and the advent of jet travel in the 1960s resulted in far more exotic travel for personal pleasure, often to the disadvantage of purely local attractions. The use of home computers for personal entertainment provided further distraction from the 1980s onwards, but the ancient inns of the locality are now being revitalised by an increasing desire to dine out.

X

Stourbridge in the Twentieth Century

Events before the First World War

The 20th century saw changes in population and living conditions in Stourbridge that would have been unimaginable to the Victorians. The town became increasingly residential, resulting in roads and houses being built over virtually every green field capable of being developed. Many older industrial sites and even land situated over mines and filled-in quarries became targets for the modern builder, sometimes with disastrous effects on the stability of the dwellings. Most of the area's small streams and pools were piped in. Amongst these were the ancient Ludgbridge and Shepherds Brooks which flowed through the Hob Green, Hay Green and Stambermill pools on their way to the Stour. The nature of Stourbridge High Street also changed rapidly as nearly all the old shop façades (many hiding interiors dating back to the 15th century) were replaced with drab and uninteresting fronts. More people now moved around

---

Stourbridge through Time: 1901 to 1945

1901	Public Baths opened; Kinver Light Railway formed; new Junction Station opens
1903	First public park at Greenfield Gardens opens
1904	Buffalo Bill brings his Wild West Show to town
1905	New free public library opens
1910	First cinema in town
1911	New police station and court buildings in New Road
1914	Regular omnibus services commence; Charter of Incorporation for Borough
1919	First council houses are built
1922	Carlisle Hall opens
1923	Town's war memorial unveiled at top of High Street
1926	Town bus depot built in Foster Street
1928	War Memorial Athletics Ground purchased for the town at Amblecote
1929	Mary Stevens Park donated to the town; the first talking pictures
1930	The last trams run and Kinver Light Railway closes
1935	First traffic lights in town; Brocksopp's Hall at Lye burnt down
1940	Stourbridge Services Club opens
1945	Second World War ends in Europe

---

the country in search of better jobs, resulting in a far greater variety of surnames in the town, but the population of Stourbridge increased only slowly in the 20th century. In 1901 there were 16,302 people living in the town, Upper Swinford, Norton and Wollaston areas, which were served by the Stourbridge Urban District Council.[1]

In 1900 Stourbridge was still a small market town intent on improving its image. In 1914 the Urban District Council was granted its Charter of Incorporation, the first mayor of the borough being Sir Henry Foley Grey Bt. (although Harry Evers Palfrey is originally named as first mayor in the charter). John Harward, a solicitor in Stourbridge, obtained a coat of arms for the town in 1917. The arms were emblazoned 'azure, the span of a bridge argent masoned sable, suspended therefrom by a chain of the last a fleece, and in chief two pears slipped and leaved all or'. The bridge signified the origin of the town's name, the fleece and chain two old industries, and the pears the borough's association with Worcestershire. The town's motto was 'One Heart, One Way'. Six major Stourbridge personalities of that era were later appointed honorary borough freemen, these being Lady Grey of Enville Hall, Henrietta Foster of Apley Park, Mary Moody, John Harward, Ernest Stevens and Harry Palfrey. Mary Moody, who died at the age of 104 in August 1985, worked at the family printers and booksellers

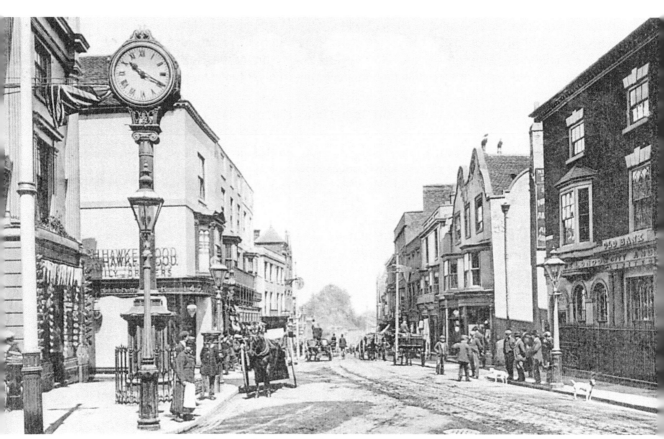

115 *The view from High Street towards the Old Bank and Lower High Street in 1900.*

116 *Lower High Street, c.1913.*

until nearly the end of her life and was reputed to be the world's oldest working company chairperson at that time. Her husband (Lt-Col. Arthur Hatfield Moody) became the seventh mayor of Stourbridge in 1921, a position he held for three years, dying in 1926.

Health and welfare continued to be a high priority. Despite initial opposition to a proposal to provide public baths, the council won the day and Isaac Nash, then chairman of the Urban District Council, laid the foundation stone on 2 August 1900 in Bath Road. On 23 May 1901 Stourbridge Public Baths were opened, enabling many local inhabitants to have their first regular weekly bath, the scheme costing £4,500. In 1902 Hayley Green Isolation Hospital was put into service for infectious diseases at a cost of £12,000 (jointly serving the towns of Stourbridge and Halesowen). The hospital was extended in 1936 but demolished in 1997 when the site was redeveloped for housing. In 1905 the Guardians erected the Cottage Homes at Norton at a cost of £11,908 for children chargeable to the Union, and two years later a new workhouse for 725 inmates was built at Wordsley, costing the ratepayer nearly £100,000. But the workhouse era was soon to draw to an end. On 1 January 1909 the first old age pensions

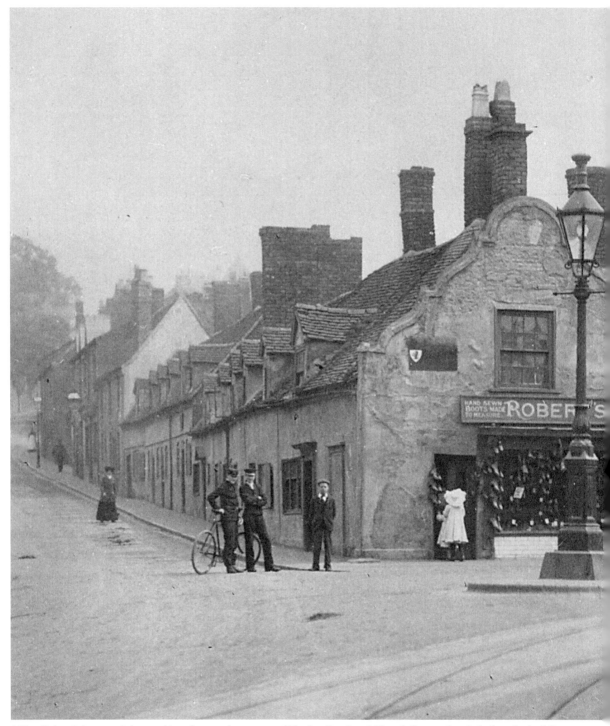

117   *Robert's boot and shoe making shop on the corner of Hagley Road and Church Street, shortly before the building of the new public library commenced in February 1904.*

118   *The old swimming baths at Bath Road in 1956. Opened in 1901, they were demolished to make way for the Crystal Leisure Centre in 1989.*

were drawn in Stourbridge and in 1911 unemployment and health insurance was introduced. The Stourbridge Waterworks were municipalised in 1910, the assets being transferred to the Stourbridge and District Water Board for a sum of £120,000. To ensure that the town was properly policed, a new police station was erected in New Road in 1911 at a cost of £8,000; an extension took place later to incorporate a juvenile court room.

The question of improved housing for the less-well-off began to be considered; the build-ing of council houses was first suggested by a forward-thinking councillor, Walter Jones, in 1898. The debate was again re-opened in 1913, with pressure being put on the council to provide houses with rents of between three and four shillings a week (suitable for workmen who were earning only one pound a week). Nothing was done and the following year war broke out, so the question was put off again. But the council had recognised that more open recreational space was needed and the first area acquired by the town was Burnt Oak Field at the western end of the recently created residential street called Greenfield Avenue. The park was opened on 6 July 1903 and, as mentioned previously, Walter Jones donated the bandstand. An additional plot was added in 1908.

Public transport was also undergoing changes. The existing Stourbridge Junction station at Chawnhill was officially opened on 1 April 1901, necessitating a slight change to the route of the Stourbridge Town branch line. The old Junction station was demolished in 1905. By the start of the First World War trams were facing competition from the petrol engine, and in April 1914 a bus service was started for the people of Stourbridge by the Midland Red Omnibus Co., and further competition was also provided by Samuel Johnson's Supreme bus fleet.

The town received a steady stream of important visitors at that time. Some were controversial figures. When David Lloyd George, the Chancellor of the Exchequer, visited Stourbridge in January 1910, elaborate precautions were taken and the time of his arrival kept secret; nearly 300 extra police were drafted into the town to protect him. He spoke at the Skating Rink and admission to the hall was by ticket only. No women were admitted because it was thought that militant suffragettes intended to demonstrate. In January 1912 Mrs. Pankhurst, founder

119 *The G.W.R. Stourbridge to Bromsgrove omnibus no. 62 in 1905, outside the entrance to Bell Hall at Bell End.*

120   *An early bus accident near the Hagley Road crossroads at Oldswinford in March 1914.*

121   *A.S. Weaver & Co.'s Central Garage at top of High Street, c.1930, later the site of a British Restaurant before becoming Housewives' Corner (an early supermarket owned by Mr. Thompson).*

of the Women's Social and Political Union, spoke in the Music Rooms. When Major-General Sir Robert Baden-Powell, founder of the Boy Scout movement, visited Stourbridge on 6 May 1911 to inspect local scouts at Old Swinford Hospital, he was received by the president of Stourbridge and District Boy Scouts Association (Sir Henry Foley Grey) and given a civic reception; various demonstrations of scouting were given by local troops.

The First World War

The calm of the area was broken when the war with Germany began on 4 August 1914. It was a holiday month, and at the Corbett Hospital fête patriotic demonstrations could be witnessed. As often happens at such times, people rushed to buy food and other goods that might be in short supply. Appeals were made for recruits for the war and the volunteers' names were made public. Tribunals were set up to hear appeals for exemption from military service and white feathers were given to those who did not willingly join up. Before the end of 1914 Stourbridge began to receive wounded soldiers at the V.A.D. military hospital run by the Red Cross inside Studley Court at The Heath, which had been specially adapted for that purpose. Jack Judge, the author of the popular song 'It's a long way to Tipperary',

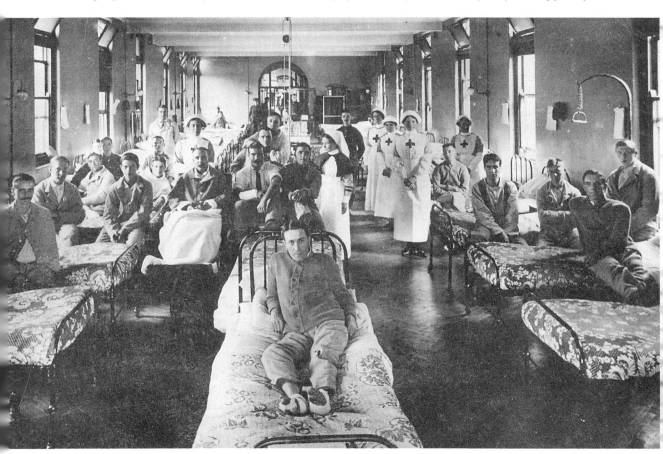

122   *The Voluntary Aid Detachment First World War military hospital at Studley Court, c.1918.*

was one famous person to visit the hospital in February 1917. Some civilian refugees were housed at Brocksopp's Hall, Lye.

The year 1915 saw the danger from air attack increasing and plans were made to warn people of any imminent strike. This was to be by the sounding of short five-minute blasts on the hooters at the works of W.J. Turney in Stourbridge, at the Providence Works in Lye and at the Stanley Works in Wollescote. People were then expected to take cover, extinguish all external lights and the fire brigade and ambulance service had to stand by. The railway station closed in March 1915 and did not open again until March 1919; that proved very unpopular with the local population. A Zeppelin raid did take place on South Staffordshire on 1 February 1916, which resulted in stricter restrictions on lighting being introduced. The following July an aeroplane actually landed on the town's golf links, but it turned out that the friendly crew of two had lost their way in thick clouds and decided to land. Despite the war, social life continued normally. Concerts were held regularly in the bandstand at Greenfield Gardens and cinemas were crowded.

News of the armistice on 11 November 1918 reached Stourbridge post office just before 11 a.m. and the postmaster informed the mayor of the exciting news. Local company hooters and railway engine whistles were sounded, church bells peeled and streets were filled with people. Official celebrations began in July 1919 with a long procession of 3,000 children from Greenfield Gardens to the Junction Fields, followed by sports and fireworks. Nine hundred servicemen who were lucky enough to have survived the war were entertained at the town hall. But the influenza epidemic that followed caused many more deaths and several schools had to be closed.

As in every other town, battle casualties were very heavy for Stourbridge volunteers. The town's memorial to the dead cost £3,000 and was designed by E.W. Pickford. It was unveiled on 25 February 1923 by the Earl of Coventry and sited at the junction of Church Street and Hagley Road near the public library; it was later moved into Mary Stevens Park when the town's ring road was built. A further tribute to the dead was the purchase in 1923 of the War Memorial Athletics Ground at Amblecote. Lye and Wollescote erected their own memorial near the parish church.

The Inter-War Years

When the war ended in 1918 the expectations of Stourbridge people were high. The years between the wars saw electricity coming into common use and cinemas and wireless providing entertainment for everyone. But very soon disillusion, trade depression and unemployment set in. The council had to act quickly to provide housing and on 1 May 1919 the first Stourbridge municipal housing estate was officially opened at The Heath. More council houses were built in the same year in the grounds of The Grange, a large house that had its own fishpond in its 39 acres; the house was acquired from the trustees of William Holcroft for under £10,000. Lye and Wollescote Council chose to build its first municipal houses at Careless Green in 1921, designed by Stourbridge architect Hugh Folkes. Each house cost about £800, and was built by direct labour. By 1932, the one thousandth council house had been opened in Turney Road. Almost 2,400 houses were on the council books by the outbreak of the Second World War, scattered around the borough on additional sites at Hodge Hill, Hay Green, Hungary Hill, Junction Road, Bridgnorth Road, Enville Street, High Park Avenue and High Street, Wollaston.

Some attempt was made to perpetuate old Stourbridge by naming roads after the ancient fields that they obliterated. This trend was particularly prevalent in Wollescote, where Birchgate was built on the ancient Birch Hill, Sensall Road after a field named Sensall (but on the opposite side of Wynall Lane). Ridge Grove, Coney Green and Parkfield Road were constructed nearer to the town. Some confusion is due to the adoption of ancient names for roads which are nowhere near the old fields that they were replacing, such as Rye Croft, Powlers Close, Murcroft Road and Dobbins Oak Road (which were all fields once close to the north side of Wollescote Hall). Other examples were Yarnborough Hill leading off Love Lane (some distance from the original hill of that name) and Studley Gate in Wollaston in a location half a mile away from the ancient town gateway that stood at The Heath.

Facilities for the public given by local councils and similar organisations included the Carlisle Hall in 1922. Named after the Countess of Carlisle, National President of the National British Women's Total Abstinence Union from 1903-21, it was officially opened by Mary Stevens on 28 September 1922. (In 1958 the hall was taken over as an old people's day club and today it serves as a centre for the Women's Royal Volunteer Service.) In 1923 a fine open-air swimming pool was added to the public baths which, in winter months, was covered over and used for meetings and dances. The Junction Road playing area was acquired from Walter Jones in 1923 (with additions in 1927 and 1929) and South Road playing fields were purchased lot by lot in 1917, 1918 and 1927. In June 1934 a large extension to the west of the original Corbett Hospital was opened, at a cost of £100,000; this included a new outpatients' department, more wards and a nurses' home. In May 1935 Sir Cedric Hardwicke opened Lye Public Library, which was designed by Frederick Woodward and cost £2,800. Cedric Hardwicke had been born in 1893 at Lye Cross House (an old Stuart building on the corner of High Street and Dudley Road, which was demolished in 1967), the son of a well-known Lye doctor, and became a famous Hollywood film star.

Some changes did take place to local government and institutions in the years between the two world wars. A Parochial Church Council was set up for Oldswinford residents in 1922 to help serve their local needs and in 1930 the workhouse organisation was placed under the Ministry of Health and administered by the County Council, Stourbridge Boards of Guardians being abolished. Once again workhouses became the homes of only the sick and the aged but they still managed to live on until 1948, before being abolished with the introduction of government social security. Stourbridge Urban District Council was enlarged on 1 April 1933 to add some 13,500 extra inhabitants in Lye, Wollescote and Pedmore to its already 20,000 residents, thus increasing the total population served by Stourbridge Council to some 33,500.

The 1920s and 1930s were memorable for the generosity of private benefactors. In August 1921 Wollaston recreation ground was opened, its eight-and-a-half acres having been given to the council by Albert Guest, a building contractor, in return for less than an acre of land occupied by a disused gravel pit, and Major G.H. Green gave Swinford Common to the people in 1928. But the inhabitants of Stourbridge should particularly remember one magnificent benefactor. Ernest Stevens lived from 1867 to 1957 and was the son of a working-class miner living in Bott Lane close to Dudley Road, Lye, but he became wealthy through his connection with the enamelled holloware trade. He purchased Prescote House, situated near the corner of Grange Lane and Wollescote Road, and lived there up to the time of his death. Following

123 *A portrait of Ernest Stevens (1867-1957), the town's greatest benefactor.*

124 *The outside of Prescote House during demolition in 1966. It was earlier home to Ernest Stevens.*

125 *The ground-floor saloon at Prescote House.*

the death of his wife Mary in 1925, in the years 1929 to 1932 he made a series of gifts to the people of the town. In 1929 he donated the attractive Studley Court at The Heath with its lake and surrounding ground. Formerly known as Heath House, it had been erected at the same time as the Heath Glassworks, in about 1690, and had belonged in turn to the manufacturing families of Jeston, Russell, Witton, Rufford and Webb. The grounds of Studley Court were renamed Mary Stevens Park in memory of Stevens' late wife and the public granted free access to the pool and the park which was laid out with ornamental gardens, two excellent bowling greens, tennis courts and cricket pitches. The large lake teemed with swans and other waterfowl. The house was extended in 1937 by the addition of offices and a council chamber for local government. Further office extensions were made in 1962. The house is still used today by the Public Works Department of Dudley Council.

In 1930 Ernest Stevens purchased for £12,000 the 17th-century Wollescote Hall with its surrounding 89 acres of ground and presented it to the Lye and Wollescote District Council, the area becoming known as Stevens Park. It had a bandstand and facilities for tennis, cricket and football. The building was leased to the Art Department of Foley College in 1971 and completely renovated in 1991, still being used for community purposes today. He also made a gift to St Mary's, Oldswinford consisting of ground for an extension to the churchyard, a new wall, gates and an improved approach from the boundary. Finally, in 1932, he donated another ancient family home, White Hall (located to the rear of Oldswinford churchyard), with the intention of turning it into a maternity home. White Hall had been the home of the Badger, Rogers and Evers families in previous centuries. The building proved to be unsuitable for its intended purpose, and so it was demolished and completely rebuilt to serve as the Mary Stevens Maternity Home, providing some two dozen beds for the Stourbridge area.

Sidney Law, a well-known local industrialist associated with the old-established chain and nail-making firm of Thomas Perrins of Careless Green, was knighted in 1938. This was in recognition of his valuable service to local charitable institutions, especially to the Corbett Hospital of which he was chairman of the Board of Governors for a number of years.

On the political scene, a champion of women's rights arrived in the person of Mary Reid MacArthur (Mrs. W. C. Anderson). She was the Labour candidate for Stourbridge in 1918 and the first woman to stand for Parliament. Amongst eminent speakers coming to Stourbridge to support Mary was George Bernard Shaw, the playwright. Mary was a champion of the local women chain makers and one of the outstanding women in the history of the British labour movement. She died on 1 January 1921 at the age of 40. Another vocal Stourbridge character and local historian was Wesley Perrins. Born in Balds Lane, Wollescote, in 1905, he was educated at Lye Valley Road School and at the age of 13 entered his father's frost cog nail shop. He served the community actively from an early age, being variously secretary of the Miners' Relief Fund (1926), founder member of Lye Town football club, Methodist lay preacher, organiser of Corbett Hospital carnivals and town councillor (1928 to 1947 and 1971 to 1974). He also represented Yardley (near Birmingham) as its Member of Parliament from 1945 to 1950, being then appointed regional secretary of his trade union. Made an MBE in 1952, for 20 years he was a Worcestershire county councillor and was honoured in Stourbridge by being made an alderman. He died in January 1990.

The years between the wars saw a revolution in transport, with motor cars and motor cycles replacing the rapidly disappearing horses in the streets. From May 1925 people were able to travel by railway directly from Stourbridge Junction to Wolverhampton (but that facility was withdrawn in October 1932). A garage and depot for buses was built in 1926 in Foster Street; this was near the town station and on a site previously used for fairs. Some inconvenience was caused to traffic in that year when four inches of rain fell in 12 hours, and people were ferried by boats from one building to another. The electric trams continued to operate for a time, but as the years went by buses began to take most of the traffic. The last tram to Kinver ran in February 1930 and the demise of the Stourbridge to Dudley service on 1 March 1930 saw the end of the tram era in Stourbridge. For a time the Midland Red Bus Company experienced keen competition from the grey Supreme buses operated by Samuel Johnson (who also had a photographer's business), but in 1932 Midland Red bought out its competitor. The continued growth of motor traffic saw the first traffic lights installed next to the town clock on 14 December 1935, the first of many measures to control traffic congestion.

126 *A tram negotiates the flooded Lower High Street in 1924.*

127 *A ladies' outing on a Samuel Johnson Supreme charabanc, c.1920.*

Buildings that disappeared from the Stourbridge scene in the inter-war years included Wollaston Hall and Brocksopp's Hall. In April 1924 the entire contents of Wollaston Hall were put up for auction; the hall itself was dismantled later but some mystery surrounds its final resting place, as the frame and panelling were probably shipped to America. On 28 July 1938 the fine old Jacobean house near Lye Cross known as Brocksopp's Hall was severely damaged by fire, and was in due course demolished. This large 17th-century brick-built house at Lye Cross had been named after Benjamin Brocksopp, a pottery maker who specialised in clay tobacco pipes in the 19th century. At the time of the fire it was being used as a headquarters for the Lye branch of Toc-H.

128   *The Wollaston tram terminal, c.1914.*

129   *Brocksopp's Hall at Lye Cross in June 1928.*

The Second World War

In 1939 the outbreak of war did not take the residents of Stourbridge entirely by surprise. A Civil Defence organisation had already been established earlier in the year. In February 1939 a decision was taken to form a local Women's Voluntary Service organisation, with the mayoress, Mrs. J.A. Mobberley, appointed local organiser. An office was opened, recruits came forward rapidly, and the WVS was able to undertake all kinds of social and relief work during the war. When war was declared on 3 September 1939, calm prevailed and business went on more or less as usual. It was only natural that local industry benefited from the demand for munitions and several firms had to expand their premises. Gas masks were distributed and Anderson air-raid shelters began to spring up on central sites and in people's own back gardens. At the start of 1940 the war still seemed a little unreal and social activities continued, albeit on a smaller scale. As the year went on more and more people spent spare time helping with fire fighting, first aid, nursing and air-raid precautions. There was an alarming increase in juvenile crime because children were left to their own devices, their fathers being in the forces and their mothers working in factories.

On 1 March 1940 a Stourbridge Services Club was opened in a building (previously used as the Conservative Club) near the junction of High Street and Church Street. The canteen was staffed by 200 voluntary women helpers and opened daily from 8.30 a.m. until 10 p.m. Extensive use was made of its facilities by the forces, including Americans billeted in and around the town. A welfare fund was opened, meals were provided and gifts given to service patients in local hospitals. In July 1940 Stourbridge launched a Spitfire Fund with a view to raising £5,000 to provide a fighter aeroplane. Money-raising events were organised and in October a Heinkel was exhibited in the St John's Road car park to arouse support for the appeal. Early in 1941 Stourbridge Council decided to open two British Restaurants (later renamed Civic Restaurants) for the provision of cheap meals for war workers. The first was situated at the corner of St John's Road and High Street in an old motor showroom and remained open until the summer of 1949. The other at Lye opened on 20 April 1942 in the premises of the *Talbot Inn*, Talbot Street, the price charged for an adult meal being one shilling. In March 1942 a Warship Week was held to raise £300,000 to provide a destroyer, which resulted in the adoption of HMS Faulkner by the people of Stourbridge. In September 1942 Viscountess Cobham opened the Victory Shop at Eagle House to raise money for war charities, and when the shop was closed in March 1945 over £7,000 had been raised.

Despite the industrial nature of the town, Stourbridge escaped without much major bomb damage, although a stray shell did badly damage the roof of Oldswinford rectory. When in the summer of 1944 London came under rocket attack, there was another exodus of evacuees and on 22 July about 350 women and children arrived in Stourbridge. After being accommodated at rest centres, they were found billets in the homes of local inhabitants. When VE Day (Victory In Europe) was celebrated on 8 May 1945, flags were hung from windows, buildings were floodlit and bonfires started.

By 1946 several German and Italian prisoner-of-war camps existed in and around Stourbridge; at Christmas the choir of Wollaston parish church visited the German camp at Studley Gate to sing carols. Some 300 cigarettes were given to the prisoners who in return gave the boys some biscuits. Some prisoners made a Star of Bethlehem and set it up in front of the

130   *A.R.P. first-aiders in gas masks at Stourbridge in October 1938.*

Christmas tree in Wollaston church. Foreign prisoners were also billeted in the rectory at Oldswinford, causing further damage to the building. On the appointment of Canon Arthur Vincent Hurley as rector in 1948, a major repair programme was carried out to make the house habitable. The Stourbridge WVS continued to devote itself to many forms of service, in particular the care of old people.

Last Years of an Independent Stourbridge

The end of the war was followed by a period of austerity, with rationing of food and many other goods. But it also saw the beginning of the Welfare State. The driving force behind the scheme was Lord Beveridge, who visited Stourbridge in August 1947 to speak at the Liberal Association fête at Prescote House, home of Ernest Stevens. He was the grandson of William Akroyd, a leading public figure in Stourbridge during the previous century. The Corbett Hospital was taken into the resulting National Health Service on 15 June 1948 and Sir Sidney Law opened a training school for nurses in Hill House the following month. In 1948 the Gas Company was transferred to the West Midlands Gas Board and later closed, although one gas holder was retained.

Other famous visitors to the town in the years after the war included Lord Beaverbrook in 1945, Sir Stafford Cripps (then President of the Board of Trade) to Stourbridge Art School in January 1946, and the Princess Royal (who was presented with a Stourbridge-made cut glass bowl by the mayor, Alderman H.P. Jones) in November 1949. The greatest honour for

---

Stourbridge through Time: 1945 to 2000

1948   National Health Service formed
1949   Church Street car park opens
1957   Queen Elizabeth II visits the town
1960   Crematorium built in South Road
1965   Stourbridge goods railway line is closed
1966   Lye Waste is redeveloped
1968   Town's ring road is built
1974   Rye Market shopping centre opens; Stourbridge Council is merged with Dudley
1976   Stourbridge Grammar School becomes a Sixth Form College
1979   New town railway station is built
1983   Market Hall demolished and Crown Centre built
1985   New public library opens in Crown Centre
1987   Bonded Warehouse re-opens by side of canal for leisure activities
1988   Victoria Passage shopping arcade opens
1989   Crystal Leisure Centre replaces public baths
1992   Princess Diana visits Mary Stevens' Hospice
1994   Redevelopment of town's bus and rail stations
1997   Security cameras installed in High Street
2000   Proposal to re-align ring road and build new supermarket

131 *Swinford Old Hall in Church Road, Oldswinford in 1983.*

Stourbridge was a visit on 23 April 1957 by a young Queen Elizabeth II with her husband Prince Philip, Duke of Edinburgh. They had an enthusiastic welcome from the townspeople of Stourbridge. On a sunny day they entered the town over its historic bridge in Lower High Street and were driven to Mary Stevens Park, where they were received in the Council House by the mayor, Alderman Howard Walker, and the town clerk, Philip Drury. They were then driven around the park in a Land Rover, to the cheers of a very large crowd.

The borough of Stourbridge continued to improve living conditions after the war. Further recreational space was provided, namely land at Norton Covert and the ground next to Wollaston Church in 1947, and four years later Ham Dingle at Pedmore. By the end of the Second World War the population of Stourbridge U.D.C. had grown to 36,290,[2] and the council created further well-laid-out municipal housing estates; one of the largest of these was on the site of the former Rufford's brickworks near the railway viaduct at Stambermill. The first houses on that Stepping Stones Estate were officially opened in April 1946 and additional estates were created at Norton, Rufford Road, Stepping Stones, Wollaston Farm, Pedmore Fields, South Road and Corser Street. In total that amounted to an additional 2,400 council houses by the 1960s. But land was now at a premium and eyes looked upwards; the result was high-rise flats. In the mid-1960s a maze of old buildings on Lye Waste was demolished to make way for new housing and blocks of flats, the first phase of that scheme being officially opened in November 1966. In the previous two years Kennedy Court and Baylie Court (on the site of Baylie's old chain works in New Street) had been built in Stourbridge and Firmstone Court at Wollaston. Older properties were also demolished or converted for housing or other community use. In the 1950s Oldswinford Castle was sold to developers who converted it into flats; an old Tudor fireplace was uncovered at that time. The ornamental pools in its grounds, which at one time were well stocked with fish and fed by a running stream, were drained for the purpose of building houses in Castle Grove. In November 1951 the Georgian house, once known as

132 *Oldswinford Castle from the southern side,* c.*1900. The pool later disappeared under the Castle Grove housing development.*

The Laurels, near Oldswinford parish church was purchased as one of the first council homes for old people at a cost of £26,000; its name was changed to Swinford Old Hall. (This home was closed in 1999 and houses built in its grounds.)

The people of Stourbridge were also becoming healthier and several extensions to the Corbett Hospital were implemented. In 1964 an out-patients and accident department, together with a further two car parks, were provided. In 1967 a new operating theatre was opened followed in 1970 by a ward block and intensive care unit. A medical services centre was built on land near Hill House in 1972 (and extended in 1989). In 1974 Dudley Health Authority replaced the old Stourbridge and Dudley Hospital Management Committee. Another former private house used for public health was West Hill in Hagley Road, Oldswinford. When William Westwood Skidmore-Westwood died on 19 August 1946 he left the property to Worcestershire County Council, together with other nearby houses called Hillville, Rose Cottage and Hillville Lodge, for use as nurseries for homeless children. Those nurseries, named Margaret Westwood in memory of his only daughter, were converted at a cost of £35,000 and were first occupied by babies and staff in December 1950. West Hill House eventually became the Westhill Annex of Stourbridge College and Westhill Clinic was erected in the grounds. In 1960 a crematorium was created out of the two former Anglican and nonconformist chapels on the site of the borough cemetery in South Road. The new chapel contained accommodation for 40 persons, a cloistered entrance and associated offices. A garden of remembrance was laid out in close proximity.

The most important changes in this period came about as a result of the vast increase in the use of motor vehicles. Car parking was already a problem in the late 1940s and this was helped to some extent by the opening in 1949 of a car park for 100 vehicles in Church Street. Much of the cost was donated by Major George Green of Oldswinford, a local magistrate who gave £500 to the Chamber of Trade. The old High Street was still much too narrow for cars and various one way systems were tried in the 1950s. The chief trouble spot was at the ancient central crossroads near the town clock, where traffic coming up Lower High Street from Amblecote and wishing to go towards Birmingham had to negotiate a sharp left corner near the old Dutch-gabled *Board Inn* to continue along the narrow Coventry Street. At the southern end of the town, the railway bridge across Foster Street was reconstructed in 1957 at a cost of £30,000 and when re-opened on 14 June 1958 the road became much easier to negotiate.

133   *The town's former bus terminus in Vauxhall Road in 1959.*

But before many more years elapsed that section of the railway line became redundant and in due course the bridge was removed.

The appearance of Stourbridge High Street in the 1950s was very different from today; virtually no local traders now remain from that period. On a walk down the town's main street from the War Memorial at the junction of Hagley Road and Church Street to the town clock at the junction of Market Street, the following traders could be encountered in the mid-1950s. At the top right was the British Restaurant (which became Thompson's Housewife's Corner) and on the left the Brierley Hill and Stourbridge Building Society and Pargeter's furniture store (trading since 1926 and one of few shops of that era still trading). Next followed the Cottage Tea Rooms (at the back of Unwin Place), the country standard red and gold-fronted Woolworths store (now a Kwiksave supermarket) and a couple of chemists (Boots, with its two-pillared Roman stone front, and Timothy Whites). The Dickensian offices of solicitors Harward and Evers with their internal ionic columns (originally the Rufford, Wragge & Griffiths Bank), the parapeted front of Longcroft House (which became Broadmeads), Stringer's Store, the Odeon Cinema and the terracotta-red post office built in 1885 (which miraculously still survives) added further interest. Further down High Street was the fascinating frontage of Walter Perry's fish shop (its coloured tiles representing a basket of fish and game and a curious Viking-looking fishing craft). There followed the 18th-century Dowson confectionery shop, Meesons who sold sweets, Paynes the tobacconist, Hepworths the clothier, Douglas the jeweller, MacFisheries and George Smith (an early 19th-century shoe shop with stucco walls). Towards the lower end of the street was Mark and Moody's impressive 1866 front. The shop traded there for 153 years, until forced to close in August 1993; it was re-opened in October of that year by its new owners under the name Paper & Pens. This was followed by Rainbow furniture stores, Yeates the chemist, Ford's Regency-period front (originally a chemist), Southern Brothers (suppliers of school uniforms), and Lawley's china shop. The Edwardian yellow terracotta and red brick Lloyds Bank is still there today. Then came the Victorian chemist Greenwood (originally Sellick), the ancient *Talbot Inn*, Craddock's shoe shop, Peplow the jeweller, the Georgian Home and Colonial Stores and Blurton the jeweller. Further along was the curved bay window of Mr. Wooldridge, the Victorian Hill and Reading's grocery shop, Alfred Preedy the tobacconist, Burton's clothes store ('the tailor of taste') and Warrilow's shoe shop. The picture was completed by the Midland Bank on the corner of Coventry Street (which in 1916 replaced the charming Old Bank) and Shirt's Tea Rooms on the corner of Market Street.

An extreme solution for the traffic problem was adopted in 1968 with the building of a clockwise ring road that virtually isolated the main shopping centre of the town; the first part became operative in November 1968 and Viscount Cobham officially opened it on 1 November 1969. The ancient Market and Coventry Streets became cul-de-sacs. Angel Street, Mill Street and several other small roads virtually ceased to exist. A one-way system for traffic came into force from south to north along the main High Street, exiting along Market Street and Bell Street. The other entrance to the town was from north to south along Lower High Street, turning west into Crown Lane to exit onto the new ring road. People were no longer aware they were crossing the ancient bridge that so long ago had given its name to the town. The scheme was very costly and many good properties had to be demolished. In due course the town also acquired two new multi-storey car parks.

Public transport tried bravely to match growing competition from the motor car. The new Vauxhall Road depot for buses was opened in 1948 and in 1959 the garage's loading bays were covered over. But rail travellers began to suffer. In July 1962 the direct rail service to Dudley came to an end and on 5 July 1965 the goods extension line from Stourbridge town was closed. From July 1967 Stourbridge town station was not staffed. In January 1972 the local railways were taken over by the West Midlands Passenger Transport Authority and in December 1973 local bus services, run formerly by the Midland Red Company, were also transferred to that body.

For the canals the news was even worse. Since the 1920s canal traffic had declined significantly, except for a time during the Second World War when there was a temporary increase because of shortage of petrol for road transport and lack of capacity on the railways. The Stourbridge Canal Company declined in importance until it was nationalised on 1 January 1948 and became part of the Docks and Inland Waterways Executive of the British Transport Commission. At that time boats were rarely seen on the canal, which had a branch from Wordsley following the course of the river Stour to Stourbridge where it ended in a basin in the railway goods yard. There followed the abandonment, silting up and closure of many miles of local waterways. In January 1964 the canals became part of the British Waterways Board; this body was more enlightened than its predecessor and encouraged volunteer groups to restore and improve the old canals, including the Wordsley to Stourbridge section.

During the last years of Stourbridge U.D.C. the population jumped, to nearly 44,000 by 1962/3.[3] On 1 April 1966 a major part of Amblecote Urban District Council with a population of some 3,000 persons was added to Stourbridge and the council now had 32 members. But between 1971 and 1981 the population of the newly defined Stourbridge increased by only 315 persons, from 54,344 to 54,659. On 1 April 1974 the Borough of Stourbridge itself was swallowed up by the neighbouring Dudley Metropolitan District, and the thousand-year link with the county of Worcester was lost as the town moved into the newly created Metropolitan County of the West Midlands. For the previous thousand years the lives of people in Stourbridge, Oldswinford, Wollaston, Lye and Wollescote had been administered by those living within the town's own boundaries and the loss of that close link was greatly mourned by the town's inhabitants.

Stourbridge controlled by Dudley

The theme of centralisation and rationalisation continued for the remainder of the century. Many of the traditional industries around the town including glass, engineering and heavy manufacturing were in decline, being replaced by smaller service industries. A new wave of immigration took place, which rivalled the arrival of the glass workers in the 17th century and the Irish in the 19th century; these people came from the old British Empire countries and enriched local skills, particularly in the eastern part of the town. At the same time new types of eating houses began to prosper, their increasing popularity resulting in Lye being nicknamed the 'Balti Capital of the Black Country'.

The physical aspect of the town continued to alter dramatically during the last quarter of the century. Previously the central focus of the town had gradually moved from Lower High Street (at one time the area with the best houses and shops) to the southern end of the High

134 *Members and officials of Stourbridge Borough Council at their final meeting in 1974.*

Street where train, tram and bus stations were situated. That trend went into reverse in the 1970s, with the opening on 22 March 1974 of the Ryemarket Shopping Precinct on the west of the High Street. In that year the High Street was completely closed to traffic at certain times on Saturdays, but the experiment had to be discontinued after a few years owing to the protests of both traders and shoppers. Many old established family businesses began to be replaced by multiple stores and supermarkets. In 1976 the former Odeon cinema in the centre of the High Street was converted into Stringer's furniture store, which in turn was taken over in the late 1970s by the Owen Owen department store. In 1983 the old market hall, built in 1827, was demolished; only the façade of the old building, which fronted onto the High Street next to the town clock, was preserved. It was replaced by the new Crown Centre complex, with its out-of-character red-brick exterior. That became the new venue for the market traders who for so long had been part of the town's life. The multi-storey car park built on the site contained the town's Register Office on its third floor, but this was not the most romantic place to have a wedding and in 1995 the office was moved to the ground floor facing Crown Lane. In 1985 a new public library opened in the Crown Centre, transferred from its old site in Hagley Road. In June 1988 a refurbished mall in Victoria Passage was developed for shopping and the offices and printing works of the County Express newspaper were demolished to make way for it. In March 1989 the town clock was removed to Bristol for repairs costing £17,000. Various proposals were made by Dudley Council to re-site the clock on its return, including using it as a traffic island in the middle of the town centre, but this caused uproar amongst Stourbridge people as the clock was symbolic of the old town. When the clock was eventually returned in April 1991, common sense prevailed and it was re-installed on its original site.

In the late 1980s the huge main mall of the Merry Hill shopping centre was developed at a cost of £150 million; it was only three miles away from Stourbridge town centre and dealt a death blow to local shops, resulting in a disastrous decline in town centre trade. Owen Owen closed their store in June 1990. The situation was not helped when in 1993 the council, in the face of great opposition, began to charge for parking in the town's major car parks. The High Street could not be easily pedestrianised because the design of the ring road made alternative vehicular access very difficult. The whole complex of the old Owen Owen store (and formerly the Odeon cinema) was demolished on 9 April 1995, watched by a crowd of people interested in seeing a piece of their history disappear. Matters began to improve slightly when the Wilkinson group built a brand new store on the site, which opened on 23 February 1996, giving the town a much needed large general store. Security cameras at strategic points were turned on in 1997 to combat vandalism, but very few shops of quality remained by that time. The condition of buildings at the foot of the eastern side of Lower High Street had also become very dilapidated by the end of the century. Plans are, however, afoot to build town houses and flats on the site of the old Congregational church. Work elsewhere in the area saw the commencement of the long-awaited Lye Cross bypass in 1999, to relieve a traffic blackspot of many years. A new town scheme was proposed in 2000 which involved expanding the Stourbridge ring road on the eastern side of the town to make space for a food superstore and realigning Birmingham Street by altering the course of the river Stour. In addition it is proposed to build a branch of the new Wolverhampton to Birmingham tram system to link up with the Merry Hill shopping complex; this may well be extended to Stourbridge in future years.

Public transport also witnessed a number of changes, but railway travellers continued to suffer. A spectacular accident happened on Grand National Day 1977 when the brakes on the shuttle train (known affectionately as the 'Stourbridge Dodger') failed as it descended to Stourbridge town station, resulting in it overshooting the buffers and brick wall at the end of the track. The train ended up balanced precariously over Foster Street, but luckily no passenger was badly injured. In February 1979 the town station buildings were demolished (this time intentionally) and replaced by a simple platform and shelter. In January 1985 the town's Bus Depot and Travel Centre were closed down and sold to the local developers for a retail garage. Early in March 1990 the brakes again failed on the Stourbridge Dodger resulting in yet another dramatic accident. It once again hit the buffers and demolished the wall at the end of the line. On that occasion there were injuries, but luckily nobody died in the crash. A £380,000 redevelopment of the rail and bus stations on the site of the old town station took place in 1994. To mark its opening and the importance of the glass industry in the life of the town, a statue of a glassblower was unveiled on the site. One benefit of canal closures was the restoration of a 200-year-old three-storey warehouse in Canal Street just north of the Stour. The redundant

135 *A boat rally on the Stourbridge canal arm in 1982.*

Bonded Warehouse had been disused since 1946 but volunteers worked on it between 1985 and 1987 and it is now popular for recreational and leisure purposes.

Further changes have benefited the health and leisure interests of the town's residents, although some of these have made services less convenient for local people. In May 1984 Princess Anne opened the first stage of the new Russell's Hall Hospital at Dudley, and many hospital services formerly provided at Stourbridge began to be transferred to that centre. In October 1987 Hill House at the Corbett Hospital was adapted as a mental health unit, followed a year later by a 20-place day unit for the elderly mentally ill. Various proposals were made to downgrade the hospital during the last decade of the century, as its valuable land was needed for extra housing. The public baths building was closed in June 1988 and demolished in 1989 to make way for the modern leisure complex known as the Crystal Leisure Centre. Mary Stevens Maternity Home was closed in 1984, and the construction of a hospice day care unit was commenced at its lodge house on the Hagley Road in November 1990. The first

136   *Looking south along Lower High Street in 2000.*

137   *View from town centre along Market Street in 2000.*

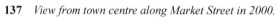

stage of the Mary Stevens' Hospice was completed in July 1991 and on 6 March 1992 the 20th century's most famous icon, Princess Diana, visited Oldswinford to open that stage of its development. Large crowds turned out to see her and the town was stunned by her tragic death in a car crash in Paris on 31 August 1997. On that Sunday morning the St Mary's parish choir were guest singers at Liverpool Cathedral and had hastily to make some re-arrangement of their music for such a momentous occasion. Further extensions to the hospice were started in September 1995 to add a unit with beds for in-patients; this was completed in April 1998. In 1998/9 the Severn Trent Water Company replaced all the piping under the roads of the town, much of which dated back to Victorian times.[4]

At the beginning of the 21st century the historic town of Stourbridge is seeking a new identity. The last published population census results taken in 1991 gave the number of people living in Stourbridge (including Amblecote) as 66,769. The make-up of that number was 12,334 in Pedmore and Stourbridge East, 11,861 in Wollaston and Stourbridge West, 11,856 in Norton, 12,024 in Lye and Wollescote and 18,694 in Amblecote. It is extraordinary that even now the role of the lord of the manor may not have completely disappeared; in December 1996 an auction was held to sell the titles of lord of the manors of Oldswinford and of Bedcote and Stourbridge on behalf of the Earl of Dudley. A Chester family paid £8,750 and £5,000 respectively for those titles.

Notes

Chapter I: The Stourbridge Area in Early Times
1. The *County Express*, Correspondence from W.W. King, George Gould and H.E. Palfrey, 3 February 1917.
2. Hooke, Della, *Worcestershire Anglo-Saxon Charter-Bounds* (1990), pp.61-3.
3. Wells, Dean & Chapter, *Liber Albus II*, fos.289v-290r; Hooke, *op. cit.*, pp.162-7.
4. *Domesday Book: 16 Worcestershire* (1982 edition), Chapter 23; 11.

Chapter II: Stourbridge in the Middle Ages
1. Cal. Inq. Misc. I, p.445.
2. Public Record Office (hereafter PRO), Anct. Doc., A9101.
3. Chan. Inq. p.m., 16 Edw. II, no.72.
4. *V.C.H., Worcestershire: The Victoria History of the County of Worcester*, Vol. III (1913), p.216 for lords of the manor quoted in this chapter. At times the manor of Oldswinford was under common ownership with Northfield (*op.cit.*, p.194) and Hagley (*op.cit.*, p.133).
5. Scott, William, *Stourbridge and its Vicinity* (1832), p.89.
6. Feet of Fines, Worcs., 25 Hen. III, no.27.
7. Birmingham Reference Library—Hagley Hall Collection (hereafter H.H.C.); land charter of 1311/12 referred to in the Oldswinford manor court held in May 1569 (377989).
8. Pope Nich. Tax. (Rec. Com.), 230a.
9. Feet of Fines, Worcs., 18 Ed I, no.17.
10. Mawer, A., and Stenton, F.M., *The Place Names of Worcestershire*, English Place-Name Society (1927), p.311.
11. Worcestershire Record Office (hereafter WRO), the Foley Scrapbooks in the Alderman Palfrey Collection (BA 3762), vol.1 p.360.
12. H.H.C., land charter of 1311/12 referred to in the Oldswinford manor court held in May 1569 (377989).
13. Razi, Zvi, *Life, Marriage and Death in a Medieval Parish* (1980), a detailed study of the manor rolls of the neighbouring manor of Halesowen in the years 1270 to 1400.
14. H.H.C., land charter of 1311/12 referred to in the Oldswinford manor court held in May 1569 (377989).
15. WRO, the Foley Scrapbooks held in the Alderman Palfrey Collection (BA 3762), vol.1, p.360.
16. Razi, Zvi, *op.cit.*

17. Feet of Fines, Worcs., 18 Ed I, no.17.
18. Hunt, J., *A History of Halesowen Abbey* (1979), p.16.
19. Razi, Zvi, *op.cit.*
20. Chambers, R.L., *Oldswinford, Bedcote and Stourbridge Manors and Boundaries* (1978), p.7.
21. Chambers, R.L., *op.cit.*, p.9.
22. Feet of Fines, *Staffs.*, 21 Hen. VI, no.37.
23. Nash, T., *Collections for the History and Antiquities of Worcestershire*, vol. II (1781/2), p.208, quoting a deed dated 46 Edw. III found in the Lyttelton MSS.
24. H.H.C., *Account Roll of the Bailiff of Oldswinford* dated 1488/9 (347135).
25. Roper, J.S., *Thomas Forest, Keeper of Dunclent Park Worcestershire* (1978), p.1; Staffordshire Record Office, D593/0/3/3.
26. WRO, BA 5672 ref. 705:222.
27. H.H.C., *Account Roll of the Bailiff of Oldswinford* dated 1488/9 (347135).
28. H.H.C., *Rentals of the Lord of Oldswinford* dated 1549 (382960).
29. H.H.C., *Court Roll of Swinford and Stourbridge* dated 3 April 1529 (347128).
30. H.H.C., *Court Roll of Oldswinford* dated April 1621 (377994).

Chapter III: Tudor and Elizabethan Stourbridge

1. Pat., 1 Hen. VII, pt. iv.
2. Rolls of Parl. VI. pp.325-6.
3. H.H.C., *Account Roll of the Bailiff of Oldswinford* dated 1488/9 (347135).
4. Nash, T., *Collections for the History and Antiquities of Worcestershire*, p.209, which quoted from material bequeathed by Bishop Charles Lyttelton (1704-68) to the Society of Antiquaries.
5. Habington, T.A., *A Survey of Worcestershire*, ed. J. Amphlett for Worcestershire Historical Society (1893-9), p.405.
6. Chambers, R.L., *The Madstard Case* (1986), p.218.
7. H.H.C., *Court Rolls of Oldswinford* dated 1569-1573 (377989-377990).
8. Chant. Cert. vol.60, no.20; vol.61, no.16.
9. H.H.C., *Rentals of the Lord of Oldswinford* dated 1549 (382960).
10. Chambers, R.L., *op. cit.*, p.210.
11. H.H.C., *Court Roll of Oldswinford* dated *c*.1578 (377992).
12. Close, 34 Eliz. pt. xxii, Persehowse and Liddeatt; William Salt Archaeological Society Collections XVIII p.6.
13. H.H.C., *Rentals of the Lord of Oldswinford* dated 1549 (382960).
14. Scott, William, *op. cit.*, p.39.
15. H.H.C., *Rentals of the Lord of Oldswinford* dated 1549 (382960).
16. Nash, T., *op. cit.*, p.208.
17. H.H.C., *Court Roll of Oldswinford* dated 22 April 1587 (377992).
18. H.H.C., *Court Roll of Oldswinford* dated 4 October 1582 (377992).
19. H.H.C., *Court Roll of Oldswinford* dated 16 March 1630 (382958).
20. H.H.C., *Court Roll of Oldswinford* dated 13 April 1592 (377993).

21. H.H.C., *Court Roll of Oldswinford* dated 6 April 1575 (377991).

22. H.H.C., *Rentals of the Lord of Oldswinford* dated 1549 (382960).

23. V.C.H. *Staffs.*, Vol. XX (1984)-Amblecote Section (pp.49-64).

24. WRO, BA 8789/(ii).

25. H.H.C., *Court Roll of Oldswinford* (377989-94, 382958-9).

26. WRO, ref. 008.7.

27. Roper, J.S., *Stourbridge Probate Inventories* 1541-1558 (1966).

28. Rental of Rowley Regis manor dated 12 April 1556.

29. H.H.C., *Court Roll of Swinford and Stourbridge* dated 3 April 1529 (347128).

30. PRO, PCC Wills, Elcoxe, Thomas, 1567 (31 Stonarde).

31. H.H.C., *Court Roll of Oldswinford* dated 19 April 1581 and 19 October 1583 (377992).

32. Roper, J.S., *op. cit.*

33. H.H.C., *Court Roll of Oldswinford* dated 3 April 1529 (347128) and 19 October 1583 (377992).

34. Chambers, R.L., *op. cit.*, p.216.

35. PRO, PCC Wills, Madstard, Thomas, 1587 (65 Spencer).

36. Chambers, R.L., *op. cit.*, pp.1-3.

37. H.H.C., *Court Roll of Oldswinford* dated 2 May 1636 (382958).

Chapter IV: The Seventeenth Century in Stourbridge

1. Archives & Local History Service of Dudley Libraries, Coseley, *Palmer and Seabright Trust Papers*, Accession 8427.

 2. H.H.C., *Court Roll of Swinford and Stourbridge* dated 3 April 1529 (347128).

 3. H.H.C., *Court Roll of Bedcote and Stourbridge* dated 17 September 1627 (382958).

 4. H.H.C., *Court Roll of Bedcote and Stourbridge* dated 4 April 1627 (382958).

 5. Scott, William, *Stourbridge and the Vicinity*, p.88.

 6. WRO, *Calendar of Quarter Session Rolls 1591-1640*, ref. 110, Vol. 16, Transactions of the Worcestershire Historical Society (151016).

 7. H.H.C., *Court Roll of Oldswinford* dated 5 September 1622 (382958).

 8. H.H.C., *Court Roll of Oldswinford* dated 16 October 1639 (382958).

 9. WRO, St Mary's, *Oldswinford parish register* (1623), BA 9150 parcel 1(i).

10. Archives and Local History Service of Dudley Libraries, Coseley, *Palmer and Seabright Trust Papers*, Accession 8427.

11. H.H.C., *Court Roll of Oldswinford* dated 1627 to 1637 (382958).

12. Noake, John, *Rambler in Worcestershire* (1848), first series, p.359.

13. Palfrey, H.E., *The Civil War Round About Stourbridge* (1943).

14. Palfrey, H.E., *Foleys of Stourbridge* (1944), p.6.

15. Stourbridge Public Library, *1699 Plan of the manor of Oldswinford*.

16. Nash, T., *Collections for the History and Antiquities of Worcestershire*, p.208, which quotes the boundaries of the manor of Bedcote set out in 1622 Court Baron of Sir Thomas Gervois.

17. H.H.C., *Rentals of the Lord of Oldswinford* dated 1549 (382960).

18. H.H.C., *Court Roll of Oldswinford* dated 12 April 1626 (382958).

19. Chambers, R.L., manuscript transcription of Oldswinford churchwardens' accounts (1603-67).

20. WRO, *Calendar of Quarter Session Rolls 1591-164*0, ref. 110, Vol. 16, Transactions of the Worcestershire Historical Society (151016).

21. Chambers, R.L., manuscript transcription of Oldswinford churchwardens' accounts (1603-67).

22. WRO, Oldswinford parish minute dated 20 March 1738, BA 3762 899:31.

Chapter V: Georgian Stourbridge

1. WRO, Oldswinford parish minutes (1723-1830), BA 3762 899:31. The references to the Oldswinford workhouse in this chapter are based on entries in these minutes.

2. Nash, T., *Collections for the History and Antiquities of Worcestershire*, p.207.

3. WRO, *Stourbridge Roads Record Book 1753-1819*, BA 3762 899:31, parcel 4(iv).

4. WRO, *Stourbridge to Colley Gate Order Book 1762-1769*, BA 3762 899:31, parcel 4(iv).

5. Goodyear, G.H., *Stourbridge Old and New* (1908), p.53.

6. WRO, *Oldswinford parish minute* dated May 1742, BA 3762 899:31.

7. WRO, BA 3762/149 (ii).

8. Stourbridge Public Library, copy of *1782 Plan of the manor of Oldswinford*.

9. WRO, BA 3762/149 (ii).

10. Scott, William, *Stourbridge and its Vicinity*, pp.41/2.

11. Scott, William, *op. cit*, p.77.

12. Hutton, William, *The History of Birmingham* (1782).

13. WRO, *Oldswinford parish minute* dated 24 May 1773, BA 3762 899:31.

14. Scott, William, *op. cit.*, p.61.

15. Haden, H.J., 'Wollaston Hall', *The Blackcountryman*, vol. 18 (Winter 1985).

16. Goodyear, G.H., *op. cit.*, p.24.

17. Melville & Co., *Directory and Gazetteer of Stourbridge* (1852), p.41.

18. Scott, William, *op. cit.*, p.42.

19. Stourbridge Public Library, copy of *Brettell's 1827 survey of the parish of Oldswinford* (with names of tenants and owners of land).

Chapter VI: Victorian Stourbridge

1. Bentley's *History, Guide and Alphabetical and Classified Directory of Stourbridge* (1841), p.7.

2. Thompson, George, *Prize Essay upon the Sanitary Conditions of the Town of Stourbridge* (1847).

3. Thompson, George, *op. cit.*

4. Thompson, George, *op. cit.*

5. WRO, *Oldswinford Road Order Book 1830-1842*, BA 3762/4 899:31, parcel 4(iv).

6. Bentley, *op. cit.*, p.6.

7. Bentley, *op. cit.*, and Melville & Co., *op. cit.*

8. Evers, Bryan, *Harward and Evers, A History* (1988).

9. Gardener, W.J., *A Brief History of Nickolls & Perks Ltd.* (1999).

10. Bentley, *op. cit.*, pp.45/6.
11. Collins, Paul (ed.), *Stourbridge and its Historical Locomotives* (1989).
12. Melville & Co., *Directory and Gazetteer of Stourbridge*, p.41.
13. Melville & Co., *op. cit.*, pp.44-53.
14. Melville & Co., *op. cit.*, p.41.
15. *V.C.H. Staffs.*, Vol. XX (1984), Amblecote Section (pp.49-64).
16. Swingle S.L., and Turner, K., *The Kinver Light Railway* (1987).
17. Haden, H.J., *The Stourbridge Scene 1851-1951* (1976); the author is most grateful to Mr. Haden for information on the years 1850 to 1900.
18. Stourbridge Public Library, reprint of *Plan of Stourbridge from Actual Survey* (1837).

Chapter VII: The Growth of Trade and Industry
1. H.H.C., *Rentals of the Lord of Oldswinford* dated 1549 (382960).
2. Guttery, D.R., 'Stourbridge Market in Tudor Times', *Transactions of the Worcestershire Historical Society* (1953), pp.16-28.
3. WRO, *Oldswinford parish minute* dated 22 June 1813, BA 3762 899:31.
4. Palfrey, H.E., *A Short Account of* The Talbot Hotel (1927), p.16.
5. Roper, J.S., *Stourbridge Probate Inventories 1541-1558* (1966).
6. H.H.C., *Rentals of the Lord of Oldswinford* dated 1549 (382960).
7. WRO, *Oldswinford Register of Burials in Woollen* (1678-1722), BA 5214, parcel 3a.
8. Chan. Inq. p.m., 16 Edw. II, no.72.
9. Dudley, Dud, *Metallum Martis* (1665), p.62.
10. Guttery, D.R., *From Broad Glass to Cut Crystal: A History of the Stourbridge Glass Industry* (1956).
11. Beard, G.W., *The History of Wollaston*, 1946.
12. Misc. Books, Land Revenue, Vol. 228, ff. 308-10.
13. Archives & Local History Service of Dudley Libraries, Coseley, *Assignment of Cradley Ironworks and its Stock on 24 June 1724*, D/DE IV 3, box 5, bundle 7.
14. Bentley, *History, Guide and Alphabetical and Classified Directory of Stourbridge*, p.24.
15. H.H.C., *Court Roll of Oldswinford* dated 7 December 1573 (377990).
16. PRO, Anct. Doc., A9101.
17. Staffordshire County Record Office, Tp. 1273/13.
18. PRO, CP 25(2)/726, 32 Chas. II, Mich. no.9.
19. Scott, William, *Stourbridge and its Vicinity*, p.65.
20. Collins, Paul (ed.), *Stourbridge and its Historical Locomotives* (1989), p.10.
21. H.H.C., *Court Rolls of Oldswinford* dated 21 October 1577 and 5 October 1581.
22. Dudley, Dud, *op. cit.*, p.62.
23. Stourbridge Public Library, *Brettell's 1827 survey of the parish of Oldswinford*.
24. Perrins, Wesley, *The Lye and Wollescote Industries* (1980), pp.70-2.
25. Melville & Co., *Directory and Gazetteer*, pp.44-53.
26. Nash, T., *Collections for the History and Antiquities of Worcestershire*, supplement p.57.
27. Bentley, *op. cit.*, pp.19-27.
28. Goodyear, G.H., *Stourbridge Old and New*, p.18.

Chapter VIII: Religion and Education
1. Worcester Cathedral Archive, Sede Vacante Register, published by Worcestershire Historical Society.
2. Chant. cert. vol.60, no.20, dated 14 February 1548.
3. Chambers, R.L., *King Edward VI School Stourbridge. The Story of a School* (1988), pp.48-52.
4. Chant. cert. vol.60, no.20, dated 14 February 1548.
5. H.H.C., *Rentals of the Lord of Oldswinford* dated 1549 (382960).
6. Simpson, Charles, *The Story of the Unitarian Chapel Lye 1790-1961* (1961).
7. Whitley, W.T., *Baptists in Stourbridge* (1929).
8. Dukes, R., *A History and Guide to St Thomas's Church Stourbridge* (1979).
9. Robertson, Revd. David, 'Recollections of the Lye Parish, 1866-1875', in a letter sent to a later incumbent, J.T. Conan Davies on 4 October 1914, typescript in Stourbridge Public Library.
10. Chambers, R.L., *op. cit.*, p.54.
11. Scott, William, *Stourbridge and its Vicinity*, p.114.
12. Scott, William, *op. cit.*, p.114.
13. Bentley, History, *Guide and Alphabetical and Classified Directory of Stourbridge*, p.36.
14. Scott, William, *op. cit.*, p.114.
15. Bentley, *op. cit.*, p.15.
16. Bentley, *op. cit.*, p.15.
17. Scott, William, *op. cit.*, p.114.
18. Robertson, Revd. David, *op. cit.*
19. Bentley, *op. cit.*, p.36.

Chapter IX: Recreation and Leisure
1. Scott, William, *Stourbridge and its Vicinity*, p.94.
2. Perrins, Wesley, *The Lye and Wollescote* (1980), p.18.
3. H.H.C., *Rentals of the Lord of Oldswinford* dated 1549 (382960).
4. H.H.C., *Court Roll of Oldswinford* dated 22 September 1594 (377993).
5. H.H.C., *Court Roll of Oldswinford* dated 8 October 1638 (382958).
6. Plot, Robert, Natural History of Staffordshire (1686).
7. Scott, William, *op. cit.*, p.61.
8. Grove, A., *A History of the Lodge of Stability No. 564 Stourbridge from 1849 to 1949* (1949).
9. Dukes, G.R., *Social Life in North Worcestershire during the XVIIIth century*, published by the Worcestershire Historical Society, p.42.
10. Palfrey, H.E., *Some Accounts of the Old Theatres of Stourbridge* (1936).
11. Bentley, *History, Guide and Alphabetical and Classified Directory of Stourbridge*, p.14.
12. Bentley, *op. cit.*, p.15.
13. Perrins, Wesley, *The Lye and Wollescote* (1980), p.22.
14. Palfrey, H.E., *The Story of Stourbridge Institute and Social Club 1834-1948* (1948).

Chapter X: Stourbridge in the Twentieth Century

1. Haden, H.J., *The Stourbridge Scene 1851-1951*; the author is most grateful to Mr. Haden for information on the years 1900 to 1950.
2. *Stourbridge Official Guide* (1947).
3. *Stourbridge Official Guide* (1962/3), p.20.
4. Stourbridge Public Library, *Press Cuttings*; much of the information for the last quarter of the 20th century comes from this source.

Bibliography

Manuscript Sources

Minutes of Oldswinford Parish Meetings 1723-1830 at Worcester Record Office (WRO), BA 3762 899:31, reference 850 Old Swinford

Oldswinford Churchwardens' Accounts 1603-1667 transcribed by R.L. Chambers

Oldswinford Parish Registers at WRO, BA 9150 parcel 1(i), reference 850 Old Swinford

Oldswinford Workhouse Accounts at WRO, BA 5214/4, reference 850 Old Swinford

Oldswinford Poor Law Documents at WRO, BA 9150, reference 850 Old Swinford

16th and 17th century Court Rolls of the manors of Oldswinford and Bedcote, The Hagley Hall Collection at Birmingham Central Library, History and Local Studies Dept.

Stourbridge Probate Inventories 1541-1558 transcribed by John S. Roper in 1966

20th century press cuttings, Stourbridge Public Library

Printed Sources

Addison, John, *The History of Stourbridge*, c.1870 (The Brierley Hill Advertiser)

Beard, G.W., *The History of Wollaston*, 1946

Bentley, *History, Guide, and Alphabetical and Classified Directory of Stourbridge*, 1841

Chambers, R.L., *Oldswinford, Bedcote and Stourbridge Manors and Boundaries*, 1978

Chambers, R.L., *King Edward VI School Stourbridge. The Story of a School*, 1988

Chambers, R.L., *The Madstard Case*, 1986

Chambers, R.L., *Thomas Milward's Seventeenth Century Daybook*, 1978

Collins, Paul (ed.), *Stourbridge and its Historical Locomotives*, 1989

Dukes, R., *A History and Guide to St Thomas's Church Stourbridge*, 1979

Dukes, R., *Schola Edwardi Sexti Stourbridgiensis. A History of the School 1430-1976*, 1987

Goodyear, G.H., *Stourbridge Old and New*, 1908

Grundy, G.B., *Saxon Charters of Worcestershire*, 1931

Guttery, D.R., *From Broad Glass to Cut Crystal: A History of the Stourbridge Glass Industry*, 1956

Guttery, D.R., *Gentlemen at the Talbot, Stourbridge*, 1954

Guttery, D.R., 'Stourbridge Market in Tudor Times', *Transactions of the Worcestershire Historical Society* (1953)

Haden, H.J., *Notes on the Stourbridge Glass Trade*, 1977

Haden, H.J., *The Corbett Hospital; A Centennial History*, 1993

Haden, H.J., *The Stourbridge Scene 1851-1951*, 1976

Haden, Joan M., *The Priest and the Prophetess*, 1981

Herbert, M.V., *The Hickmans of Oldswinford*, 1979

Hooke, Della, *Worcestershire Anglo-Saxon Charter-Bounds*, 1990

Hunt, J., *A History of Halesowen Abbey*, 1979

Palfrey, H.E., *A Short Account of the* Talbot Hotel, 1927

Palfrey, H.E., *Foleys of Stourbridge*, 1944

Palfrey, H.E., *Some Accounts of the Old Theatres of Stourbridge*, 1936

Palfrey, H.E., *The Story of Stourbridge Institute and Social Club 1834-1948*, 1948

Perrins, Wesley, *The Lye and Wollescote Industries*, 1980

Perrins, Wesley, *The Lye and Wollescote*, 1980

Perry, N.R., *The Poor Law & Settlement Documents of St. Mary Oldswinford 1651-1794*, 1977

Perry, N.R., *The Story of St. Mary's Church and the Parish of Oldswinford*, 1989

Plot, Robert, *Natural History of Staffordshire*, 1686

Roper, J.S., *Thomas Forest, Keeper of Dunclent Park Worcestershire*, 1978

Scott, William, *Stourbridge and its Vicinity*, 1832

Simpson, Charles, *The Story of the Unitarian Chapel Lye 1790-1961*, 1961

Swingle S.L. and Turner, K., *The Kinver Light Railway*, 1987

Thompson, George, *Prize Essay upon the Sanitary Conditions of the Town of Stourbridge*, 1847

Whitley, W.T., *Baptists in Stourbridge*, 1929

Index

Numbers in **bold** refer to illustration page numbers.